PICTORIAL HISTORY OF
ENGLISH FOOTBALL

Biographies and Dedications

For Andy Sayer of Wimbledon and Slough Town.
Robert Jeffery worked on local newspapers before helping to launch *Sky Sports Magazine*. He has contributed to several books on individual soccer stars, alongside his regular reporting for *Four Four Two,* Britain's best-selling football magazine. He supports Wimbledon and Slough Town.

To Sue, Emma and Nick for putting up with my sports mania.
Mark Gonnella has been a sports journalist for 20 years since realizing his football prowess would never allow him to play for a living. His career has spanned local newspapers, radio and national newspapers. Now working freelance, he is married with two children. Mark holds an FA coaching badge and admits to being a lifelong fan of his home town club Reading.

Jimmy Armfield won 43 England caps. He captained his country from 1962-64, and was a member of the World Cup squads of 1962 and 1966. He played almost 700 games for Blackpool – his only club – skippering the Seasiders for 13 years in their heydays of the 50s and 60s. He managed for nine seasons, shared almost equally between Bolton Wanderers and Leeds United – taking the Yorkshire side to the European Cup Final in 1975. A BBC Radio sports commentator, he is now the FA's Technical Consultant, and Head of the Professional Footballers' Association Coaching Department.

ISBN 1 84084 214 8

First published in 1998 by
Dempsey Parr
13 Whiteladies Road
Clifton
Bristol
BS8 1PB

Copyright 1998 © Dempsey Parr

Produced for Dempsey Parr by Foundry Design and Production, Crabtree Hall, Crabtree Lane, Fulham, London, SW6 6TY.

A CIP catalogue record for this book is available from the British Library.

PICTORIAL HISTORY OF
ENGLISH
FOOTBALL

Robert Jeffery
with Mark Gonnella

Introduction by
Jimmy Armfield

DP

DEMPSEY
PARR

CONTENTS

Special Note

The Pictorial History of English Football contains an in-depth overview of the beautiful game, running chronologically from football's origins to a look at what the future holds. The reader can approach the text in several ways:

▶ For a historical perspective, the book can be read from start to finish concentrating on the decades and eras documented, such as '1914-18: The First World War' or '1970-1980: Taking on the World'.

▶ Important individual moments, such as the White Horse FA Cup Final or the 1966 World Cup Final, can be explored as separate elements.

▶ There are team profiles, such as the Corinthian Casuals or the Euro 96 squad, and individual player profiles (Alf Common to Alan Shearer).

▶ Throughout the book, reaching out from the main entries, there are many features boxes. These contain invaluable snippets of football trivia and historical facts, providing the opportunity to browse through the book, picking up on points of interest.

The extensive index also helps with reference and the glossary explains terms some readers may be unfamiliar with.

INTRODUCTION

I have always believed that football is the greatest game ever invented by man. I say this after four decades of involvement as player, manager, journalist, broadcaster and finally as a member of the FA staff. But, whatever the title, I have also been proud just to be a good, old-fashioned fan.

Football is in fact more than a game to most of us. It is a way of life. Certainly it has captivated the world more than any other sport. When soccer, every four years, celebrates its World Cup, then every continent is involved. Europe and South America have always been regarded as the traditional bedrocks of the sport, but in the latter part of this century Africa, Asia, Australasia and

even the North Americas have been forced to capitulate to the powerful force that drives football on.

One of the great attractions of football is that every so often the Davids do beat the Goliaths. Yet even when the giant is winning there is still the beauty of the game to behold, the physical confrontations, and the disputes surrounding decisions that go on long after the final whistles have been blown.

For players and spectators alike, football is built into the structure of our lives. It can just as easily induce ecstasy as despair and it can take us through all of the emotions known to mankind. Never

will I forget watching Burnley beat Leyton Orient on the final day of the season in 1987. The Lancashire club had to win to ensure its survival in the Football League. At the end of what had been a nerve-wracking 90 minutes for the Burnley fans, I sat in the stand and watched men and women crying. They were not tears of joy, just because Burnley had survived, they were tears of relief -- the tension-packed last 15 minutes with Burnley hanging on at 2-1 proved just too much. Long after the teams had left the field, most of the fans were still anchored to their seats -- expressionless faces reflecting bodies that were physically and emotionally drained. But football can do that; it can be vindictive and even cruel, but for most of the time it brings an excitement to our lives that those who don't follow the game find difficult to comprehend.

Of course, you can enjoy football for its own sake if you are neutral, but to experience the whole range of emotions you need to be committed, either as a participant or supporter. But as we move deeper into the age of space, computers and television even the committed must prepare for a change. Television has altered our League structure already, and it hasn't finished in its demands just yet. The moguls who govern our viewing have to compete for soccer rights, and the massive sums involved have elevated the game way beyond its foundations when it was considered the game of the working classes.

Mass media coverage, sponsorship, new stadia, corporate boxes at matches, big clubs becoming Plcs, it has all taken football into a finance world that none of us could have dreamed about only a decade ago. Top players' salaries have rocketed them into the superstar bracket, and it is this intervention of the big money that has probably brought the biggest single change to the game in my lifetime. But as football fills its coffers, it should never forget its roots, or the many millions who have put it where it is today. It should remember that the human element, both on and off the field, is still the key ingredient to the successful product. Football should make certain that it never prices the fan out of the football ground. If it does it will soon discover that television will find another bedmate very readily. Every community that boasts a football club should be aware of its responsibilities towards the club, and at the same time every professional club should never lose sight of its own responsibility to the community it serves.

There's nothing wrong with the game itself. Administrators may tinker with it over the years, but it has a quality that will see it through. We should treasure it. It is part of our heritage … and our future.

JIMMY ARMFIELD, *BBC commentator, former Blackpool & England manager.*

THE ORIGINS OF FOOTBALL

A global game

Trying to pinpoint the exact starting point for what is now the world's most popular sport is like trying to find a needle in a haystack. England may have been the home of football, but the first instances of foot meeting ball may well have taken place thousands of miles away; and as time moved on, the formative game was being adopted and invented in various guises all across the globe. Nobody took football to the world; the world discovered it in dozens of locations over thousands of years.

The China link

Traditionalists often talk of the early game being played out with hollow pigs' bladders which could burst at any moment. Certainly there is some truth in this assumption – today, we believe the earliest incarnation of football to have been played with animal skins in ancient China around 2500 BC. The 'ball' was kicked between poles some thirty feet high, and may have served a military purpose; soldiers were trained using the rough-and-tumble of gameplay and matches were held to mark important dates in the calendar.

▲ *England was only one of many countries that played an early version of football. This anonymous painting, entitled* The Game of Football, *in the Stanza Gualdrada, is kept in the Palazzo Vecchio in Florence.*

A game of peace

By AD 50, the Chinese had named the game 'tsu chu' and early records compare the round ball and square goal to

▼ *Inflating the bladder of an early Italian football (known as a 'Pallone'). This illustration dates from pre-1700.*

Yin and Yang, the ancient symbols of harmony – an interesting contrast to the distinctly unharmonious scenes that followed as the game developed. Historians have also suggested that ancient Egyptian fertility rites may have been linked, in some way, to a form of football; however a more plausible stage of development was a Mexican game in AD 600 which involved forcing a ball through a hole in the wall of a specially designed court. Certainly, the Mexicans came up with the first synthetic footballs.

> **The basic equipment worn by players has changed radically in design over the decades but remains essentially that as laid down by Law IV of the Laws of the Game. It states: "the basic compulsory equipment of a player shall consist of a jersey or shirt, shorts, stockings, shinguards and footwear."**

Gang warfare

By the time the game was developing in England, it had taken a strangely comic – and occasionally tragic – turn for the worse. The earliest stories of football, date from around AD 1100 and involve a crude chasing of a ball through city streets by gangs of youngsters egged on by their parents. There was little organization either in terms of fixtures or rules, yet the foundations for the development of the game in its host country had been laid.

Nineteenth-Century Inventions:

1874	Shin-guards invented by Samuel Widdowson – he was first to wear them, while playing for Nottingham Forest.
1875	Crossbars installed.
1878	First floodlit match played in Sheffield.
1878	Whistle used for first time by umpire of match between Nottingham Forest and Sheffield Norfolk.
1890	Goal nets invented and patented by Liverpool-based Mr Brodie.
1890	Old Etonians first to use goal nets.

▼ *An illustration of street football in medieval England. Games such as this were unorganized and often ended in gang violence.*

Breaking the rules

Throughout the next 700 years or so, football became a source of inspiration for the masses and of great consternation to the authorities. Edward II was the first monarch to call for curbs on the 'uproar' the game caused – and it seems he may well have had a point. What began as a game of chasing soon developed into near warfare, with scores of players forming sides and causing havoc in urban areas as they rampaged through pitches hundreds of yards long. There are reports of serious injuries and even deaths, as well as complaints from more sedate residents alarmed by the disruption football caused.

FA CUP HOOLIGANISM

In 1889 the semi-final replay between Sheffield United and Liverpool was abandoned at half time following a series of pitch invasions. The game had been halted so many times that it took 90 minutes to complete the first half, after which the referee called proceedings to a halt.

Country troubles

In rural areas the problem was exacerbated by the vast amounts of space afforded to the game. Whole villages would come out to chase the makeshift ball, and the absence of rules meant kicking, punching and crushing were all acceptable. The traditional Shrove Tuesday clashes were particularly troublesome. Successions of English rulers and lawmakers issued edicts attempting to crack down on the game, but it proved near impossible to stop. At the same time, the American Indians had developed a beach version of the game – in which players would disguise themselves in masks to evade blame for dangerous challenges – and the Inuits had begun playing on ice, shooting balls stuffed with grass through goals placed miles apart. Football was taking off in many different ways all over the world.

The most players sent off in one match is five: three Plymouth players and two from Chesterfield were ordered off following a mass last-minute brawl in their Second Division fixture at Saltergate, 22 February 1997.

Saved by the schools

Somewhat ironically, it was the public schools who gave the whole affair some order. Oxford and Cambridge had accepted football as a competitive sport as early as the seventeenth century, and Eton, Harrow, Shrewsbury and Rugby quickly followed suit. The implementation of rules worked both ways: with Victorian values gradually disappearing, the schools saw the sport as a vital way to instil discipline, while also disassociating the young gentlemen who played it from the lower classes and their street games. Many still considered football too 'vulgar' a game for the upper classes, but by the 1800s it was common practice in public school life. As a result, the people's game began to take shape in the last bastions of the aristocracy.

▶ *Harrow School football team, photographed in 1867.*

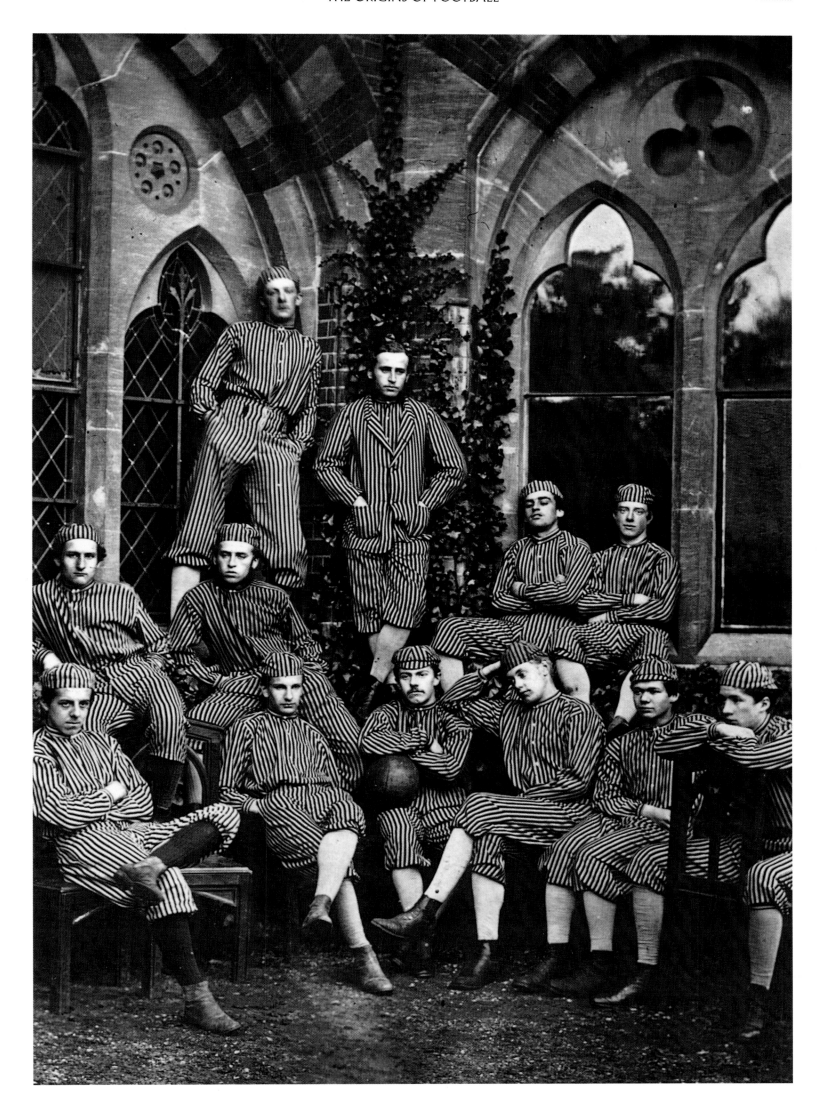

HOW FOOTBALL IN ENGLAND BEGAN

Other schools required three defenders to be between the attacking player and the goal for him to be onside, a rule enforced by the Football Association until as late as 1925. Today, only one defender is required, thus encouraging attackers to go one-on-one with opponents.

Reading the Riot Act

The development of the game, from a crude kick-around involving 200 or more players to an organized team sport of 11-a-side, is shrouded in mystery and confusion. What is clear is that by the 1830s, the previously popular mass public matches – which often resulted in injury and occasionally death – were well on their way to being stamped out by the conservative Victorian authorities. It was also the time that football was finding an accepted home in the public schools. Not that the schools themselves were strangers to the odd outbreak of violence: Winchester had to call in the Army to quell one particularly dangerous riot in 1818, and many other schools required the Riot Act to be read to pupils at one time or another.

A bar to progress

The random nature of football's rules at this time was not a problem for individual schools, but when boys left for the outside world and took their footballing traditions with them, it became near impossible to agree on a single set of regulations with team-mates. In addition, it became very difficult for inter-school matches to be played when the two sides involved may have had wildly different versions of the rules. Particularly contentious was the offside trap. Many schools did away with it entirely, allowing the opposition simply to plant 'goal-hangers' around the goalkeeper to tap the ball in when it came their way.

▲◄ *This illustration of boys playing football dates from 1868 – five years after the Cambridge Rules were accepted.*

▲ *Rugby football as played at Rugby School in the early nineteenth century.*

MILESTONES OF THE NINETEENTH CENTURY

1862	School master Mr Thring draws up Cambridge Rules.
1863	Football Association launch and produce first official rules on 1 December.
1865	Tape stretched between goal posts eight feet high.
1871	Goalkeepers mentioned in rules for first time.
1871	FA Cup launched.
1872	Size of ball regulated.
1872	Corner kicks introduced.
1883	Two-handed throw-in introduced.
1888	Football League comes into existence.
1891	Referees and Linesmen replace umpires.
1891	Penalty kicks awarded.
1891	Goal nets made compulsory.

different colour shirts was only established in the 1840s – and many matches were played in top hats before the widespread introduction of 'caps' (still awarded today for international matches).

▶ *It was not uncommon for early school football matches to result in serious foul play.*

Serious foul play

The early public school matches were often marked by the sort of foul play that would give many a modern referee nightmares. It was considered fair play to trip an opponent while they had the ball and whole groups of players would huddle down to 'scrummage' for the ball when it ended up in no man's land. It was often difficult to tell the players apart – the requirement that the two teams wear

MILESTONES UP TO 1939

1912	Goalkeepers stopped from handling outside the area.
1913	Ten-yard rule at free-kicks.
1914	Ten-yard rule at corners.
1924	Goals allowed straight from corners.
1925	Offside changed to require two defenders between attacker and goalkeeper.
1938	Laws re-written.
1939	Numbers on shirts made compulsory.

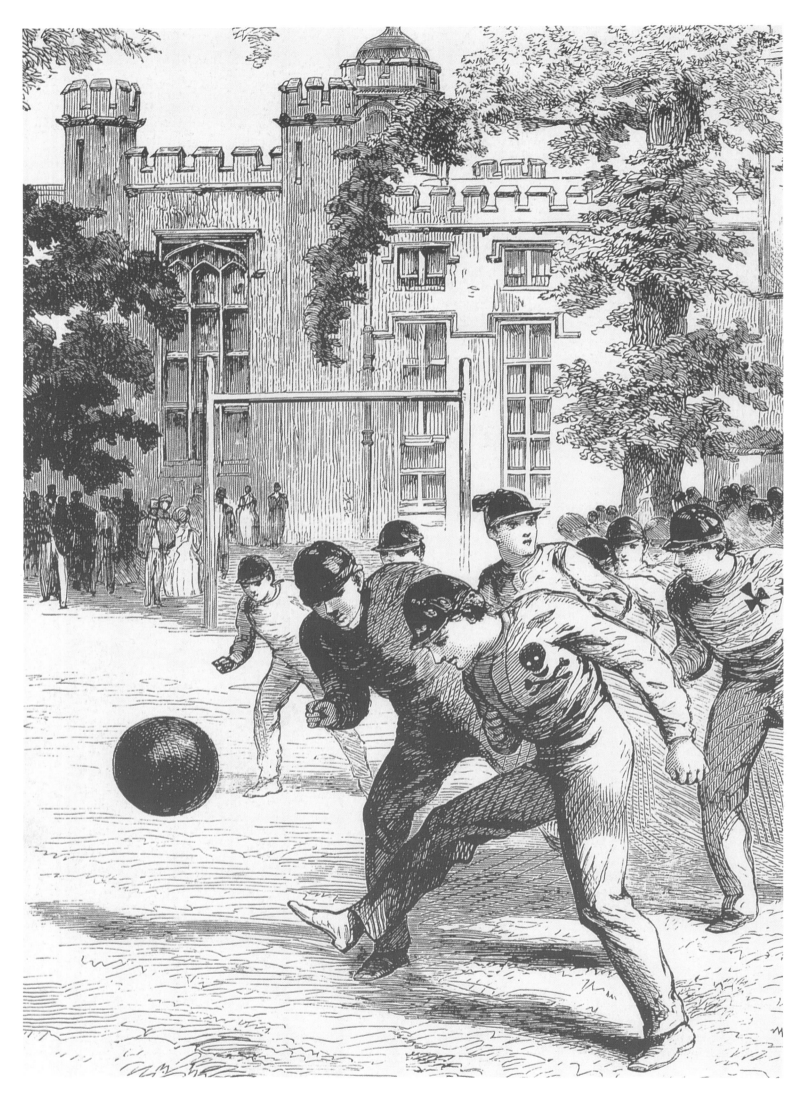

Rugby breaks away

The handling debate also took several decades to be decided. The common belief is that a player named William Webb Ellis first picked up and ran with the ball during a Rugby School game in 1923, thus first giving rise to the concept of the game of rugby. This story is unsubstantiated, but what is known is that many schools allowed the playing of a football-rugby hybrid into the 1860s. When the Football Association finally decided to keep the amount of handling to a bare minimum, the practice still continued in several locations, including Blackheath, which later formed the first rugby club. Thus football regulation as a whole remained something of a murky issue for many a year.

Order is established

The first stab at a definitive set of rules is believed to have been initiated in 1848 by a pair of enthusiastic Cambridge house masters. However, persuading rival schools to drop many of their own long-running traditions and adopt uniform rules proved problematic. Two further attempts in the 1850s also met with little success.

It was not until 1863 that the celebrated 'Cambridge Rules' were drawn up and accepted by the major schools (bar Blackheath). At last, eager pupils who had enjoyed the game at school could go out and form their own teams with unanimous regulations in mind. Just days after the rules were laid down, it was decided to set up a Football Association to administer the game; in those few days the whole of the modern-day game was made possible.

FA CUP HOOLIGANISM

The fifth-round tie between Cup holders Aston Villa and Preston North End in 1888 was abandoned when spectators invaded the pitch in the second half. Preston were 3-1 up at the time and the result was later allowed to stand. Preston went on to lose 2-1 to West Bromwich Albion in the final.

IN JANUARY 1963, MANSFIELD TOWN HAD THE MOST PLAYERS BOOKED IN ONE GAME – TEN NAMES WERE TAKEN IN THE FA CUP THIRD-ROUND MATCH AT CRYSTAL PALACE.

▲ *A scrum at Winchester College. Boys playing rugby football in 1886.*

◄ *Football being played at Rugby School; the illustration is from* The Boy's Own Annual *of 1863.*

THE CAMBRIDGE RULES

▲ *An early Oxford v Cambridge match at the beginning of the twentieth century.*

The need to unify

The failure of Cambridge's attempt to formulate a clear set of rules in 1848, meant that matches between different schools and colleges were near impossible. Somebody had to take a lead, so, in 1862, Cambridge tried again. This time, their attempts were more widely accepted and, although they were never made law, formed the basis of the first Football Association set of rules in 1863. Today, however, there is no surviving copy of the Cambridge Rules and historians can only make rough guesses at what those first regulations allowed and forbade.

Pitch requirements

Certainly the pitch itself would have been very different to those played on by today's footballers. Goal posts were joined together only by a crossbar made of string and there was no definitive size for either the field of play or the equipment used. If a player 'touched' the ball down behind his opponent's goal he was awarded a free-kick – a strange parody of what was to become American football.

West Bromwich Albion's Scottish international winger Willie Johnston has the dubious distinction of being sent off more times in his career than any other footballer in history. He got his marching orders 21 times – seven with Rangers, six with WBA, four with Vancouver Whitecaps, three with Hearts and one for Scotland.

much discussion they decided to abolish it. The official FA rules later backed up this decision, leading to a breakaway group forming what was to become rugby union. One Cambridge chancellor later famously commented: 'Football is a gentleman's game played by ruffians, and rugby is a ruffian's game played by gentlemen.'

Offside or onside?

The offside problem was cleared up by the three-players-to-a-goal rule pioneered by Cambridge, while handling was deemed legal in small amounts. Throw-ins could be taken one-handed, allowing the ball to be propelled for long distances across the pitch. However the most controversial point, and one which led to splits among all the rule-making bodies of the 1850s and 60s, was hacking. This practice of scything down players from behind caused deep divisions among the Cambridge committee and after

To hack or not?

Those in favour of hacking saw it as a manly practice necessary to keep football quintessentially English; its opponents thought it barbaric. It would be difficult to imagine the game today, however, were such blatant fouls considered the norm. Certainly, the skills of some of the all-time greats would never have been nurtured without protection from crude and dangerous challenges.

▼ *The third FA Cup, as it looked in 1973. This particular cup was 'retired' in 1992, but the current cup is an exact replica of it.*

THERE HAVE BEEN FOUR TROPHIES SINCE THE FA CUP WAS LAUNCHED IN 1871. THE FIRST WAS SNATCHED FROM A SHOP WINDOW IN BIRMINGHAM WHERE IT WAS ON DISPLAY FOLLOWING ASTON VILLA'S 1-0 WIN OVER NEIGHBOURS WEST BROMWICH ALBION. THE SECOND WAS PRESENTED TO LORD KINNAIRD WHEN HE CELEBRATED 21 YEARS AS PRESIDENT OF THE FA IN 1911. THE THIRD CUP WAS "RETIRED" IN 1992 AFTER 80 YEARS' SERVICE – THE FA CLAIMED IT WAS "FALLING APART" – AND THE FOURTH TROPHY IS A REPLICA OF THE ONE IT REPLACED.

THE CLUBS ARE FORMED

The ancient origins

Football today is dominated by big business, by chairmen who often boast larger personalities than those of their players, and by the constant need to see a return on investment. So when delving into the origins of many of today's biggest clubs, it is frequently intriguing to find their formations dominated not by financial concerns but by the principles of socialism, Christianity and togetherness.

NEAR DOUBLES – RUNNERS-UP IN BOTH LEAGUE AND FA CUP

1928 ▶ Huddersfield Town
1932 ▶ Arsenal
1939 ▶ Wolverhampton Wanderers
1962 ▶ Burnley
1965 ▶ Leeds United
1970 ▶ Leeds United
1986 ▶ Everton
1989 ▶ Liverpool
1995 ▶ Manchester United

From pulpit to pitch

In recent years, the Church has frequently criticized football for staging Sunday fixtures and for the unsportsmanlike behaviour of many of its participants, yet it was the Church which launched so many of the clubs on their way to prosperity. Past religious leaders saw football as an important way of filling the additional leisure time so many workers found at their disposal – considering it better for them to be charging around a pitch than being idle or indulging in crime.

Everton: the early years

Everton is a prime example of these principles. The team was formed when an enthusiastic group of Merseyside churchgoers asked their Reverend if they could set up a football team. He agreed, and the new side played local matches under the name St Domingo's. Their first year was such a success that they decided to widen their catchment area and attract even better players. After changing its name to Everton, the club joined the local Football Association; joining the Football League in 1888. The Methodists who started the original St Domingo's were no longer in the side, but their principles remained in the new outfit.

Liverpool are born

Ironically, Everton also spawned their great city rivals, Liverpool. After an internal row, Everton chairman John Houlding walked out of the club and decided to form his own side. Everton switched grounds to Goodison Park, and the new 'Liverpool' team took over their Anfield site just a few hundred yards away. Many refused to believe that one city could support two big sides, but they were proved dramatically wrong. Between them, the two teams have 27 League titles, although Everton have generally existed in the shadow of the newer team since Liverpool entered the League in 1893.

MANAGER OF THE YEAR – MULTIPLE WINNERS

6 ▶ Bob Paisley (Liverpool 1976, 1977, 1979, 1980, 1982 & 1983)
4 ▶ Kenny Dalglish (Liverpool 1986, 1988 & 1990; Blackburn 1995)
4 ▶ Alex Ferguson (Manchester United 1993, 1994, 1996 & 1997)
3 ▶ Don Revie (Leeds, 1969, 1970 & 1972)
2 ▶ Jock Stein (Celtic 1966 & 1967)
2 ▶ Ron Saunders (Aston Villa 1975 & 1981)
2 ▶ Howard Kendall (Everton 1985 & 1987)
2 ▶ George Graham (Arsenal 1989 & 1991)

▶ *Since Liverpool began, formed after an internal row at Everton, they have become one of the country's top teams. One of Liverpool's star players of the 90s is Robbie Fowler.*

A church affair

As many as a quarter of all major nineteenth-century football clubs were started in the churches. These include Southampton, Wolves, Blackpool, Bolton and Fulham (whose 'aristocrats' tag stems from their formation in West Kensington in 1880). Bolton, however, split from their church founders when the local Reverend demanded attendance at Sunday services in return for playing on a Saturday.

Cricket helps soccer

Many clubs also grew from rugby and cricket organizations. Sporting sides saw football as a useful way of filling the idle winter months, as well as earning extra money through the use of their grounds. When one group of keen north-east cricketers decided to form a supplementary football side in 1881, they can scarcely have guessed the implications. The Newcastle-based Stanley FC played their first match against Elswick Leather Works Second XI, and later went on to amalgamate with neighbours Rosewood. This partnership went on to become Newcastle United, one of the most successful and fashionable clubs in the game today. Tottenham Hotspur followed a similar path, forming in 1882 from members of

▼ *The Royal Arsenal Football Club as it looked in the 1888–89 season.*

Hotspur Cricket Club – named after the Harry Hotspur character of William Shakespeare's plays. The early Spurs drew many of their players from the local YMCA.

▲ *FA Cup winners: the Preston North End Football Club of the 1888–89 season.*

The following players all scored hat-tricks in three successive matches

FRANK OSBORNE, Tottenham, 1925

▼

TOM JENNINGS, Leeds, 1926

▼

ALF LYTHGOE, Stockport, 1934

▼

GILBERT ALSOP, Walsall, 1939

▼

JACK BALMER, Liverpool, 1946

Nothing stirs up the passions more than a full-blooded local derby. This table shows who rules in the major derby matches:

Arsenal v Tottenham	Played 120	Arsenal 48	Tottenham 44	draws 28
Everton v Liverpool	Played 156	Liverpool 56	Everton 52	draws 48
Manchester City v Manchester Utd	Played 124	United 48	City 32	draws 44
Middlesbrough v Newcastle	Played 90	Newcastle 35	Middlesbrough 31	draws 24
Newcastle v Sunderland	Played 118	Newcastle 43	Sunderland 39	draws 36

Factory teams

Derby County, Sheffield Wednesday and Preston were also formed from cricket sides, and Sheffield United originated as a recreational side for Yorkshire cricketers. Alongside these, there were the works teams. Royal Arsenal – later to drop the 'Royal' tag – began in 1886 when two Nottingham Forest players moved south to work for the Woolwich Arsenal munitions factory in south-east London. Workers there had previously been denied permission to use the works' cricket pitch for footballing purposes, but the new pair of players got together a squad of eager footballers who paid two-and-a-half pence each to buy a ball. The cricket club faded into obscurity, and seven years later Arsenal were in the Football League.

United on the rails

Manchester United began life in 1878 as Newton Heath, a side formed by workers from the Lancashire and Yorkshire Railway Company. The original club went bankrupt in 1902, but today's team earn more in merchandise and prestige than any other club in the world. West Ham, meanwhile, earned their 'Irons' nickname from an early incarnation as Thames Ironworks FC, formed from the workers of a huge iron factory on Victoria Dock Road. The club progressed quickly through the Southern League, and might have settled in their original East Ham home had local residents there not objected to football being played on their doorsteps.

NEAR DOUBLES – LEAGUE RUNNERS-UP AND FA CUP WINNERS

1904 ▶ Manchester City
1913 ▶ Aston Villa
1948 ▶ Manchester United
1954 ▶ West Bromwich Albion
1960 ▶ Wolverhampton Wanderers
1972 ▶ Leeds United
1974 ▶ Liverpool
1989 ▶ Liverpool

▼*Scoring a goal – an illustration from* The Boys Own Paper *in 1896.*

▲ *The Wolverhampton Wanderers team who beat Newcastle United in the FA Cup Final, 25 April 1908.*

Official blessings

Nineteenth-century employers began to view football as an important way of relieving workplace tension and of increasing morale. Thames Ironworks owner Arnold F. Hills spoke of the game as part of 'the co-operation between workers and management', and others were quick to follow his example. Coventry City, for example, began life as a cycle factory team, while Stoke City were started up by railwaymen and teachers in 1863.

Down the pub

Many of the early clubs relied on local pubs to meet, advertise for players and, on occasion, change before matches, and the role pubs played in the growth of the game has often been overlooked. Blackburn were formed directly from a pub team, while many others began as groups of neighbourhood friends who gathered together in local hostelries and eventually decided to cement their love of football by beginning a side. With an element of luck, some financial backing and success on the field, the transition from pub side to League side was nowhere near as impossible as it would seem today.

Still going strong

Many modern supporters remain unaware of the influence their team's origins exert on their own allegiances and habits. Many families still support the same teams their ancestors first adopted, while chants and nicknames from the nineteenth century are still in evidence today. Furthermore, the very basis of support remains drawn along the same lines as of a century ago, particularly in cities where there is more than one team. Liverpool and Everton originally divided the city between Protestant and Catholic, although that is less relevant today. Spurs' Jewish connections are still strong and Manchester United, who have consistently overshadowed their neighbours City on the pitch, remain significantly less popular in Manchester itself, where City are seen as the traditional side. Old habits, whether we are aware of them or not, die hard.

THE FORGOTTEN CLUBS

Where are they now?

For every success story, there is a club time has forgotten. Over the 110 years of the Football League, dozens of sides have simply disappeared: some were closed down early on due to lack of success or spectator interest, some were amalgamated into other teams and others still were never heard of again for a variety of reasons.

Darwen go down

Darwen were among the earliest victims of this phenomenon. The Lancashire-based club were a top-flight side from 1891 to 1899, although throughout their history they were regularly to be found at the wrong end of the table as well. In 1879 they took Old Etonians to two replays in the quarter-finals of the Cup, but in the League they always struggled, losing by a record 12-0 to West Brom in 1892 and 11-1 to Arsenal shortly afterwards. Their end was a merciful one.

A recipe for disaster

Several notable sides followed Darwen's example in the latter part of the twentieth century, among them the constantly-troubled Workington, who at one point had

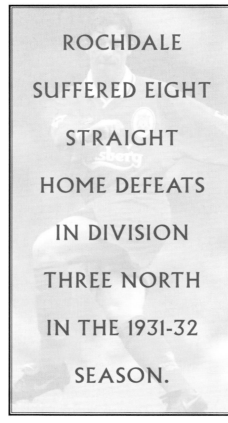

ROCHDALE SUFFERED EIGHT STRAIGHT HOME DEFEATS IN DIVISION THREE NORTH IN THE 1931-32 SEASON.

more directors than full-time players. They dropped out in 1977, to be replaced by Wimbledon. New Brighton left in 1951, and Bradford Park Avenue disappeared in 1970. They had been generally more successful than rivals City, but were eventually forced to share their ground when they hit hard times. The club reformed in 1988 and still dream of regaining their League status.

Hope springs eternal

Southport might do just that soon. The Seasiders were founder members of the Third Division, but gave up on the League in 1978 to join the Northern Premier League. Today they are hovering around the top of the Vauxhall Conference, the top flight of non-League football. Barrow, too, have regrouped since their eleventh application for re-election to the League was refused in 1972 and Aldershot are currently in the Isthmian League, after folding in 1992. The club were almost saved at the last minute by an investment of £200,000 from 19-year-old whizz-kid Spencer Trethewy, but could not afford to go on. Maidstone left in the same year, and have never recovered. They had been in the League for just three years.

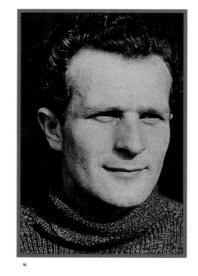

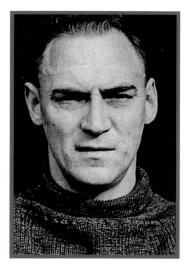

'Who are they?'

With promotion and relegation between the Conference and the Third Division much more prevalent in the 1990s, more new teams will continue to enter the League, and those at the bottom face a real struggle for survival. They will be hoping to avoid the fate of Accrington Stanley, the most famous League drop-outs, who departed in 1962. They were notoriously immortalized in a 1980s advert for milk, in which a young boy told his friend he should drink more milk or he would end up playing for Accrington Stanley. 'Who are they?' asked the boy. 'Exactly,' replied his friend.

Darwen had the worst defensive record ever when they let in 141 goals in 34 Division Two matches during the 1898–99 season.

▼*Barrow Football Club, 19 October 1947. Bottom left l-r: W. Phillipson, A. McIntosh, L. Hall, W. Lee; top right l-r: G. Forbes, E. O'Donnell, G. Summerbee, J. Henderson; bottom right l-r: E. Miller, A. Burnett, J. Dendal, W. Leach. Today, Barrow are hoping to be re-elected to the League.*

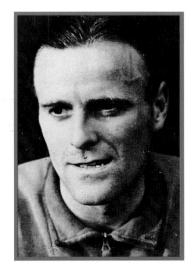

THE 1860S: THE DECADE OF INVENTION

Getting it together

It was apparent that football needed a focus and some sense of organization to keep it moving. As a result, on 26 October 1863, representatives and captains of 15 clubs gathered at the Freemasons' Tavern in Great Queen Street, London, to form what would become England's most important sporting body – the Football Association. Today, the area where they met is the heart of the country's legal profession, a hive of lawyers' offices and after-work bars. Back then, it seemed the natural focal point for such a historic moment in the game's development.

Southern bias

The clubs present at that 1863 meeting were drawn from the Home Counties and the public schools – neither of which are seen today as the traditional strongholds of the game – Manchester, Liverpool, Sheffield, Nottingham and Birmingham were represented. Sheffield later wrote to the FA applying for membership; they did not even get a reply. It was not until the turn of the century that the industrial north was on an even footballing keel with the prosperous south.

Establishing order

The clubs wanted a uniform set of rules to clarify how football was to be played. It took another five meetings to decide on just 14 regulations, and even then the subject was one of frenzied debate and frequent argument. The majority of those present were exponents of the 'kicking' game rather than the 'handling' game, and by the time they had decided on a definitive code, Blackheath – leaders of the handlers – had stormed out. Later they formed the Rugby Football Union.

The end of hacking

The newspapers by and large ignored those formative meetings, and the clubs' membership fee of a guinea a year was cheap even by 1860s standards. Yet the decisions they made were crucial, particularly the outlawing of 'hacking', a practice whereby a player running with the ball could be legally tripped at the ankles by an opponent. The rugby pioneers saw this as an integral part of football,

▼*An illustration from 1892 showing a player running with a ball – according to legend a player running with the ball led to rugby evolving from football.*

although it was later banned from their own game, while the football clubs saw it as ungentlemanly and a barrier to genuine skill. There was also significant opposition to the handling of the ball, although the clubs eventually voted overwhelmingly in favour of allowing it to be caught and run with on the volley or half-volley.

TWENTIETH-CENTURY INVENTIONS

1933	**FA Cup finalists Everton and Manchester City wear numbers 1-22 on shirts.**
1951	**White ball first used.**
1956	**Floodlights become a regular fixture after being used for League match between Portsmouth and Newcastle, 22 February.**
1958	**Everton install under-soil heating at Goodison Park.**
1979	**Red and yellow cards introduced; scrapped in 1981.**
1981	**QPR install first artificial pitch at their Loftus Road ground.**
1987	**Red and yellow cards return.**
1993	**Premier League clubs introduce squad numbering system.**

▲ *First view of the new artificial pitch installed at Loftus Road ground. Admiring Queen's Park Rangers's new turf are* (l-r): *Peter Borota (Chelsea's goalkeeper), Barry Davis (director of Omnisport International, who laid the turf), Terry Venables (Q.P.R.'s manager) and Mick Leach (Chelsea's Youth Team coach).*

▼ *Yellow Card – Bradford City's goalkeeper, Gary Walsh, being booked in 1998, 11 years after the red and yellow card system was reintroduced.*

11-a-side

Even after the meeting, there was still no uniform rule dictating the number of players on each team, although Cambridge later pioneered the 11-a-side rule. By the end of the decade, the offside rule, goal kicks and corner kicks were all adopted and 50 clubs had joined the FA. Sheffield formed its own regional association in 1866, and was later affiliated to the national body. Those initial pioneers had truly set the ball rolling, although football was still largely unrecognizable from the game we enjoy today. A challenge match between Sheffield and London three years after the FA began was credited at the time with being the first 'disciplined' and 'enjoyable' fixture; Nottingham Forest and Notts County's derby match in that same year drew similar plaudits, despite finishing goaless.

> THE 26 GOALS PRESTON NORTH END SMASHED PAST HYDE WITHOUT REPLY, IN THE FA CUP FIRST ROUND ON 15 OCTOBER 1887, REMAINS THE BEST SCORING PERFORMANCE IN A COMPETITIVE FIXTURE.

▲ *Michael Owen, number 11, demonstrates the squad numbering system that was re-introduced for Premier League clubs in 1993.*

Saturday is freed

Most crucially, the 1860s saw changes to the working week all over the British Isles. Led by concerned liberal crusaders, industrialists freed up the weekend for recreational pursuits; by the 1870s workers all over the country would down tools at midday on a Saturday and use the free period in the afternoon to relax, drink or play sport. Thus the traditional Saturday afternoon football fixture, that remains in place to this day, was born.

Bridging the divide

At the same time, important social changes were taking place to make the development of football easier than during the previous century. The working classes became increasingly empowered and the gulf between the public schools and the general public was slowly closing. Eventually, the schools who had first adopted football were to abandon it for rugby, yet the masses preferred 'the beautiful game' for its simplicity and the ease with which it could be played: all that was required was a ball, a goal and a handful of willing participants.

> **Arthur Rowley is the top scorer in League history. He rattled in 434 goals in 619 League games between 1946 and 1965 – four for West Bromwich Albion, 27 for Fulham, 251 for Leicester City and 152 for Shrewsbury. No-one else has passed the 400-goal mark.**

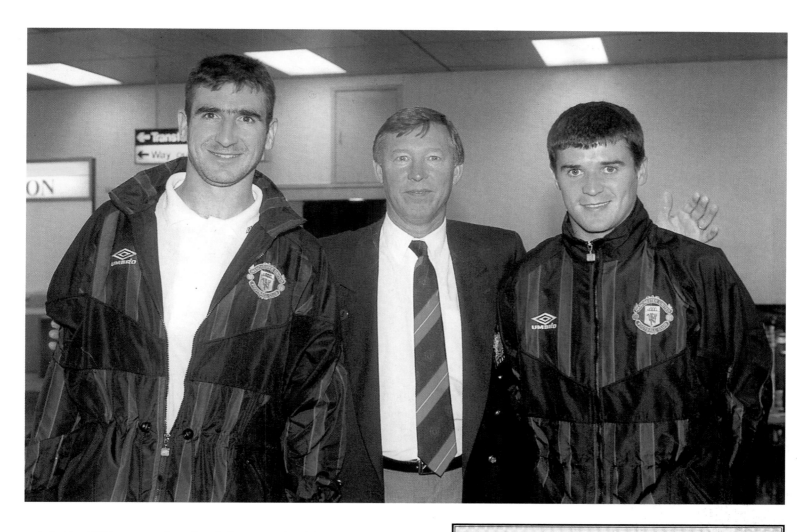

▲ *In the 1860s teams chose local players; today it is common to employ foreign players, such as Eric Cantona (photographed when he was with Manchester United).*

The birth of 'soccer'

It is also worth noting that during this period, the game also gained its own distinctive name. Its invention is credited to Charles Wreford-Brown, a member of the rebel Blackheath club, who when asked whether he was going to play 'rugger' answered that he would prefer to play 'soccer' instead. This play on the phrase 'association football' remains in place 130 years on, although it is more widely used today in emerging sporting nations. In England, the word will always take second place to the more simple – and self-explanatory – 'football'.

FIRST WORLD WAR FOOTBALL RESTRICTIONS

No midweek matches were allowed to avoid interrupting munitions manufacture.

Games were reduced to 80 minutes.

All players were expected to take up work for the benefit of the country.

The presentation of cups and medals was banned.

In 1915 the FA ruled no wages should be paid to footballers.

In 1917 the FA decreed cups and medals could be awarded – but solely in matches for War Funds and charity and as long as they were not paid for from gate receipts.

THE FA THROUGHOUT HISTORY

The first success story

The success of football in England has been down to many factors – the skill of its players, the fervour of the public and the ability of its coaches. But it is all too easy to overlook the contribution made by the ultimate controlling body of the game, the Football Association.

THE FIRST HAT-TRICKS WERE SCORED IN THE FIRST ROUND OF THE FA CUP IN 1874: KINGSFORD, WHO GOT FIVE GOALS, AND WOOLASTON (FOUR) WERE THE HEROES IN WANDERERS' 16-0 TRIUMPH OVER FARNINGHAM; WHILE OXFORD UNIVERSITY'S PARRY SCORED THREE GOALS IN HIS TEAM'S 6-0 WIN OVER BRONDESBURY.

Over the years, the FA have kept a steady head through the incredible changes the game has seen. Their first and most important challenge was to administer successfully the onset of professionalism – appeasing both those who wanted to see players rewarded fairly for their efforts and those who did not want to see the original amateur spirit of the game betrayed. The FA even went so far as withdrawing from Fifa in protest at their support for professionalism, but they could not resist the tide of progress.

▶ *An FA press officer sporting his distinctive uniform, including the England three lions crest.*

Resisting commercialism

The traditional stance was repeated in the late 1980s, when a group of top-flight chairmen proposed wide-ranging changes to the distribution of funds and revenue. Although, in an important change with the past, the FA allowed home sides to keep all gate receipts, they remained loyal to the game's non profit-making principles. Perhaps the FA's most controversial decision was the introduction of Sunday football at both professional and amateur level during the early 1980s.

The hardest job

Today, the FA are still working hard to shed their image as 'men in suits'. Their main role is in administering the England team and acting as a disciplinary body for players, officials and clubs, unfortunately a series of high profile charges against big-name players has to done little to help them. The Association's future was secured by the creation of the FA Premiership in 1992 – there had long been talk of complete breakaways by leading clubs,

but by keeping a lid on the rebels' activities they were able to stamp their authority and influence on proceedings.

A century of growth

And so, from the clutch of clubs who formed the first Football Association in 1863 has grown an organization covering over two million players (at all levels) and over 40,000 members. Such a rate of growth has made the FA one of the most high-profile governing bodies in the world – and now almost every country where football is played has its own equivalent.

▼ *The England team. Today the FA spends much of its time administering England's footballing heroes and acting in a disciplinary role.*

LEAGUE GIANT-KILLERS

In 1933 Walsall (Division Three North) beat League Champions Arsenal 2-0.

In 1955 York City (Division Three North) beat Tottenham 2-1.

In 1959 Norwich (Division Three) beat Manchester United 3-0.

THE 1870S: INTRODUCING THE CUP

Alcock the innovator

The public schools' final impact on football was to inspire its greatest competition. Charles Alcock, a notable player, journalist and administrator, proposed the first ever FA Cup after noting the success of inter-house challenges during his own Harrow schooldays. In July 1871, in the offices of *The Sportsman* newspaper, Alcock and five FA colleagues decided a knockout Cup would provide the excitement and edge so far lacking in the game. They were to be proved right.

Can't pay, don't play

Only 15 of the 50 FA members approached to enter the first tournament actually accepted. Of those, three clubs were unable to fulfil a fixture and Queen's Park – the great Scottish side – were not required to play until the semi-final stage due to the huge cost of travelling south from Glasgow. They drew their semi-final game with The Wanderers and could not afford the cost of a replay in London. Their exploits in the competition not only led to the setting up of a Scottish FA Cup but also inspired the formation of dozens of new clubs north of the border.

Betts wins the Cup

The Wanderers were therefore left to face The Royal Engineers in the final at London's Kennington Oval. Only 2,000 spectators turned up to see that historic first match – the county cup competitions were at first more popular than the national event – but they witnessed an exciting and evenly-matched game. It was finally settled by a Matthew Betts goal for The Wanderers, set up by the interestingly-named Reverend R.W.S. Vidal. Fittingly, it was Charles Alcock who, as captain, accepted the first ever trophy on behalf of his team.

▲ *C. W. Alcock, the founder of the FA Cup.*

The first hat-trick

The Wanderers dominated the Cup for the rest of the decade, and won it three times in a row from 1876 to 1878. FA rules decreed that they had therefore won the trophy

Blackpool's Stan Mortensen is the only player to score an FA Cup Final hat-trick. He found the back of the net three times as his side overcame Bolton 4-3 in 1953. Yet the match is remembered as the "Matthews Final" because of Stanley Matthews' sensational display on the wing.

▶ *Old Etonians beating Blackburn Rovers in the final tie of the Challenge Cup contests at Kennington Oval, London, in 1882.*

outright, but Alcock handed it back and asked that no club should ever be able to keep it. Royal Engineers, Oxford University and Old Etonians provided the only other 1870s winners, while Nottingham Forest became the first club from the north of England to enter in 1878-79, reaching the semi-final.

FREDERICK AND HUBERT HERON WERE THE FIRST BROTHERS TO PLAY TOGETHER FOR ENGLAND WHEN THEY APPEARED IN THE 3-0 DEFEAT AT THE HANDS OF SCOTLAND ON 4 MARCH 1876. THE PAIR ALSO APPEARED FOR THE WANDERERS IN THEIR 3-0 FA CUP FINAL REPLAY VICTORY OVER OLD ETONIANS IN THE SAME YEAR.

A crucial decade

There were further innovations during the decade: 1878 saw the first ever floodlit match between two Sheffield teams, while Wales and Northern Ireland both adopted the game. Referees were given whistles to bring attention to their decisions, and shin-guards were brought in to protect players from injury. But it will be the introduction of the FA Cup that will stand as the milestone of the 1870s; had the competition not arrived, would the game ever have come so far?

THE MAGIC OF THE CUP

The best in the world

The FA Cup has risen from its modest beginnings at Kennington Oval to become the most exciting and celebrated sporting competition in the world, beamed live to almost every country and eagerly anticipated when its Final arrives each May. Its magic remains undiminished to this day – the Cup has a unique ability to create stars overnight, and to allow even the smallest of teams to beat the big clubs over the course of one 90-minute contest.

The first star

The Cup had its first ever superstar by its second competition, in 1873. Lord Kinnaird, a Scottish aristocrat who was to appear in nine Finals overall, scored The Wanderers' second goal in their victory over Oxford University and proved a colourful character in the early game. With long white trousers and an impressive red beard he was an imposing figure who delighted the crowds by standing on his head while celebrating the 1882 victory.

A new home

Stamford Bridge, Crystal Palace, Old Trafford and Goodison Park all played host to the Final before it found its Wembley home in the 'White Horse' final of 1923, meanwhile the tradition of Royal attendance at the game was started by King George V in 1914. Since then, the occasion has grown ever greater – and more controversial. Kevin Moran of Manchester United received the fixture's first red card in 1985, while Dave Beasant of Wimbledon saved the

first Final penalty in 1988; and then there are the Cup heroes: Ronnie Radford, Lawrie Sanchez, Matthew Hanlon, Stan Mortensen, Robert Di Matteo – all of whom entered the record books by their exploits in the competition.

Grass roots glory

Manchester United now hold the all-time competition record with nine wins, but it is at the lower end of the spectrum where the FA Cup continues to prosper. Entry has grown over 100-fold since those first 15 clubs took part. A club entering at the very first stage would need to win 12 matches to reach Wembley, and could take part in the odd penalty shoot-out along the way. The route may have changed since The Wanderers fought their way to that first win in 1872, but the magic remains the same.

FA CUP HOOLIGANISM

▶ **Ugly scenes at St James Park in March 1974 brought a sixth-round tie between Newcastle United and Nottingham Forest to a halt. 23 fans needed hospital treatment and a further 103 received first aid at the ground. There were 39 arrests. Forest were 3-1 up when the game was stopped and went on to lose 4-3. The Football Association ordered a replay which ended 0-0. Newcastle eventually won 1-0 in a replay.** ◀

▼ *Wimbledon FC celebrating their FA Cup win in 1988 – Dave Beasant saved the first Final penalty. Their open-top bus drove them to Wimbledon Town Hall, with fans cheering all along the route.*

The fastest ever FA Cup Final goal came from John Devey after 30 seconds of Aston Villa's 1895 victory over West Bromwich Albion. Chelsea's Roberto Di Matteo scored after just 43 seconds against Middlesbrough in 1997.

Maidenhead United and Marlow are the only two sides to have been involved in every FA Cup competition from the first to the present day.

▼ *Aston Villa's FA Cup-winning team of 1895. John Devey scored the fastest ever FA Cup Final goal during the match.*

THE FIRST INTERNATIONAL

The challenge concept

As Scotland grew ever more interested in football, so it became natural that they should challenge their English counterparts to an 'international' fixture to test the weight of their respective nations's prowess. The concept of this match was both an extension of the historical rivalries between the two countries and the start of one of the most established and entertaining games in the soccer calendar.

England's biggest international win is 13-0 against Ireland in Belfast on 18 February 1882.

Unofficial fixtures

It was FA secretary Charles Alcock who first initiated an England v Scotland match in 1870, arranging four games in London which resulted in three victories and a draw for the host side. The Scots, however, were unhappy by the fact that Alcock – an Englishman – picked the Scottish side, which was composed not of players based north of the border but of 'exiles' plying their trade down south.

With only 10 established clubs in the whole of Scotland, an international fixture was vital to kick-start a public interest in football, and it worked. On 30 November 1872, a genuine Scottish side took to the field at the West of Scotland cricket ground in

— KEEPING WARM — — NEMO ME IMPUNE &c — — A HARD STRUGGLE —

— DRIBBLING —

— WELL KICKED —

— SOFT FALLING, FORTUNATELY — — HOW'S THAT UMPIRE — — WELL DONE MAC !! —

SKETCHES AT THE INTERNATIONAL FOOTBALL MATCH, GLASGOW

▶ *Images of the first international match between England and Scotland; the illustrations were printed in* The Graphic, *14 December 1872.*

Scotland used the gate receipts of the first international to travel to The Oval for a return leg in 1873 – England won 4-2.

Partick, playing before over 2,000 spectators who paid a total of £102. The profit margins were a mere £38, and the English travel expenses were paid by donations from FA members. Six of the Scots came from Queen's Park, who competed in the English FA Cup.

No-goal show

The game ended goaless, but was generally considered entertaining by the partisan fans, many of whom were watching the sport for the first time. Alexander Bonsor of Old Etonians made history as the first ever international goalscorer, and the concept of a regular fixture between the two sides was born. Scotland improved as the century wore on, and beat their rivals 7-2 at Queen's Park in 1878.

A regular fixture

By the next century the England-Scotland match had expanded into a Home International championship which included Wales and Northern Ireland. The two larger nations continued to dominate and the fixtures gained a reputation for extreme competitiveness; sadly, they were discontinued due to fears of crowd violence during the 1980s. However, there is still a substantial and vocal campaign calling for the reinstatement of the Home Internationals – not least because they helped fend off demands for the four British sides to be amalgamated into one team.

England's Geoff Hurst is the only player to score a World Cup Final hat-trick. His triple salvo fired England to the 1966 trophy in a 4-2 victory over West Germany.

▼ *The victorious England team in 1966. Geoff Hurst is the only player to have scored a hat-trick in a World Cup Final.*

THE 1880S: BIRTH OF THE LEAGUE

The north rises up

The balance of power was shifting gradually from the gentlemen of the south to the working class north, and it was the 1880s that were to provide a blueprint for future trends in the game. In fact, it is possible to pinpoint the culmination of these important changes to just one game of football in 1883.

From its inception, the game had been dominated by the public schoolboys of Old Etonians, The Wanderers, Royal Engineers and their ilk, and the poorer northern clubs were slow to catch up both in terms of sporting prowess and financial organization. Blackburn was the very epitome of the poverty-stricken north, a weaving, industrial town – one of the largest exporters of clothing

NON-LEAGUE GIANT-KILLERS

Tottenham Hotspur, then in the Southern League, lifted the cup by beating Sheffield United 3-1 in a replay in 1901.

▼ *The Royal Engineers, photographed in the latter half of the nineteenth century.*

▲ *Blackburn Olympic photographed in 1883, the year they became the first northern team to win the FA Cup.*

materials in the world. Wages were low and unemployment rife, yet football was to provide a vital outlet for the downtrodden population.

Poor v Rich

Blackburn Rovers created a mini-sensation when they reached the 1882 Cup Final; although Old Etonians disposed of them by a single goal. Their neighbours, Blackburn Olympic, were more dogged, however, and the following year faced the Etonians in the second North-South Final. Olympic's collection of poorly-paid tradesmen could scarcely have provided more of a contrast to the upper-class gentlemen they faced – indeed, the club had only been in existence for five years. But Blackburn Olympic had done their homework, and had prepared for the final in a professional manner with an away trip to Blackpool and a strict dietary and fitness regime. When Lord Kinnaird saw a goal disallowed for the Old Etonians, and they went on to lose a player to injury (there were no substitutes in the 1880s), the tide turned and the underdogs eventually won 2-1 in extra time. The game, and the form book, had been well and truly turned on its head.

Wither the south

So dramatic was the change thereafter that no southern club was to win the Cup for the rest of the century. Blackburn Rovers took over Olympic's mantle as champions of the north, and won the FA Cup three times in a row between 1884 and 1886, echoing Wanderers' achievements of the previous decade. Aston Villa opened the Midlands account in 1887, and WBA and Preston took the final two trophies before 1890.

LEAGUE HOOLIGANISM

The first recorded incidence of crowd violence came in 1885. Players were attacked with stones, sticks and spit after Preston North End beat Aston Villa 5-1. One player, Ross of Preston, was knocked unconscious. Newspaper reports of the day described the hooligans as "howling roughs".

The first scandal

Many southern clubs attributed the northerners' success to their attraction of accomplished players through 'expenses' payments or other inducements. This caused considerable resentment among the fiercely amateur public schools, and when Londoners Upton Park lodged an official complaint against Preston in 1884, the matter came to a head. Preston, Burnley and Great Lever were all suspended from competition, but the dissenters threatened to form a breakaway British Football Association of sympathetic northern clubs. The FA sensibly agreed to allow professional football under strict conditions, and thus the modern million-pound player was made possible. James Forrest became the first professional England player in 1885.

DOUBLES WINNERS – LEAGUE CHAMPIONS AND FA CUP WINNERS

1889	▶	**Preston North End**
1897	▶	**Aston Villa**
1961	▶	**Tottenham Hotspur**
1971	▶	**Arsenal**
1986	▶	**Liverpool**
1994	▶	**Manchester United**
1996	▶	**Manchester United**
1998	▶	**Arsenal**

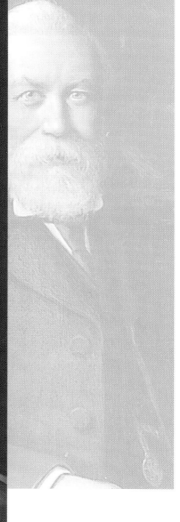

◀ William McGregor, founder of the Football League in 1888.

The League kicks off

There were other reasons for the rise of the north: the public schools now preferred rugby, and a definitive set of laws of the game had provided a level playing field at last. A league had long been argued for by clubs eager to provide supporters with definite dates for competition, and 12 teams entered the inaugural competition set up by William McGregor, a director of Aston Villa: Accrington, Villa, Blackburn Rovers, Bolton, Burnley, Derby, Everton, Notts County, Preston, Stoke, WBA and Wolverhampton Wanderers. Significantly, none were southern.

Preston go goal-crazy

Preston earned themselves the tag 'The Old Invincibles' for their achievements in that first 1888-89 season. Coached by the formidable Major William Suddell they were champions by January and didn't lose a single League match. Indeed, they failed to score only once and did not concede a goal in any round as they romped to a 3-0 FA Cup Final victory over Wolves, thus completing the first and most dominant 'Double'.

Bad news for Bon

It seemed football had been turned on its head in the space of just a few years. Bon Accord, however, may wish they had never taken up the game in the first place. They lost their first-round Scottish FA Cup match against Arbroath by a record 36-0, the largest score ever recorded in a British first-class match. Bon Accord had to field a defender in goal and were so poor they did not have a pair of boots between them. These were interesting times.

▶ *Kenny Dalglish raising the FA Cup for Liverpool in 1986 – the year they won the Double.*

TRANSFER FEE MILESTONES

Player	From	To	Date	Fee
Alf Common	Sunderland	Middlesbrough	February 1905	£1,000
Syd Puddefoot	West Ham	Falkirk	February 1922	£5,000
David Jack	Bolton	Arsenal	October 1928	£10,890
Tommy Lawton	Chelsea	Notts County	November 1947	£20,000
Trevor Ford	Aston Villa	Sunderland	October 1950	£30,000
John Charles	Leeds	Juventus	April 1957	£65,000
Denis Law	Manchester City	Torino	June 1961	£100,000

THE FOOTBALL LEAGUE

Early struggles

The early days of the Football League could not have been more different from today. After agreeing to set up a League system in the 1880s, it was a constant struggle to balance the books and those early pioneers were all volunteers. Today, the Football League raises millions of pounds every year and has earned worldwide respect for its administration of the game.

An American idea

It was clear right from the start that a League was needed, although the principles themselves were imported from American sport. Organizing teams on a competitive basis provided interest for spectators and players every week, as well as a guaranteed income. The Football League presided over a huge rise in attendances over the first few years of its existence and by the 1980s had 90 members.

Liverpool's Bob Paisley holding the League Cup in his ▲ last season as manager; Liverpool and Manchester United have dominated the championship since it began.

Northern soul

The main power base of the League Championship has always been the north – the League's winners have been from the north almost two-thirds of the time. Today, there are more southern clubs in action than ever before, but Liverpool and Manchester United have taken the top prize more often than any other clubs.

▶ **Albert Mundy's strike for Aldershot against Hartlepool on 25 October 1958 was officially timed at six seconds.**

▶ **Newport County's Barrie Jones struck in six seconds against Torquay United on 31 March 1962.**

▶ **Keith Smith also hit a six-second goal for Crystal Palace v Derby County on 12 December 1964.**

Premiership pains

The formation of the Premiership finally ended the Football League's stranglehold on the game, and today it is reduced to the lower three divisions. The League has had to ensure its members receive a fair share of all television and sponsorship revenue, and that what money it does receive is distributed evenly among all clubs – an important principle crucial to the organization's ethos.

The League's challenge

The challenge as we enter a new century is for the League to retain its power while also keeping up with the times. Many would like the lower divisions to be reduced or regionalized to cut down on travel costs, while there have been threats for some time of a second Premiership of First Division teams breaking away. Those at the top of the tree feel too much of the vital TV revenue is eaten up by those Third Division clubs rarely seen on television, while several clubs remain in constant danger of liquidation as they suffer in the shadow of their bigger neighbours. The next century will be far more difficult for the oldest footballing Championship of them all.

NEAR DOUBLES – LEAGUE CHAMPIONS AND FA CUP RUNNERS-UP	
1905 ▶	Newcastle United
1913 ▶	Sunderland
1957 ▶	Manchester United
1977 ▶	Liverpool
1985 ▶	Everton
1988 ▶	Liverpool

▼ *The Manchester United squad of 1994, celebrating their FA Cup win at a packed Old Trafford. This was the year of their first Double.*

THE 1890S: INTO THE MODERN ERA

Football on the rise

The excitement of those 1880s League and Cup tussles, as well as the advent of professional, competent players, made football a booming industry in the last decade of the nineteenth century. It seemed the game had truly captured the imagination of the general public, and its inexorable rise towards becoming the nation's favourite past-time had truly begun.

Boom time

Attendances were up all over the country, and clubs responded by improving the facilities at their grounds to include the provision of covered areas and basic fencing around some pitches. By the middle of the 1890s, a total of two million people were watching the championship race progress. That figure was up to a massive seven million by the end of the century. Many supporters simply left their workplaces and risked the sack to watch matches. Soccer also provided a number of lucrative spin-off industries, including the manufacture of boots and balls.

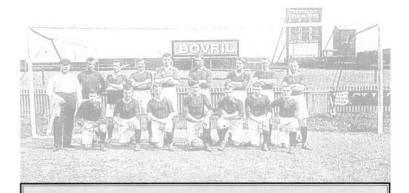

OLD TRAFFORD, THE HOME OF MANCHESTER UNITED, CAME INTO BEING IN 1911 AT A COST OF £60,000. IT WAS BOMBED DURING THE SECOND WORLD WAR AND WAS EXTENSIVELY REBUILT IN 1949. IT WAS TURNED INTO AN ALL-SEATER STADIUM IN 1994.

▼ *A selection of caps awarded to international players between 1895 and 1905.*

▲ *Woolwich Arsenal FC of 1903–04. Arsenal were the first London side to join the League.*

New contenders

It was only natural that new clubs should emerge and in 1892-93 a Second Division of the Football League was added to accommodate them. Small Heath, Sheffield United, Darwen, Grimsby, Ardwick, Burton Swifts, Northwich Victoria, Bootle, Lincoln, Crewe, Burslem and Walsall were its first members, but the make-up of the divisions changed drastically before the First World War as new sides broke through and others quickly dropped out due to financial constraints.

London joins in

By 1893, Woolwich Arsenal had become the first London side to join the League, and Luton and New Brighton continued the southern interest in future years. Promotion and relegation issues between the two divisions were settled by 'test matches' where the bottom three Division One teams played the top three of Division Two for the right either to stay in the top flight or be replaced by their lower League rivals. This created an embarrassing situation for Notts County in 1894, when they won the FA Cup with an impressive 4-1 demolition of Bolton Wanderers but then failed to gain promotion when Preston beat them 4-0 in a test match.

Wembley Stadium opened in time to host the 1923 FA Cup Final. It was built in 300 working days and was described by officials as being 'as big as the biblical city of Jericho'. The famous twin towers are now recognized around the globe. The stadium is regarded by many as football's spiritual home.

New powers emerge

However, Preston's early powers were on the slide and over the next century they were never again to regain their place at the top of the football tree. Today they reside in the lower divisions, but in the 1890s they hung on in the top flight while Sunderland and Aston Villa shared seven of the 10 available titles between them. Sunderland had only joined up in 1890, but they won three titles in four years, including a brilliant 13-match 100 per cent run in 1891-92. Their only English player was their captain; Scotland continued to provide most of the finest individuals in the League and their national side remained superior to England's for the latter part of the century.

Where's the Cup?

Villa added the 1895 FA Cup to their haul, but managed to lose it just a few months later. The trophy was put on display in a local shoemaker's shop and was promptly stolen from the window; it is now believed to have been melted down to make counterfeit coins. Villa offered £10 reward for the Cup's return, but to no avail; they guarded it a little more carefully after winning it again in 1897. Blackburn, West Brom, Wolves, Sheffield Wednesday, Sheffield United and Nottingham Forest also lifted the Cup during the decade.

Refs go it alone

The 1890s also saw a number of important rule changes on the pitch. Referees were allowed on to the field of play, and their 'umpires' became the equivalent of modern-day Linesmen on the sidelines. This speeded up matches and did away with the need for constant conferring between officials. The refs were also given whistles to alert players to their intentions. A goal-line handball during a Notts County match in 1891

> Everton moved into their Goodison Park stadium in 1892. They previously played at Anfield, the eventual home of local rivals Liverpool.

> *Arsenal's impressive Highbury ground was built in 1913. Henry Norris, who had saved the Woolwich Arsenal from financial ruin, paid £125,000 to have the stadium constructed.*

led to the introduction of penalties for foul play in the area, although many amateurs were incensed by the inference that they could possibly cheat and refused to acknowledge the existence of the penalty spot-kick.

Changes for the better

Stoppages were also allowed at the end of normal time to take account of injuries and time-wasting, while goalkeepers' handling was restricted to their own penalty area. Most importantly, the primitive tactics which saw as many as eight men chasing the ball upfront were refined to a 2-3-5 system that remained in place well into the next century. The modern game was taking shape, and the papers noticed too: the first sports newspaper was set up in the mid-1890s, and coverage of football filled many a page. Everything was ready for the challenges the turn of the century would bring.

▲ *A spectator's view of Arsenal's Highbury Stadium, built in 1913.*

▶ *Illustration of the 1898 FA Cup Final, taken from* The Graphic, *13 April 1898.*

THE WOMEN'S GAME

A constant struggle

Misunderstood, mocked and frequently undermined, women's football was forced to exist for years as a second-class compartment of soccer culture. And, even to this day, the female infiltration of a predominantly male sport is still far from complete. Right from the very beginning, football – in common with its public school roots – was considered a bastion of male strength and athleticism; and so the process of acceptance of the women's game has been a slow and laborious one.

IT WAS A HISTORIC DAY WHEN WENDY TOMS TOOK HER PLACE ON THE OFFICIAL FOOTBALL LEAGUE LINESMEN LIST AT THE START OF THE 1997-98 SEASON. THE 33-YEAR-OLD FROM POOLE, DORSET, EARNED PROMOTION AFTER SPENDING TWO YEARS RUNNING THE LINE AT CONFERENCE GAMES. SHE IS THE FIRST, AND STILL THE ONLY, WOMAN REFEREE OPERATING AT A NATIONAL LEVEL.

Beginning the fight

The first recorded female match was an 1895 challenge game between northern and southern XIs in London, but within a year the FA had instructed its existing members to discourage the hosting of such matches. Doctors were called on to explain the medical 'drawbacks' of football and the damage it could do to female players, and the mostly male spectators who paid to watch it did so mostly to mock rather than encourage.

▼ *Teams such as the Llanelly Women's FC (pictured here in 1921) endured constant derision from male players, fans and the media.*

◀ The face of women's football today – a player from Arsenal Ladies battles it out with one of the Liverpool Ladies, 27 April 1997.

public. The FA took over its running in 1993. By the 1980s, Doncaster Belles had emerged as the first women's superteam, matching for some time Manchester United's recent dominance of the men's game. Large clubs such as Arsenal and QPR set up their own women's teams and their annual Cup Final was shown for the first time on domestic television.

A long way to go

Still, however, the problems persist – exhibited in Ron Atkinson's now famous remark that 'a woman's place is in the boutique or the discotheque, not on a football pitch' – while scores of commentators and male pros have continued to deride the female game. It will take a considerable change in the attitudes of the media in particular before further headway can be made in this important area of football, but the ever-growing number of female players and fans, coupled with the ongoing social changes in this country, can only be good news.

The Preston pioneers

It was the Dick, Kerr Ladies team who perhaps saved the game and bucked the trend of male domination. Formed pre-war in a Preston factory, they began playing large-scale games to keep fans entertained during the First World War and drew huge crowds to their popular matches. By the 1920s their endeavours had inspired hundreds of other teams to form all across the country.

ENGLAND'S FIRST OFFICIAL WOMEN'S INTERNATIONAL WAS STAGED AGAINST SCOTLAND AT GREENOCK, IN NOVEMBER 1972. ENGLAND WON 3-2.

On to the world stage

Though the next 40 or so years were difficult, by 1969 the game had become a major force. England's women's team played their first semi-official international in Italy that year and a fully-fledged Women's Football Association was formed to oversee organization and administration of Leagues and Cups, as well as promoting the cause to the

IN 1992, THE DONCASTER BELLES TOOK THE FIRST NATIONAL LEAGUE TITLE AFTER BEATING 11 SETS OF OPPONENTS IN RAPID SUCCESSION.

1900-14: THE PROFESSIONAL ERA

A whole new game

As the new century got underway, football was becoming ever more professional both on and off the pitch. By the time the First World War interrupted the game's progress in 1914, every side in the top flight, as well as the entire English and Scottish national sides, was composed entirely of pros, and the innovations around the game at the time reflected its growth.

Attendances were growing all the time, and football had been adopted as the principal past-time for working class men. The social changes that were also taking place at the time, including the increasing prosperity of all the social classes and the ever greater emancipation of the poor, only contributed to their willingness to enjoy the game. When the War began, football took on a vital role that would further endear it to the nation.

THREE CLUBS HAVE WON 14 MATCHES IN SUCCESSION: MANCHESTER UNITED WAS THE FIRST IN 1904-05, BRISTOL CITY FOLLOWED SUIT THE FOLLOWING SEASON AND PRESTON MANAGED IT IN THE 1950-51 CAMPAIGN. ALL THREE WERE IN THE SECOND DIVISION AT THE TIME.

Wages are curbed

The 1900s began with the introduction of a maximum wage for footballers, set at £4 per week, and designed to curb worries over the eroding of the 'amateur' ethos of the previous century. Signing-on fees when players first joined clubs were to be pegged to a maximum of £10, while match bonuses were abolished in favour of players being given a benefit match when they retired from the game. Such issues were to become central to the whole professionalism debate as the pre-war period moved on.

The big names

On the pitch, the next 14 years were to see the development of a 'great eight' of clubs who took the lion's share of the available trophies: Aston Villa, Everton, Liverpool, Newcastle, Sheffield Wednesday, Sunderland and both the Manchester sides were richer and more successful than the sides below them who yo-yoed between the top two divisions. But that is not to say that nobody else was allowed a look-in.

FA CUP FINAL ROYAL GUESTS

1923	▶	King George V, The Duke of Devonshire
1924	▶	Duke of York
1925	▶	Duke of York
1926	▶	King George V
1927	▶	King George V
1928	▶	King George V and Queen Mary, Duke and Duchess of York
1929	▶	Prince of Wales

▶An illustration of how football was played in 1903.
Football's professionalism increased as the century progressed.

Mighty Spurs

Football took second place in England's priorities early in 1901, as the game all but closed down for several weeks to mourn the death of Queen Victoria. All forms of public entertainment were postponed for the period, but when football got underway again it was to see the traditional hierarchy temporarily thrown into turmoil. Tottenham Hotspur were a Southern League side back then, outside the Football League and minnows by any standards, but 1901 was to start them on the road to fame and give further impetus to the south's charge to power. Nobody expected them to make any progress when they began their FA Cup campaign that year, but they managed to beat four First Division sides under the astute leadership of player-manager John Cameron, aided by the goals of mercurial striker Sandy Brown. They made their way to the final of football's oldest and biggest competition not knowing quite what to expect.

> ▶
> **Sir Stanley Matthews is the oldest England international and oldest scorer.**
>
> ▶
> **He won his last cap aged 42 years and 104 days, against Denmark on 15 May 1957.**
>
> ▶
> **He was 41 years, 248 days when he found the net against Northern Ireland in Belfast on 6 October 1956.**

controversial equalizer to salvage a 2-2 draw for the northern giants. The replay drew a crowd of just 20,000, but saw one of the most famous giant-killing acts in the competition's history, as Tottenham recovered from a 1-0 half-time deficit to win 3-1. Brown was among the scorers, adding to his two strikes in the first Final, and he became the only man to score in every round of the Cup. No other non-League has equalled their achievement, nor are they ever likely to – the club were granted a Second Division place in 1908, and won promotion in their first ever season.

'Pool of dreams

Liverpool were also shaking up the old order. They took the League for the first time in 1900-01, denying Aston Villa the chance to win their second championship hat-trick. The Merseysiders chalked up a run of 12 games unbeaten to revive what had initially looked an average season and pip Sunderland at the post. Villa were lucky not to be relegated.

SOCCER DISASTERS

Ibrox	▶▶▶▶▶	1902
Bolton	▶▶▶▶ ▶	1946
Munich	▶▶▶ ▶	1958
Bradford	▶ ▶▶	1985
Heysel	▶ ▶	1985
Hillsborough	▶	1989

Glory, glory Tottenham

Spurs' opponents Sheffield United had become a major top-flight force and were widely expected to obliterate them in front of over 100,000 spectators at Crystal Palace. But the Londoners did not oblige, and it took a late,

◀ Alf Common who helped Sunderland to their win in 1902; photographed in his time playing for Middlesbrough and England.

▲ The aftermath of one of football's worst disasters: a Hillsborough survivor leaving Anfield after a memorial ceremony held on 22 April 1989.

Common people

Sunderland, with Alf Common in their side and a plethora of Scottish internationals at their disposal, made amends with a title win in 1902, while Southern League Southampton came breath-takingly close to repeating Spurs' achievement of the previous year before eventually succumbing to Sheffield United in an FA Cup Final replay. Sheffield Wednesday took the title in both 1903 and 1904, despite scoring a mere 48 goals in the latter season. Relative newcomers Newcastle could have won the Double in 1905, but had to content themselves with the title alone, leaving Villa to take their fourth Cup in five Finals.

SINCE IT BEGAN IN 1960, ENGLAND HAVE ONLY CONTESTED THE LATTER STAGES OF THE EUROPEAN CHAMPIONSHIP (FORMERLY THE NATIONS CUP) ON THREE OCCASIONS: 1968, 1972 AND 1996. THEY HAVE YET TO REACH THE FINAL ITSELF.

England rejects Europe

For all the excitement on the pitch, those running the game off it were still stuck firmly in the 1880s. As football developed throughout the rest of the world and Europe in particular, several countries began to toy with the idea of an overall international governing body. The FA, however, were not among them – they had already rejected offers from Holland and Belgium to co-operate more closely and establish small club tournaments, and when Fifa was formed in Paris in 1904, England was not represented. The FA reluctantly agreed to join the party two years later, but it was an uneasy alliance and was to cause further problems in years to come.

▼*Kings of the pitch: Aston Villa FC as they looked in 1905, the year they took their fourth FA Cup title.*

NON-LEAGUE GIANT-KILLERS

COLCHESTER UNITED BEAT HUDDERSFIELD TOWN 1-0 IN 1948.

YEOVIL TOWN UPSET SUNDERLAND 2-1 IN 1949.

HEREFORD UNITED BEAT NEWCASTLE UNITED 2-1 IN 1972.

WIMBLEDON, THEN STILL SEEKING LEAGUE STATUS, BEAT BURNLEY 1-0 IN 1975.

SUTTON UNITED BEAT DEFENDING CUP HOLDERS COVENTRY 2-1 IN 1989.

Branching out

The England team was grudgingly allowed to branch out into the rest of the world for the first time in 1907-08, touring Austria, Hungary and Bohemia over eight days and thrashing all three opponents. The Home Internationals, however, in which all four home nations competed annually, were a more mixed affair and both Wales and Ireland walked away with the title in the 1900s. England saw greater success in the 1908 Olympics; these were held in London and featured football for the first time. Despite fielding an entirely amateur side, the hosts swept the other five teams involved aside to take their first world title. They defended their title successfully in 1912.

World champions

Even the minnows were in on the act. West Auckland, members of the Northern Amateur League, accepted an invitation to take part in businessman Sir Thomas Lipton's 'World Cup' in Turin in 1910 after the FA refused to send a professional side. The County Durham team, who were mostly miners by trade, beat Red Star Zurich and Stuttgart en route to a final against Juventus. They beat the Italian giants 2-0 to become unofficial World Champions!

TROUBLE AT THE FA CUP FINAL HAS BEEN RARE, HOWEVER THE VERY FIRST WEMBLEY FINAL IN 1923 WAS MARRED BY THOUSANDS OF GATE-CRASHERS WHO SWELLED THE 127,000 CAPACITY CROWD TO AN ESTIMATED 200,000. MORE THAN 900 PEOPLE WERE HURT AND POLICE REINFORCEMENTS WERE BROUGHT IN FROM ACROSS LONDON.

The first disaster

There was tragedy, too, for the national team. Playing against Scotland at the newly-built Ibrox Stadium in 1902, England became part of football's first disaster when a stand collapsed under spectator pressure. Twenty five people died and over 500 were injured, yet the match continued in order to prevent any further panic and many fans were not aware of the tragedy until they left the ground. The incident forced clubs to think again about stadium design and safety, and many also took out insurance to cover themselves in the event of another such disaster.

Gunning for glory

In the domestic game, the south was continuing to exert pressure on the northern clubs who had become so dominant in the 1890s. Arsenal became the first southern side to enter the First Division when they won promotion in 1904, and a few months later Chelsea were formed by entrepreneur and football fan Gus Mears. He knew the Second Division was to be expanded by three teams and wanted his West London side to have a piece of the action.

A new superpower

Mears built Stamford Bridge to house his side, a huge stadium to rival Scotland's showcase Hampden Park and capable of holding 100,000 people, including 5,000 seated. Despite the whole set-up only having been in operation for a matter of months, Chelsea were awarded their prized League place and have been there ever since – the first instance of a rich chairman buying his side success. Chelsea's first star was the former Sheffield United keeper Bill 'Fatty' Foulke, a 22-stone giant who became the largest man ever to play professional football in England.

Foulke's party piece was to pick opposing forwards up by the scruff of the neck and throw them into his goal – he was temperamental, but an excellent netminder, not least because he filled up so much of the target. Chelsea placed two small boys behind the goal to draw even greater attention to his girth – they became the first ever ballboys.

Stars of the decade

There were other stars beside Foulke – Billy Meredith was dubbed the 'wing wizard' for his prowess with both Manchester clubs, while Albert Iremonger was a 6'6" giant between the sticks of Notts County. Bob Crompton of Blackburn won 41 caps for England and was widely accepted as the best defender of the pre-war era – his nearest rival was Manchester United's skipper Charlie Roberts, a physical centre half with a classy touch. Roberts' involvement with the players' union restricted his England career to just three caps.

▲ *Bill 'Fatty' Foulke who weighed over 20 stone throughout his career. Foulke kept goal for Sheffield United, Chelsea and the England team.*

▶*A poignant illustration of Britain's first soccer disaster at Ibrox Stadium. Those unhurt carried off the injured on stretchers made from pieces of the collapsed stand.*

▲ *A caricature of Everton's Sandy Young. Everton were a major force in English football at the turn of the century, though they rapidly became eclipsed by hometown rivals Liverpool.*

Mighty Merseyside

By 1906, Merseyside had assumed temporary command at the heart of the English game. While Liverpool took the title by four points from Preston – thanks largely to the efforts of their young keeper Sam Hardy – Everton were defeating Newcastle 1-0 to land the Cup. Newcastle were to win the 1907 and 1909 titles, sandwiched between the first win for the game's most celebrated club, Manchester United. They took the championship by some nine points, before moving to their new home at Old Trafford. The superstadium contained a billiard room, massage room, gym and plunge bath for players to train and relax in and was the envy of their smaller rivals. United had arrived.

▶ *The 1910 FA Cup Final: Newcastle United and Barnsley drew at Crystal Palace; Barnsley won the Cup two years later.*

United in glory

The Mancunians won the title again in 1911. Cups went to Sunderland, Blackburn, Everton, Bradford, Villa, Burnley and Sheffield United, but it was Barnsley's 1911-12 victory that really caught the imagination. The Second Division Yorkshiremen needed 10 games to reach the final, where they tired out West Bromwich Albion in a replay to win 1-0 with two minutes remaining.

Amateur defeat

Few could have foreseen the problems around the corner in those heady days; attendances were as high as they were in the 1980s, and standards of play were improving all the time. The old guard had even grudgingly accepted professionalism. Alf Common's £1,000 transfer prompted the FA to impose a £350 limit on all transfer fees, but such was the opposition from clubs it was dropped after just a few months. The amateurs broke away to form their own football association, and the majority of public schools finally made the switch to rugby, which remained amateur. The growth of the players' union showed that professionalism had truly won the day.

Royal approval

The final piece of the jigsaw fell into place at the 1914 FA Cup Final. King George V became the first ruling monarch to attend such an important match, and it gave football a much-needed seal of approval in the public eye for the King to be involved in a working-class sport. The whole route from Buckingham Palace to Crystal Palace was lined with cheering supporters, and over 70,000 fans watched both the game and the royal spectator as Burnley beat Liverpool 1-0. From then on, the attendance of a monarch became a regular fixture at all Cup Finals.

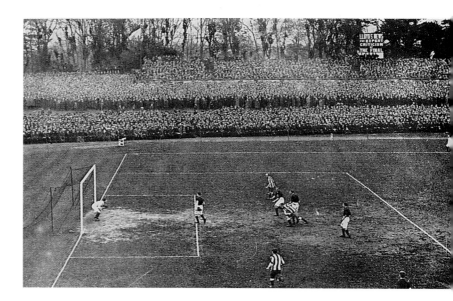

LEAGUE GIANT-KILLERS FROM THE 1960S ONWARDS

IN 1964 ▶ FOURTH DIVISION ALDERSHOT BEAT ASTON VILLA 2-1.

IN 1965 ▶ THIRD DIVISION PETERBOROUGH BEAT ARSENAL 2-1.

IN 1969 ▶ THIRD DIVISION MANSFIELD BEAT WEST HAM 3-0.

IN 1971 ▶ FOURTH DIVISION COLCHESTER UNITED BEAT REIGNING CHAMPIONS LEEDS 3-2.

IN 1980 ▶ FOURTH DIVISION WIGAN BEAT CHELSEA 0-1.

IN 1980 ▶ FOURTH DIVISION HALIFAX BEAT MANCHESTER CITY 0-1.

IN 1984 ▶ THIRD DIVISION BOURNEMOUTH BEAT MANCHESTER UNITED 2-0.

IN 1985 ▶ THIRD DIVISION YORK BEAT ARSENAL 1-0.

IN 1992 ▶ FOURTH DIVISION WREXHAM BEAT ARSENAL 2-1.

IN 1994 ▶ SECOND DIVISION BRISTOL CITY BEAT LIVERPOOL 0-1.

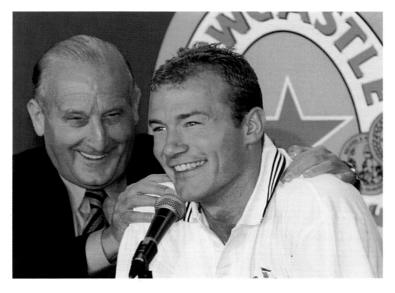

▲ Alan Shearer with Newcastle United chairman Sir John Hall, photographed after Shearer's record signing in July 1996.

▲ The fundamental changes that took place in football during the first decades of the twentieth century paved for way for star players such as George Best.

TRANSFER FEE MILESTONES

PLAYER	FROM	TO	DATE	FEE
Trevor Francis	Birmingham	Notts Forest	February 1979	£1,000,000
Bryan Robson	West Brom	Manchester United	July 1980	£1,500,000
Mark Hughes	Manchester United	Barcelona	May 1986	£2,300,000
Ian Rush	Liverpool	Juventus	June 1987	£3,200,000
Chris Waddle	Tottenham	Marseille	July 1989	£4,250,000
Paul Gascoigne	Tottenham	Lazio	June 1992	£5,500,000
Andy Cole	Newcastle	Manchester United	January 1995	£7,000,000
Stan Collymore	Nottingham Forest	Liverpool	June 1995	£8,500,000
Alan Shearer	Blackburn	Newcastle	July 1996	£15,000,000

CORINTHIAN CASUALS: AMATEURS TO THE END

History makers

Throughout history, one team and one name has come to symbolize the great amateur spirit which pervaded the early English game: Corinthians. Founded in 1882 by N. Lane Jackson, the club has remained to this day staunchly opposed to professionalism and payment of any kind and has provided domestic football with some truly memorable achievements.

Dedicated amateurs

The early Corinthians team was made up of celebrated and competent players who shunned the moves towards professionalism. They refused to enter Cup competitions, as they were deemed against the amateur spirit, but still won some notable matches. In 1884, for instance, they thrashed the Cup holders Blackburn 8-1, and 10 years later repeated the trick against Bury 10-3. The England side that met Scotland in 1886 was composed of an incredible nine Corinthians, a record which stands to this day.

Football's ambassadors

Perhaps their most important role has been as footballing ambassadors. In the early part of this century, the club took football to Europe and South America, beating the

One of the most unusual dismissals came in an FA Cup third-round tie on 9 January 1979 when Charlton strikers Mick Flanagan and Derek Hales got their marching orders – for fighting each other!

domestic champions in several countries with style and dignity. The Corinthians refused to indulge in foul play and always played a traditional passing game.

The club was amalgamated in 1939 with the lesser-known Casuals, but their spirit did not die. To this day they play on in the

▼ *A gentlemanly line-up: the Corinthian Casuals at Crystal Palace in 1905.*

lower echelons of the non-League pyramid and have made their base in Kingston, south-west London. Even now they refuse to pay players, and receiving a red card is a sackable offence. Swearing or questioning a referee's decision is met with a hefty fine.

Paying the penalty

One of the most curious aspects of the Corinthian game was their refusal to take penalty kicks, a practice which continued well into the latter part of this century. When awarded a penalty, a Corinthian player was ordered to miss a spot-kick deliberately, likewise if a penalty was awarded against them the goalkeeper would stand to one side of the goal and let his opponent score.

Samba successes

When they celebrated their centenary in the 1980s, the Corinthians toured in Brazil and faced their namesakes of that country, who were christened in honour of their English counterparts. Countless sides in dozens of countries have been inspired by this great amateur side, and it is a constant source of comfort to those who resist the money-mad modern game that at least one side remembers the principles on which football is founded: a love of the game and, above all, sportsmanship at all times.

ENGLAND INTERNATIONALS HAVE SCORED FIVE GOALS IN ONE GAME ON FIVE OCCASIONS

- ASTON VILLA'S OLIVER VAUGHTON IN A 13-0 WIN OVER IRELAND ON 18 FEBRUARY 1882.
- DERBY COUNTY'S STEVE BLOOMER IN A 9-1 VICTORY AGAINST WALES ON 16 MARCH 1896.
- CORINTHIANS' G.O. SMITH IN A 13-2 WIN OVER IRELAND ON 18 FEBRUARY 1899.
- TOTTENHAM'S WILLIE HALL IN A 7-0 VICTORY AGAINST IRELAND ON 16 NOVEMBER 1938.
- NEWCASTLE'S MALCOLM MACDONALD IN A 5-0 VICTORY OVER CYPRUS ON 16 APRIL 1975.

▼*Receiving a red card is a sackable offence if you play for Corinthian Casuals.*

ALF COMMON: RECORD BREAKER

The unlikely hero

Alf Common did not even look like a footballer: at just 5'8", he was small even for the 1900s, and he had great difficulty keeping his weight down even to 13 stone. Yet in 1905, the Sunderland centre forward caused nothing short of a scandal when he moved to Middlesbrough for the princely sum of £1,000.

A storm brewing

Middlesbrough were languishing just above the First Division relegation zone and in serious need of a proven goalscorer, and 25-year-old Common fitted the bill to a tee. In desperation, the club agreed to pay the first four-figure fee in return for his services, but could never have predicted the outcry that followed. Traditionalists bemoaned the demise of the amateur days when players played for free, while others feared that transfer fees would soon spiral and smaller clubs would no longer be able to compete. Charles Clegg, Football League chairman, was particularly enraged as his club Sheffield United had

MIDDLESBROUGH'S
GEORGE CAMSELL HIT
NINE HAT-TRICKS IN THE
1926-27 SEASON, THE MOST
IN ONE CAMPAIGN.

▲ Alf Common as he looked when he helped Sheffield United win the FA Cup in 1902.

TRANSFER FEE MILESTONES

Player	From	To	Date	Fee
Allan Clarke	Fulham	Leicester	June 1968	£150,000
Martin Peters	West Ham	Tottenham	March 1970	£200,000
David Nish	Leicester	Derby	August 1972	£250,000
Bob Latchford	Birmingham	Everton	February 1974	£350,000
Kevin Keegan	Liverpool	Hamburg	June 1977	£500,000

sold Common to Sunderland for a more acceptable £375 just a few months earlier. They were furious at the profit they could have made – a slightly hypocritical school of thought.

The goalscorer

The player himself certainly did the trick for Middlesbrough. His goals proved enough to keep them on top and he became a hero to the fans. Later on, the club narrowly escaped a ban when it was found they

FA CUP FINAL ROYAL GUESTS

1930	▶	**King George V**
1931	▶	**Duke of Gloucester**
1932	▶	**King George V and Queen Mary**
1933	▶	**Duke of York**
1934	▶	**King George V**
1935	▶	**Prince of Wales**
1937	▶	**King George VI and Queen Elizabeth**
1938	▶	**King George VI**
1939	▶	**King George VI**

had made illegal payments to their players above the accepted limits. The critics were further outraged. They could never have dreamt of the huge transfer fees and payment scandals that were to follow years later, when players could move for over £20 million and managers found themselves before the FA for transfer irregularities.

A practical joker

Common left Middlesbrough for Arsenal in 1910 and found himself relegated for the first time in 1912. A practical joker who wrestled in his spare time, he went on to appear briefly for Preston before giving up football to become a publican. Despite the indignation that surrounded his career, he liked nothing better than to laugh at all the fuss he had started back in 1905.

◀ *Seventy-two years after Alf Common's £5000 transfer, Liverpool's star player, Kevin Keegan, was sold to Hamburg for £500,000.*

BILLY MEREDITH: THE FIRST FOOTBALL GREAT

Humble beginnings

A deeply religious and reserved Welshman from the tiny village of Chirk, Meredith was working down the mines as soon as he finished school at 12 and never intended to enter football as a profession, due to his family's wishes. Yet eventually Manchester City persuaded him to join them in their first season after breaking away from Ardwick FC, and what followed made soccer history. Meredith became the club's first-choice right-winger and a prolific goalscorer feted for his strength and skill – and known for the toothpick he kept in his mouth during games. By 1904, the 30-year-

◄ *Billy Meredith photographed in his Manchester kit c. 1906.*

A dash of colour

There have been more talented players than Billy Meredith, but in a century of English football there can have been few more colourful or controversial. Meredith outraged the authorities, was banned for bribery, became ostracized by his fellow professionals and laid the foundations for today's Professional Footballers' Association. And in the middle of it all, he lit up the game in a dazzling career spanning 30 years.

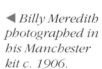

FOOTBALLER OF THE YEAR– DOUBLE WINNERS

Stanley Matthews ▲ **(Blackpool 1948, Stoke 1963)**

Tom Finney ▲ **(Preston 1954 & 1957)**

Danny Blanchflower ▲ **(Tottenham 1958 & 1961)**

Kenny Dalglish ▲ **(Liverpool 1979 & 1983)**

John Barnes ▲ **(Liverpool 1988 & 1990)**

The oldest player to appear in a League match is New Brighton manager Neil McBain. He was aged 51 years and 120 days when he played in goal away to Hartlepool United (Division Three North) on 15 March 1947.

old was captain; he lifted Manchester's first FA Cup following a glorious victory over Bolton at Crystal Palace.

Courting controversy

Meredith, however, quickly became famous for the wrong reasons. In 1909, he was banned for eight months for reportedly attempting to bribe an Aston Villa player before an important League game. He always maintained his innocence, but left the club to join Manchester United when the suspension was lifted.

A United man

Across the city, Meredith won one FA Cup and two League titles and enjoyed a celebrity status afforded to no player before him. He used it to campaign for the lifting of the maximum wage and to set up a players' union which, though unsuccessful in its aims, was an important step forward for the game. At the time, though, many were unhappy he

failed to deliver his promises.

The veteran years

Meredith returned to City during the war and joined them full-time in 1915: even as a 50-year-old in 1924 he was still playing, being controversially recalled for the club's Cup run, which ended in the quarter-finals. The authorities were far from upset at his eventual retirement, but the concessions gained – more than a quarter of a century later – over wages proved the Welsh wonder right. He

The Footballer of the Year title is awarded by the Football Writers' Association since 1948 to the 'player who, by precept and example, on the field and off, shall be considered to have done most for football'.

died in 1958, still remembered by many as the first superstar of the game.

◄ *Players of Billy Meredith's calibre led to the creation of the Player of the Year award. Kenny Dalglish is one of a few double recipients of the award.*

1914-18: THE FIRST WORLD WAR

War sets in

War inevitably sets cultural development back by decades, and football was severely affected by the First World War, declared in August 1914. The game had begun to boom, in terms of attendances and the emergence of the first superstars, so the small amount of poor-quality football played during the war years was a major blow.

The 1914-15 season was completed, with Everton pipping Oldham to the title by just one point in an incredibly close race, and members of the armed forces turned out in their thousands for the Cup Final at Old Trafford, which was later dubbed the 'Khaki Cup Final'. Sheffield United beat Chelsea 3-0, but many of the players present would never again perform on such a stage. These included Steve Bloomer, who had gone to Germany beforehand to take up a coaching position but was instead interned, and Bradford star Donald Bell, recipient of the Victoria Cross.

▶Soldiers and civilians using posts to rise above the rest of the crowd; 1914 FA Cup Final.
▼A selection of medals from the Billy Wright collection.

SECOND WORLD WAR FOOTBALL RESTRICTIONS

▶ **In July 1940 the Football League ruled there would be no trophies or medals.**
▶ **Crowds were limited to 8,000 or half a ground's capacity due to evacuation procedures.**
▶ **Clubs were allowed to choose their own opponents although each First and Second Division club had to play at least two Third Division teams.**
▶ **No points were awarded for wins or draws.**
▶ **The League tables were compiled purely on goal average.**
▶ **All the leagues had reverted to a traditional points system by the 1942-43 campaign.**

▲ *King George V was the first monarch to attend a Cup Final. He appeared amongst the 100,000 strong crowd wearing the red rose of Lancaster in his buttonhole.*

ONE OF THE LONGEST-SERVING MANAGERS WAS FRED EVERISS, HE WAS SECRETARY-MANAGER OF WEST BROMWICH ALBION BETWEEN 1902 AND 1948.

A day to remember

In an amazingly memorable act, the hostilities of war were temporarily stopped on Christmas Day 1914 for a historic football match between British and German troops, which the Allies won. Many Battalions also took footballs with them as they went 'over the top'.

Change is needed

By the summer of 1915, it was clear that the continuation of ordinary football would be near impossible. Already, many star players had been called away to war and the general public were growing resentful at the many young men paid to play football when they could have been serving their country. The 1915-16 season was greatly scaled down, and a national championship abandoned in favour of three regional tournaments – Lancashire, Midlands and Southern.

Football under attack

Several high-profile political figures began to speak out against the game and gained considerable support. They claimed football was setting a bad example to young men and wanted it scrapped entirely – one even went so far as to claim the remaining players were 'playing for the enemy and helping Germany win'.

The Footballers' Battalion

Football responded to criticism over its continuation by starting a Footballers' Battalion, the 17th Service Battalion of the Middlesex Regiment, in which a number of high-profile players fought. This encouraged fans to join up, too, and the players were allowed leave on Saturdays to play for their original clubs. Within a year, the entire League programme had been restricted to weekends to allow players who remained at home to take part-time jobs. Soon, national service had been made compulsory and the police would scour football matches looking for draft-dodgers.

The Buckley babes

If war was disastrous for players, it was a godsend for the coaching system. A number of successful future managers were groomed in forces football, most notably Major Frank Buckley, who was second-in-command of the Footballers'

Battalion. He coached a star-studded side during the war and later became manager of Wolves' greatest ever team, which included Stan Cullis and Billy Wright and was nicknamed the 'Buckley Babes' some years before Sir Matt Busby laid claim to a similar title for his great Manchester United team.

THE 8TH BATTALION THE EAST SURREY REGIMENT, WHO FAMOUSLY PLAYED FOOTBALL DURING THE BLOODY BATTLE OF THE SOMME, WERE AWARDED SEVERAL MEDALS FOR WARTIME BRAVERY: TWO DSOS, TWO MCS, TWO DCMS AND ONE BAR AND EIGHT MMS.

The depleted schedule

By 1916, the awarding of cups, medals and championships had been outlawed altogether. Games were to last only 80 minutes, without a half-time interval, and as games became increasingly irregular it was decided to cut players' payments drastically to just three pounds a week. There were problems finding enough players to fulfil fixtures, and teams often had to make up the numbers with members of the crowd or the opposition.

▶ The 1998 version of the Buckley Babes show off Manchester United's new kit: (l-r) Ole Gunnar Solskjaer, Nicky Butt and Andy Cole.

Football continued during the First World War. The Lancashire and Midland Leagues were formed with the winners meeting each other home and away for the title of League Champions in 1917 and 1918; a London Combination League served the South.

Winners were:

SEASON	LANCASHIRE	MIDLAND	LEAGUE CHAMPIONS	LONDON
1915-16	Manchester City	Notts Forest	Not played	Chelsea
1916-17	Liverpool	Leeds City	Not played	West Ham
1917-18	Stoke	Leeds City	Leeds	Chelsea
1918-19	Everton	Notts Forest	Notts Forest	Brentford

Brink of disaster

Under the circumstances, many clubs struggled to survive. They were forced to hand over large amounts of their gate receipts to charity, and their grounds fell into disrepair. The golden age was coming to an end, and it would take years for football to recover. Not so women's football, which flourished as many women worked full-time to keep the country running smoothly. They took up football as a past-time during their lunch breaks or after hours, and important matches staged during the war regularly drew crowds into the five-figure bracket.

One famous game staged around this time was between a women's charity XI and a group of Canadian soldiers who kept their hands tied behind their backs to make up for their physical advantage. The ladies won 8-5, and went on to surprise many who doubted their prowess over the next few years.

IN THE 1914-1915 SEASON, SHEFFIELD UNITED WON THE FA CUP AFTER BEATING CHELSEA 3-0 AT OLD TRAFFORD. PRESENTING THE TROPHY LORD DERBY TOLD THE SIDES: 'YOU HAVE PLAYED WITH ONE ANOTHER AND AGAINST ONE ANOTHER FOR THE CUP. IT IS NOW THE DUTY OF EVERYONE TO JOIN WITH EACH OTHER AND PLAY A STERNER GAME FOR ENGLAND'.

THE SMALLEST POST-WAR ATTENDANCE FOR A LEAGUE MATCH CONSISTED OF JUST 450 FANS WHO TURNED UP TO WATCH ROCHDALE TAKE ON CAMBRIDGE UNITED IN DIVISION FOUR, 2 FEBRUARY 1974. THE LOWEST CROWD TO WATCH A MATCH IN THE TOP FLIGHT WAS THE 3,039 WHO WATCHED WIMBLEDON V EVERTON IN A PREMIER LEAGUE CLASH ON 26 JANUARY 1993.

Scandal for United

The game was also hit, in 1915, by a scandal of titanic proportions. A bookmaker claimed that the Easter fixture between Manchester United and Liverpool, which United had won 2-0, had been fixed by the players. An immediate investigation by the Football Association found that huge bets had been placed on the outcome all across the country, and that both teams were fully aware of the scam.

Eight players in all were banned for life, although United's Enoch West was the only member of his team on the day to be punished. He protested vehemently at the ban, and continued to plead his innocence until he died. There were many who felt West had been made a scapegoat while the real ringleaders had escaped unpunished. The whole incident was a chilling forerunner of later, greater, match-fixing scandals.

Time to regroup

The competitive game was re-established in time for the 1918-19 season, when Nottingham Forest won a hastily-arranged Championship. The standard of football, however, suffered greatly for several years as clubs rebuilt their depleted playing staff, nurtured previously untapped new talent and tried to lead the nation in recovering from what had been a gruelling and tragic four years.

◄ In the 1990s, Bruce Grobbelaar was involved in a scandal of similar proportions to the 1915 match-fixing controversy.

▲ *Illustration showing* The British Ladies Football Club *at the turn of the century.*

1918-30: BIGGER AND BETTER

No clear leaders

In the 1980s and 1990s we have become accustomed to the concept of a 'Super Team' who dominate the League and Cups for several seasons at a time. The nature of such a team is cyclical; from Tottenham through Liverpool, and on to Manchester United, the baton of near-invincibility has been passed each few years. Yet football in the post-World War One era was very different.

Chasing Preston

Not since that great Preston side of the previous century had any one outfit really stamped their authority on the game, and it was a trend that was to continue right up until the 1930s and the emergence of Arsenal as a genuine force. In the meantime, it was left to a whole host of different clubs to make the era one of the most memorable, genuinely exciting and unpredictable in history.

A time of expansion

The advent of peace brought with it a new mood of expectation and relief which, inevitably, filtered through to football. As the game kicked off again in 1919, it was immediately decided to expand the top two divisions from 20 to 22 clubs each. Most expected the top flight to remain the same and be extended by the introduction of the top two teams from the Second Division. In fact, Arsenal – who finished a mere fifth in Division Two – were added to the list after their chairman exerted significant pressure on the authorities, and Tottenham were relegated at their expense. It heightened the rivalry between the two teams and saw the start of an enviable record for the Gunners – from 1919 to this day, they have never left the First Division. Spurs bounced back, but remained bitter.

A Third Division

It was also decided, a season after that initial expansion,

> Queen's Park flew the Scottish flag in the early years of the FA Cup, twice reaching the final. The Glasgow-based club was regarded as the best team around in the 1880s. In 1884 they reached the final after beating Crewe Alexandra 10-0 in the first round, Manchester 15-0 in round two, Oswestry 7-1 in round three, Aston Villa 6-1 in the fourth round, Old Westminster 1-0 in the quarter-finals and the holders Blackburn Olympic 4-1 in the semis. They lost 2-1 to Blackburn Rovers in the final after a controversial offside goal was allowed to stand. Two years later Queen's Park were back in the final where they again met Blackburn Rovers who repeated their previous feat with another 2-1 success.

to add yet another division to the fray. The quality and competitiveness of the Southern League had long been noted, and the 1920-21 season kicked off with all 22 clubs joining up en masse as a new Division Three. Crystal Palace won that first season, followed closely by Southampton, QPR and Swindon. By the time 1921-22 rolled around, the north had won itself its own Division Three, running in parallel to its southern equivalent: Stockport, Darlington and Grimsby led the way there, along with the more quickly forgotten Barrow, Stalybridge, Ashington and Durham City.

PLAYER OF THE YEAR – DOUBLE WINNERS

Mark Hughes
(Manchester United 1989 & 1991)
Alan Shearer
(Blackburn 1995, Newcastle 1997)

▲ *Alan Shearer playing for Blackburn in 1995, the same year he won the Player of the Year award for the first time.*
▶ *A crowd of expectant football fans, photographed in the 1920s.*

The League takes off

Both new leagues were generally welcomed, but some critics claimed a further increase in club numbers could only weaken the overall quality of the English game. Whether they were right is a matter still up for debate today, but the general public – particularly in the south – loved the new Division Three, and its opening weekend was welcomed by crowds of between 20-25,000 at several grounds. The North and South format was to stay in place until the two leagues were amalgamated into Third and Fourth divisions in 1958 – as a new century looms closer, there is talk of once again regionalizing them to maximize local derbies and minimize travelling costs for the country's smaller clubs.

Super Town

If there was one outstanding team of the era, it was Huddersfield Town. However, when the war ended, they were lucky to still be in existence. A series of crippling debts had left them almost bankrupt, and they were only allowed to stay in the Second

> **JUST FOUR MANAGERS HAVE WON THE LEAGUE CHAMPIONSHIP WITH DIFFERENT CLUBS**
>
> ▶ **Tom Watson with Sunderland in 1892, 1893 & 1895; with Liverpool in 1901.**
> ▶ **Herbert Chapman with Huddersfield in 1924 ,1925 & 1926; with Arsenal in 1933, 1934 & 1935.**
> ▶ **Brian Clough with Derby County in 1972; with Nottingham Forest in 1978.**
> ▶ **Kenny Dalglish with Liverpool in 1986, 1988 & 1990; with Blackburn in 1995.**

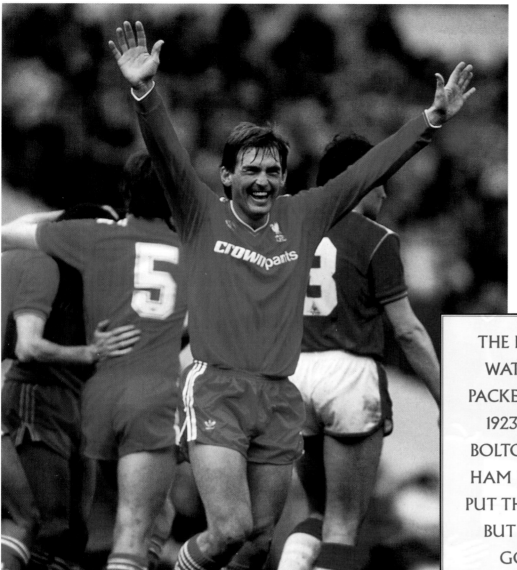

Aston Villa. Herbert Chapman joined them as manager in their next season, and they went on to win three titles in a row in the 1920s under his astute leadership. Chapman's success in purchasing and motivating the right players made him the first genuine managerial star.

Scandal and surprise

And yet Chapman might never have made it to Huddersfield had it not

> THE BIGGEST CROWD EVER TO WATCH AN ENGLISH MATCH PACKED INTO WEMBLEY FOR THE 1923 FA CUP FINAL BETWEEN BOLTON WANDERERS AND WEST HAM UNITED. OFFICIAL FIGURES PUT THE ATTENDANCE AT 126,047 BUT UP TO ANOTHER 70,000 GOT INTO THE GROUND WITHOUT PAYING.

▲ *Like Herbert Chapman, Kenny Dalglish (seen here celebrating Liverpool's second FA Cup Final goal in 1986) has won the League championship with two different clubs.*

Division on condition they merge with Leeds United and move to Elland Road. The Huddersfield public were outraged and rallied round to raise the cash needed to keep the club going: they succeeded, and the new players and staff turned things around in double-quick time.

Huddersfield finished as runners-up to Newcastle that season, and had been transformed from relegation favourites to a First Division side. Furthermore, they knocked out two top-flight teams to reach the 1920 Cup Final, where it took an own goal to separate them from

◄▲ *Brian Clough, photographed in his time as manager of Derby County.*
◄ *Huddersfield Town FC in the 1924–25 season – one of the years they were League champions under Herbert Chapman.*

been for the bizarre demise of Leeds City. Found guilty of making illegal payments to players during the war, the Yorkshire side were wound up in 1919 and expelled from the Second Division. Chapman, their manager at the time, was suspended from the game and could not even turn up as a spectator; his punishment was lifted to allow him to take over at Huddersfield. His former players were less fortunate; they were sold off in an auction at a Leeds hotel, fetching bargain prices.

Town on top

At Huddersfield, Chapman was a colossus. He took his first title in 1924, when his side beat Cardiff on a goal difference of 0.024 – the Welsh side missed a crucial penalty in their final game of the season against Birmingham, which ended goaless. Town's 3-0 victory against Nottingham Forest edged them ahead, even though the two sides were level on points. A year later, it was easier to call, as Chapman's team dominated from start to finish, remaining undefeated in their last 17 matches. Chapman left for Arsenal at the start of the 1925-26 season, seeking new challenges down south, but the side he left behind made it a hat-trick of championship wins.

Wales can't win

It was all bad news for Cardiff, who in 1924-25 sought to make up for their League disappointment by becoming the first Welsh side to win the FA Cup. Sadly, they lost 1-0 to Sheffield United because of a momentary lapse of concentration and had to wait another two years for another chance, when they beat Arsenal 1-0 with a controversial Hugh Ferguson goal. Yet there were other unlikely heroes that decade: Burnley won the 1920-21 championship despite losing their opening three matches, and Sheffield Wednesday emerged from mid-table mediocrity to take the title in 1929. Bolton Wanderers took the Cup three times and Liverpool took the League twice, in 1922 and 1923, thanks largely to the goalkeeping heroics of the great Elisha Scott.

Wembley steps in

The FA were taking notice of football's growing popularity and decided the game need a new venue to showcase both the FA Cup Final and the England national team. In 1921 they rejected the idea of expanding Crystal Palace and instead drew up plans for a new stadium at Wembley, north-west London, which they

ENGLAND WORLD CUP SQUAD, BRAZIL – 1950

POSITION	NAME	CLUB	AGE	CAPS	GOALS
GOALKEEPERS	TED DITCHBURN	TOTTENHAM	28	2	0
	BERT WILLIAMS	WOLVES	28	7	0
FULL-BACKS	JACK ASTON	MANCHESTER UTD	28	14	0
	BILL ECKERSLEY	BLACKBURN	23	0	0
	ALF RAMSEY	TOTTENHAM	30	5	0
	LAURIE SCOTT	ARSENAL	33	17	0
HALF-BACKS	JIMMY DICKINSON	PORTSMOUTH	25	7	0
	LAURIE HUGHES	LIVERPOOL	24	0	0
	BILL NICHOLSON	TOTTENHAM	31	0	0
	WILLIE WATSON	SUNDERLAND	30	2	0
	BILLY WRIGHT (C)	WOLVES	26	29	2
FORWARDS	EDDIE BAILY	TOTTENHAM	23	0	0
	ROY BENTLEY	CHELSEA	27	4	2
	HENRY COCKBURN	MANCHESTER UTD	27	10	0
	TOM FINNEY	PRESTON	28	25	18
	WILF MANNION	MIDDLESBROUGH	32	19	9
	STANLEY MATTHEWS	BLACKPOOL	35	30	10
	JACKIE MILBURN	NEWCASTLE	26	7	6
	STAN MORTENSEN	BLACKPOOL	29	18	15
	JIMMY MULLEN	WOLVES	27	4	2
	JIM TAYLOR	FULHAM	32	0	0

hoped would be among the most impressive in the world. Wembley took just over 300 working days to finish and was rigorously tested by battalions of soldiers in anticipation of its first ever match, the 1923 Cup Final.

The Old Lady

The new venue was an immediate success and quickly became the home of the English game. With its famous Twin Towers, Wembley was an imposing structure, vast in both its capacity and its sheer size. It was certainly big enough for the Olympics to be held there, but it was the endearing design of the great stadium that has made it such a fond memory for fans all across the world. With a strong sense of tradition and the regular patronage of the Royal Family, Wembley is a bigger star than many of the teams who frequent it: today it is nicknamed the 'Old Lady' and will need to be modernized considerably to take it into the next century.

◄ An oil painting by Charles Ernest Cundall (1890–1971) showing the Arsenal-Sheffield FA Cup Final of 1936, played at Wembley Stadium.
► One of England's best-loved players: Stanley Matthews during his time at Blackpool.

Transfer trials

Meanwhile, as Wembley was being prepared for action, the transfer market yet again spiralled. In 1922, one Syd Puddefoot became the first ever £5,000 footballer when he moved from West Ham to the small Scottish side Falkirk. The Hammers did not believe Falkirk would stump up a huge fee, and so demanded £5,000 just to test the water. To their amazement, they had a deal, and the furore surrounding the transfer prompted Arsenal to suggest a £1,650 ceiling on deals. That was rejected, but the maximum wage was reduced to £8 a week two years later, despite the threat of strike action from the Players' Union.

Scots savour victory

In spite of what was perceived as a greater-than-ever level of skill in the English game, the national side had a dismal decade. Scotland dominated the Home Championship, and it took England until 1930 to get a win under their belts. Even Wales were rubbing their noses in it, twice pipping their neighbours to the British crown. But the lowest point of all for England came in 1928, when Scotland's visit to the Twin Towers was to yield one of the most humiliating defeats the host nation had ever suffered.

A masterful display

The match itself was not important, as neither side could win the Championship that year. But Scotland put on a masterful display of attacking football, outclassing their opponents in every part of the pitch, and walked off 5-1 winners, with Alex Jackson grabbing a hat-trick. They rubbed salt in the wounds with a 1-0 victory at Hampden Park the season after, the only goal of the game being scored direct from a corner.

FA CUP FINAL ROYAL GUESTS:

1946	▶	**King George VI, Queen Elizabeth, Princess Elizabeth**
1947	▶	**Duke and Duchess of Gloucester**
1948	▶	**King George VI**
1949	▶	**Princess Elizabeth, Duke of Gloucester**
1950	▶	**King George VI**

The Player of the Year is selected from votes cast by fellow professionals.

Turn up the heat

Yet if England were woeful on the home front, things were going from bad to worse on foreign fields. In 1929, a shattered side lost 4-3 to Spain in searing heat in Madrid, their first defeat against a foreign side. It was Spanish coach Fred Pentland, a former England international, who had plotted the defeat, and it

Two shots of Dixie Dean showing off his world-class skills.

Dixie Dean has the highest tally of goals in one season. He scored 60 goals in 39 First Division games for Everton during the 1927-28 season. On top of that he also scored three FA Cup goals and 19 in international and representative matches, making a total of 82.

gave the popular press further ammunition as they bemoaned the passing of England's footballing dominance. In truth, the side were not helped by a dispute between the FA and Fifa which curtailed development for several years. The British authorities were incensed when their international governing body passed a motion allowing amateur players to be 'compensated' for their time when playing with professionals, and they walked out of Fifa under a cloud. They only rejoined in time for the 1950 World Cup, by which time England were no longer a major force in the world game.

Change in the law

One important development the FA were on top of was the offside law. In 1925, it was decided that only one player had to be between a forward and the opposing goal to keep him onside – previously it was three. The result was an increase in attacking football, and an explosion of goals in the 1925-26 season, up by an amazing 50 per cent. But the new law's greatest legacy was to change completely the way we think about the game tactically.

Chapman comes clean

Arsenal boss Herbert Chapman and his legendary defender Charlie Buchan are between them credited with inventing the modern sweeper (or stopper) system, when in 1925 – after a humiliating 7-0 defeat at Newcastle – the pair introduced a deep-lying midfielder to help marshall the offside trap and pick up players breaking from the middle of the field. Welshman Herbie Roberts filled the role admirably, and the Gunners' subsequent success is

> JAMES ROSS SCORED SEVEN GOALS FOR PRESTON NORTH END V STOKE, DIVISION ONE, 6 OCTOBER 1888. TED DRAKE ALSO SCORED SEVEN FOR ARSENAL V ASTON VILLA, DIVISION ONE, 14 DECEMBER 1935.

testament to Buchan and Chapman's tactical understanding.

The astute signing

Newcastle were among the clubs to follow Arsenal's lead, and they took their fourth League Championship in 1927. Hughie Gallacher, a

> Alec and David Herd were the first father and son duo to play in the same side. They lined up for Stockport County and celebrated a 2-0 Division Three North victory over Hartlepool on 5 May 1951.

▼*Arsenal photographed in 1927; Herbert Chapman is on the far right in the front row.*

£5,500 signing from Airdrie, was the side's inspiration, and averaged more than a goal every game during his time there. Meanwhile, Middlesbrough completed a fine season for the north-east by winning promotion to the First Division and scoring 122 goals – 59 of them from forward George Camsell.

> WANDERERS' LORD KINNAIRD, WHO PLAYED IN NINE FINALS, WAS CREDITED WITH THE FIRST OWN GOAL IN THE 1887 FINAL AGAINST OXFORD UNIVERSITY.

Full circle?

And so, as the first ever World Cup kicked off in Uruguay without the country that popularized football, it was a time of transition for England. The old order had been cast aside, and the death in 1930 of that first Cup Final superstar, Lord Kinnaird, was a genuine milestone. That same year, the Graf Zeppelin hovered above Wembley as Arsenal and Huddersfield played and appeared to salute the King. The game had come a long way in a very short space of time.

▼ *Newcastle supporters welcoming Alan Shearer back to St James's Park in 1996.*

DIXIE DEAN: THE COMPLETE CENTRE FORWARD

A striker without peers

There are, it is said, not enough superlatives in existence to describe the talents of Dixie Dean, the Everton and England centre forward whose devastating goalscoring skills dominated the British game for the best part of a decade. Dean was a colossus in the air, a clinical finisher and an amazingly powerful striker, and although relatively few people alive today ever had the chance to see him play, he is still talked off as one of football's first legends.

Dynamic Dixie

Dean, whose real name was William but who adopted the nickname 'Dixie' from a popular song of the early 1920s, lived for Everton. A lifelong fan, he always dreamed of playing for the Goodison Park outfit, but instead began his career with Merseyside's third team, Tranmere Rovers. There he scored 27 goals in 27 matches as a 17-year-old and attracted the attention of almost every leading First Division side – but there could be only one victor, and Everton paid a weighty £3,000 for his services in 1925.

> ROBERT (BUNNY) BELL SCORED NINE GOALS IN TRANMERE ROVERS' 13-4 WIN OVER OLDHAM ATHLETIC IN DIVISION THREE NORTH ON 26 DECEMBER 1935.

Into the record books

The stocky centre forward was an instant hit. Everton were languishing in the wrong half of the First Division for his first couple of seasons up front, but in 1927-28 they were chasing for the title and Dean was leading the way. By May Everton had the championship sewn up and Dean had 57 League goals to his credit. The three more scored

▲ *Dixie Dean is one of football's greatest legends. His skilful playing is still an inspiration for footballers today.*

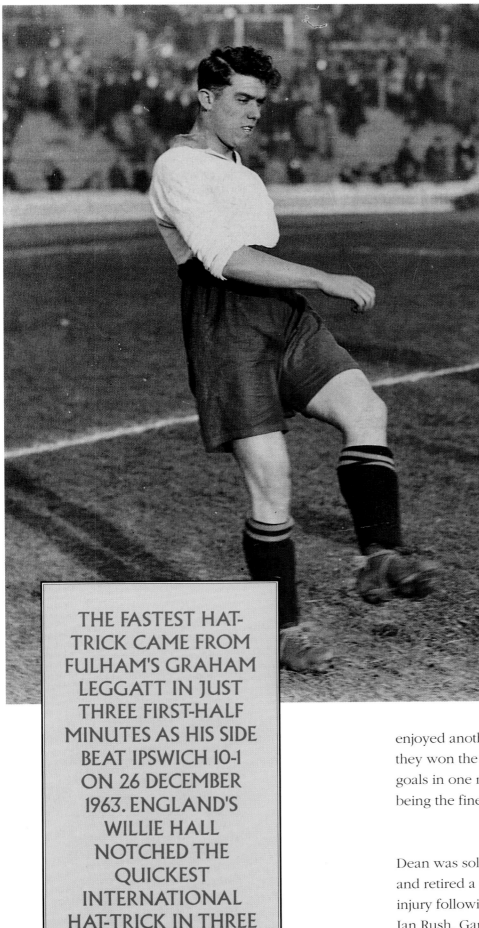

◄ Dixie Dean, seen scoring one of his many goals for Everton.

when second-placed Arsenal visited would put him into the record books, overhauling George Camsell's total of the previous year. The two men enjoyed a healthy rivalry, but it was Dean who took the record when he got a hat-trick in Everton's 3-2 win that day. It is unlikely anyone will beat his 60-goal mark in the top flight, particularly the 40 he scored with his head.

A natural scorer

Many believe Dean was able to score so many goals because he took advantage of the new relaxed offside rule: that is true, but he was also a natural finisher who would have found the net at any level. He averaged more than a goal a game for England in one of their more barren periods, and was still smashing them in past his 30th birthday. Everton were relegated at the turn of the decade, but Dean helped them bounce straight back and enjoyed another Indian summer the next season when they won the title again. He twice scored five goals in one match, and cemented his claim to being the finest striker of his generation.

A fitting end

Dean was sold to Notts County in 1938 and retired a year later through injury following a spell in Ireland. Ian Rush, Gary Lineker and Kenny Dalglish may also have been Merseyside legends, but they had nothing on Dean. He died in 1980, fittingly after watching his beloved Blues play Liverpool at Goodison Park.

THE FASTEST HAT-TRICK CAME FROM FULHAM'S GRAHAM LEGGATT IN JUST THREE FIRST-HALF MINUTES AS HIS SIDE BEAT IPSWICH 10-1 ON 26 DECEMBER 1963. ENGLAND'S WILLIE HALL NOTCHED THE QUICKEST INTERNATIONAL HAT-TRICK IN THREE FIRST-HALF MINUTES AGAINST IRELAND ON 16 NOVEMBER 1938.

THE WHITE HORSE FINAL

The Twin Towers

When the Football Association announced plans for a new national stadium in 1921, they anticipated building the greatest arena of its kind in the world. But when Wembley Stadium finally opened in 1923, after a mammoth construction job costing hundreds of thousands of pounds, the occasion proved to be larger than the organizers could ever have dreamed it to be.

▲ *The FA Cup Final of 1923 made headlines worldwide; this is an Italian illustration of crowds invading the pitch.*

That year's FA Cup Final between Bolton Wanderers and West Ham was chosen as the match to mark the opening of Wembley. It was claimed the new venue could hold over 125,000 spectators, but such was the hype and publicity surrounding the event that on 28 April, almost double that turned up – and most of them managed to get in.

A near-disaster

Back in the 1920s, the idea of holding an all-ticket match was unheard of, and so fans were able to pour into Wembley, often overturning barricades and barging past officials to get in. By the time the players emerged from the tunnel to try and begin the match, the pitch was swamped with people and kick-off was delayed for 45 minutes as police attempted to clear the field. As a result, the referee dispensed with the formality of a half-time break.

The White Horse

The game was later to become known as the 'White Horse Final' because one of the most recognizable of the policemen present was Constable George Scorey on his white horse Billy; ironically, he wasn't a football fan and could never understand the publicity he received. When he got home that night and was asked how his day had been, the modest hero merely replied: 'ordinary.'

A controversial match

Even when things finally got underway, the Final became increasingly difficult to play as the ball was continually lost in the crowds swelling round the edges of

FA CUP FINAL ROYAL GUESTS

1961	▶	Duchess of Kent
1962	▶	Queen Elizabeth II and Duke of Edinburgh
1963	▶	Queen Elizabeth II and Duke of Edinburgh
1964	▶	Earl of Harewood
1965	▶	Queen Elizabeth II and Duke of Edinburgh
1966	▶	Princess Margaret
1967	▶	Duke and Duchess of Kent
1968	▶	Princess Alexandra
1969	▶	Princess Anne
1970	▶	Princess Margaret

▲ *The police, memorably including Constable Scorey on Billy, attempt to move the crowd back to the sidelines.*

the pitch. Bolton's first goal was scored while a Hammers player was lost in the melee trying to retrieve the ball; the Lancashire side went on to win the game 2-0 and were presented with the Cup by King George. The FA, meanwhile, made sure that every Cup Final from that day onwards was an all-ticket affair. They knew a disaster had been narrowly averted that day, and it was only the good humour of the crowd and the actions of the police that had prevented injuries, and quite possibly fatalities.

FA CUP UPSETS

Yeovil Town have beaten League opposition 17 times during their FA Cup career. They have reached the Third Round on eleven occasions, more than any other non-League club. The clubs to have suffered at their feet are:

1924-1925	▶	**Bournemouth 3-2**
1934-1935	▶	**Crystal Palace 3-0, Exeter 4-1**
1938-1939	▶	**Brighton 2-1**
1948-1949	▶	**Bury 3-1, Sunderland 2-1**
1958-1959	▶	**Southend 1-0**
1960-1961	▶	**Walsall 1-0**
1963-1964	▶	**Southend 1-0, Crystal Palace 3-1**
1970-1971	▶	**Bournemouth 1-0**
1972-1973	▶	**Brentford 2-1**
1987-1988	▶	**Cambridge 1-0**
1991-1992	▶	**Walsall 1-0**
1992-1993	▶	**Torquay 5-2, Hereford 2-1**
1993-1994	▶	**Fulham 1-0**

BROADCASTING FOOTBALL

The radio era

The Arsenal v Sheffield United fixture on 22 January 1927 was an unremarkable match – but off the pitch, history was being made at Highbury that day. The BBC had finally given in to pressure from listeners and made the First Division game the first ever to be broadcast live on radio, thus beginning a tradition which is continued to this day.

Football had never really been considered as a suitable source of radio material until then, but the success of the Arsenal game led to many further broadcasts during the remainder of that season, culminating in a live radio relay of the Cup Final, where future Arsenal manager George Allison commentated on Cardiff's 1-0 victory over the Gunners. Broadcasting had arrived in the game, and would never leave it.

The calling game

The BBC initially tried to get round the problems of visualizing the game through the radio by employing a second commentator to call out numbers which related to

MIDFIELDER VINNIE JONES HOLDS THE RECORDS FOR THE QUICKEST BOOKINGS IN LEAGUE AND CUP. HE WAS BOOKED WITHIN FIVE SECONDS OF SHEFFIELD UNITED'S FIRST DIVISION AWAY FIXTURE AT MANCHESTER CITY ON 19 JANUARY 1991. IN CHELSEA'S FA CUP FIFTH-ROUND TIE AGAINST HIS FORMER SHEFFIELD UNITED TEAM-MATES ON 15 FEBRUARY 1992, JONES HAD HIS NAME TAKEN AFTER THREE SECONDS.

the position of the ball on the pitch. A grid printed in the *Radio Times* enabled listeners to follow the action at

▼ *Sky TV's outside broadcasting studio, used for exclusive sports coverage.*

CAREERS AFTER FOOTBALL – COMMENTATORS/JOURNALISTS (PLAYING CAREERS IN BRACKETS)

CHARLES BUCHAN
(Sunderland, Arsenal 1909–28) – now deceased
DENIS COMPTON
(Arsenal 1936–49)
JACKIE MILBURN
(Newcastle 1946–56)
LEN SHACKLETON
(Bradford PA, Newcastle, Sunderland 1946–57)
IVOR BROADIS
(Carlisle, Sunderland, Manchester City, Newcastle, Carlisle 1946–58)
DANNY BLANCHFLOWER
(Barnsley, Aston Villa, Tottenham 1948–63) – now deceased
JIMMY HILL
(Brentford, Fulham 1949–60)
JIMMY MCILROY
(Burnley, Stoke, Oldham 1950–67)
JIMMY ARMFIELD
(Blackpool & England 1954–70)
IAN ST JOHN
(Motherwell, Liverpool, Coventry, Tranmere 1956–72)
DENIS LAW
(Huddersfield, Manchester City, Manchester Utd, 1956–73)
JIMMY GREAVES
(Chelsea, Tottenham, West Ham 1957–70)
JOHNNY GILES
(Manchester Utd, Leeds, West Brom 1959–76)

introduced *Match Of The Day* – a compilation of League highlights and goals from each Saturday's play – to huge success a few years later.

Pay-per-view?

The advent of the Premiership in the 1992-93 season saw television rights granted to Sky TV, a satellite service paid for by subscription. While many were dismayed by the prospect of paying to watch football, Sky's cash became crucial to clubs and its service is generally regarded as second-to-none. The next venture,

home, although many found the practice too confusing and it was dropped as the game got ever faster. The distinctive style of the commentators and the vital service they provided, however, made BBC football an important and lasting institution. It even survived a 14-year ban which began in 1931 – Third Division clubs complained that live broadcasting of matches was hitting their attendances and, for a while, only the World Service was able to carry games.

Enter television

Almost inevitably, television entered the fray soon afterwards, and in 1937 a limited number of viewers were able to see an Arsenal practice match from Highbury. As picture quality and transmission improved, so did the coverage of football, and by the late 1940s the Cup Final was a regular fixture in the schedules. The 1960s saw the first broadcasting of international matches, and the BBC

▲ *One of sport's best-known faces, TV personality Desmond Lynam.*

however, will be more controversial still: the 21st century is almost certain to usher in pay-per-view football with a fee for each match. Eventually, it may be possible to stage your own action replays or view the match stats of your choice from the comfort of your armchair.

1930-39: ARSENAL DOMINATE

Heading south

It was a sign of the changing face of football that the League title made its first journey to the south of the country almost as soon as the 1930s had begun. Arsenal were the side who took the trophy to London, and it was no flash in the pan – the Gunners, thanks largely to the efforts of their iconic manager Herbert Chapman, were to become the team of the decade.

The country was in the grip of depression in those pre-war years, and the previous inexorable rise in attendances was halted as recession hit hard on the average family. But

on the pitch at least, the 1930s saw some of the most entertaining and skilful football of the century, much of it emerging from north London.

Herbert leads the way

Arsenal took the 1931 championship in style. Under Chapman's inspired tactical leadership, which encouraged attacking football while keeping the back-line simultaneously tight, they failed to score in only one of their matches, finished the season with a record 66 points (in the days of two points for a win) and hit the net some 127 times in the League. Ironically, this was not a record as second-placed Aston Villa managed 128 in the same season.

Bastin the best

Alex James, shifted from forward to playmaker, was the lynchpin of the side, but its star was winger Cliff Bastin, a fast and nimble player who shone both for the Gunners and England. With Jack Lambert putting the goals away and David Jack imposing himself on the other

▲ *Highbury Stadium, the home of Arsenal. Inside the club is a statue of Herbert Chapman, manager extraordinaire.*

◀ *Today Arsenal are still one of the best teams around, as their 1998 Double proves.*

EIGHT MEN HAVE ACHIEVED THE ULTIMATE FEAT OF PLAYING FOR AND MANAGING A CHAMPIONSHIP WINNING SIDE

Ted Drake	Player	▶	**Arsenal, 1934, 1935, 1938**
	Manager	▶	**Chelsea 1955**
Bill Nicholson	Player	▶	**Tottenham 1951**
	Manager	▶	**Tottenham 1961**
Alf Ramsey	Player	▶	**Tottenham 1951**
	Manager	▶	**Ipswich 1962**
Joe Mercer	Player	▶	**Everton 1939, Arsenal 1948, 1953**
	Manager	▶	**Manchester City 1968**
Dave Mackay	Player	▶	**Tottenham 1961**
	Manager	▶	**Derby County 1975**
Bob Paisley	Player	▶	**Liverpool 1947**
	Manager	▶	**Liverpool, 1976, 1977, 1979, 1980, 1982, 1983**
Howard Kendall	Player	▶	**Everton 1970**
	Manager	▶	**Everton 1985, 1987**
Kenny Dalglish	Player	▶	**Liverpool 1979, 1980, 1982, 1983, 1984**
	Player-manager	▶	**Liverpool 1986, 1988**
	Manager	▶	**Liverpool 1990, Blackburn 1995**

wing, Arsenal had a formidable side. The south's new might was comparable only to the dismal season suffered by the previous doyens of the north, Manchester United. The great club lost their opening 12 matches, a record to this day (including a 7-0 thrashing by Aston Villa) and were cut well adrift of proceedings by the New Year. Relegation was a merciful release that season at Old Trafford, and the club languished in the doldrums until the arrival of Sir Matt Busby.

A unique Double

West Brom achieved an unusual Double in that same year, becoming the first club ever to be promoted and win the Cup in the same year. They defeated high-flying Everton in the semi-finals, before beating local rivals Birmingham 2-1 in the Final. Meanwhile, Southport of the Third Division (North) went all the way to the quarter-finals, before succumbing 9-1 to Everton.

▶ *Liverpool's world-class player-manager Kenny Dalglish in his heyday.*

The giant-killers

Southport's achievements were overshadowed by one of the greatest giant-killings of Cup history in 1933, when Third Division Walsall humbled League leaders Arsenal in the third round. Robbed of several players through injury, the Gunners were outplayed by their minnow opponents and lost 2-0, the second goal coming through a Bill Sheppard penalty. Tommy Black, the debutant defender who gave away the spot-kick, was transferred after the match for bringing shame on the club. Few games since have sent the same sort of shockwaves through the football community.

No Double at Highbury

Arsenal missed out on the Double in 1933 after collapsing in the final month of the season. Everton – newly promoted to the top flight and fired by the record-breaking Dixie Dean – capitalized on the Gunners' slip-up and their own superb home form, to take the championship by two points. And Arsenal could not even savour the consolation of an FA Cup win – 1-0 up in their final with Newcastle, they conceded a Jack Allen goal that modern technology has proved should not have stood. The Arsenal players stopped, certain Newcastle's winger Richardson had taken the ball out of play, but the referee thought otherwise and the Geordies went on to win 2-1.

Glory days for England

The Thirties saw the national team steadily improving, after the setbacks of the 1920s tussles with Scotland. In 1932, England defeated the Scots 3-0 at Wembley to clinch the International Championship outright, despite fielding five debutants in the one match. Austria arrived at Stamford Bridge a year later, billed as one of the finest teams in the world. But although they generally outplayed their hosts and gave England a major scare, they lost 4-3. It would be a few years yet before any non-British team could win on English soil.

No-go Italy

Even world champions Italy were unable to do it in 1934, in a fixture that was to become known as 'The Battle of Highbury.' An early skirmish between the two sides left the visiting Italians furious, and they went 3-0 down as they fouled their way through the first half. Two goals after the break were not enough to prevent an

> The best team tally of goals in the top flight was Aston Villa's 128 in 42 games in the 1930-31 season.

> HERBERT CHAPMAN LED HUDDERSFIELD TO THREE STRAIGHT TITLE VICTORIES IN 1924, 1925 AND 1926. REMARKABLY, HE ACHIEVED THE SAME FEAT WITH ARSENAL IN 1933, 1934, AND 1935.

England victory, and the Press were particularly critical of the visitors' conduct. England should have rounded off a fine series of results by beating Scotland at Hampden Park in 1937, but instead managed to lose 3-1 in one of the finest pre-war derby matches. The official attendance figure of 149,547 supporters was a world record at the time, and more spectators may have got in without paying.

▶ *Dennis Bergkamp one of Arsenal's top players of the 1990s.*

Sudden death

Arsenal were definitely the nation's greatest side in 1934 and were heading for their second title when, on 6 January of that year, disaster struck: Herbert Chapman, their brilliant, innovative manager, died of pneumonia after catching a chill watching his third team play. His demise left the club in utter disarray. Many of the players hadn't even heard the news when they turned up at Highbury for their next match. It was left to George Allison, a club director and popular commentator with BBC Radio, to step into the breach, despite never having played League football. He steered Arsenal to the title that year, with centre forward Ted Drake scoring seven in the last 10 games.

Swift goes faint

There was more drama in the Cup Final of 1934, when Manchester City's young goalkeeper Frank Swift – a future England player – fainted on the final whistle and had to be helped to the Royal Box to collect his medal. The 19-year-old had blamed himself for allowing Portsmouth to take the lead, and was overcome with emotion when his side hauled back the deficit to win 2-1. Arsenal completed a hat-trick of Championships when they took the top honour in 1935, with Ted Drake scoring 42 goals in the League. It was a fitting memorial to the man who had built the Highbury side, Herbert Chapman – particularly as it was Chapman who had engineered the last triple League success, with Huddersfield in the 1920s.

▼ *The face of Wembley in 1934; Manchester City playing Portsmouth in the FA Cup Final.*

Luton, who hit the back of the net some 10 times for his side as they beat Bristol Rovers 12-0 in the Third Division (South).

◄ *Some of Arsenal's top players of 1935* (l-r): *Male, Drake, Hapgood, Bastin and Copping.*

Pools for fools?

It was gambling that was to provide the 1930s' main talking point. The pools – in which punters tried to guess which games would be drawn in return for a cash prize – had become

Drake roams free

Sunderland interrupted the Gunners' progress in 1935-36, denying them a fourth title when they won by 10 clear points, but the season's outstanding player was once again Drake. The free-scoring striker entered the record books again by scoring all seven goals in his side's 7-1 away win at Aston Villa, despite playing with a knee injury. He was upstaged in the strike stakes, however, by Joe Payne of

unbelievably popular in the 10 years since their introduction, but the FA were concerned about the

> In the 1939 Cup Final, Wolves were rumoured to be using monkey gland potion to boost their fitness before the match.

involvement of gambling in football and a possible repeat of the 1915 match-fixing scandal. They first tried to outlaw the practice in 1934, and in 1936 invoked a 'Pools War' when they tried to outfox the betting companies by refusing to announce which away team would be playing where until a couple of days before the game, thus scuppering any attempts to predict the outcome of matches in advance.

> Individual tragedies: Roy Harper died while refereeing a Division Four match between York City and Halifax Town at Bootham Crescent on 5 May 1969.

NEWCASTLE UNITED'S ALBERT SHEPHERD SCORED THE FIRST FA CUP FINAL PENALTY IN THE 1910 REPLAY AGAINST BARNSLEY.

A stunt gone wrong

The public, however, were furious at the decision, which also led to a huge decline in attendances due to the lack of publicity over fixtures, and the idea was dropped after just a few weeks. The authorities eventually gave way and were later to receive cash in return for the use of their fixture lists. It was an important victory for the fans.

Super City

Frank Swift was the driving force behind Manchester City's surprise title win in 1936-37, as the Maine Road outfit outscored second-placed Charlton by 49 goals following a season of dynamic attacking football and solid defending. But they were upstaged by Millwall in the FA Cup – no team could beat the south Londoners at The Den, and they defeated Chelsea and Derby before dismissing City 2-0. The first basement side to make it to the semi-finals, Millwall eventually lost to Sunderland, who went on to beat Preston in the Final thanks to the inspiration of the great Raich Carter.

LEN SHACKLETON SCORED SIX GOALS ON HIS DEBUT FOR NEWCASTLE UNITED IN A 13-0 SECOND DIVISION WIN OVER NEWPORT COUNTY ON 5 OCTOBER 1946, JUST THREE DAYS AFTER ARRIVING AT THE CLUB FROM BRADFORD PARK AVENUE.

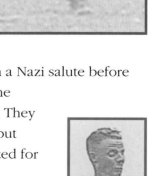

THE POOLS

▲ LAUNCHED IN 1923 BY LITTLEWOODS WHEN THEY DISTRIBUTED 4,000 COUPONS OUTSIDE OLD TRAFFORD.

▲ THE FIRST PAY-OUT WAS JUST £2-12S.

▲ THE TREBLE CHANCE WAS INTRODUCED IN 1946.

▲ THE FIRST MILLIONAIRE WINNER LANDED HIS JACKPOT IN 1986.

▲ IN NOVEMBER 1994 A SYNDICATE FROM WORSLEY, MANCHESTER WON THE BIGGEST PAYOUT SO FAR – £2,924,622.

Last-gasp win

Arsenal were back in business by 1938, although they only won the Championship from Wolves on the final weekend of the season. Everton took over the ascendancy in the final championship before war set in, but it was the 1939 Cup Final that really captured the imagination – in-form Wolves were beaten 4-1 by unfancied Portsmouth in what was a major shock.

Salute of danger

By then, however, the sceptre of war was looming. When England played in Berlin's Olympic Stadium in 1938, they were ordered to perform a Nazi salute before the game, despite the players' uneasiness. They beat Germany 6-3, but were heavily criticized for bowing to Hitler's demands. At home,

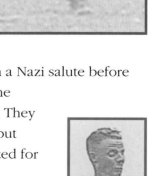

▲ *Arsenal's Bryn Jones demonstrating the kind of playing that made them such a top club; 13 August 1938.*

Arsenal smashed the transfer record by paying £14,000 to sign Bryn Jones from Wolves. It was hoped he would replace Alex James at Highbury, but Arsenal's decade of dominance was to be severely interrupted by the hostilities that shortly followed. For better or for worse, the game would never be the same again.

HERBERT CHAPMAN: BREAKING THE MOULD

A revolutionary

Football management before the arrival of Herbert Chapman was an archaic institution. Sides were selected by committee and looked after by the club secretary. Tactics and motivation were crude, if they existed at all. It was Chapman who single-handedly dragged the system into the modern era.

Like so many fine managers, Chapman was nothing more than an average player. His best days were spent with Northampton (for whom he appeared in three different spells), Sheffield United and Spurs, but his most significant action was to take charge of Northampton as his playing career came to an end in 1907. Chapman introduced different forms of tactics for individual matches instead of the usual all-out attack and handed out much-needed advice to his sides.

Between 1975 and 1983, Liverpool's Bob Paisley led the club to 20 trophies — six League Championships, three European Cups, three League Cups, one UEFA Cup, one European Super Cup, six Charity Shields (one shared).

Glory days

Northampton, and Chapman's next club Leeds City, both came desperately close to a Football League place, and larger clubs soon came sniffing after him. Huddersfield – an unfashionable side in the wrong half of the First Division – won the race and he won them the 1922 FA Cup. After four years in Yorkshire, Arsenal tempted him to London for a glorious career at Highbury. A bust of Chapman now takes pride of place in the club's famed Marble Halls.

Highbury high jinks

Arsenal were pipped only by Huddersfield for the championship in a halcyon first season. They finally got their hands on the silverware in both 1931 and 1933, as well as winning an FA Cup with the likes of Eddie Hapgood, Alex James and the legendary Cliff Bastin, dedicated players of unprecedented skill. When Chapman died suddenly in January 1934, the team he moulded went on to their third title in a row, allowing them to keep the trophy outright.

Five managers have suffered the misery of being involved with two clubs relegated in the same season: John Bond managed Swansea and Birmingham in the 1985 to 1986 season; Ron Saunders was in charge of West Bromwich Albion and Birmingham in the same campaign; Bob Stokoe worked with Carlisle and Sunderland in 1986 to 1987; Billy McNeill was at the helm during Manchester City and Aston Villa's 1987 relegation season and Dave Bassett managed Watford and Sheffield United in 1988.

Change for the better

Chapman's greatest legacy was the changes he introduced in the overall organization of the managerial system and the game as a whole. Never before had anyone considered compensating for the offside trap, arranging special medical treatment for injured players, motivating players on a one-to-one basis or playing friendlies abroad to gain greater knowledge of the game. Chapman did them all, and his legacy helped make football what it is today.

The Chapman legacy

By all accounts, Chapman was generally a reserved man with few vices. What he possessed in abundance, however, was a vast intellect utilized to the full for the good of football. Alex Ferguson, Kenny Dalglish and co. have more than they probably realize to thank Herbert Chapman for. Without him, who knows where we would be now?

▲ *The face of Arsenal's most revered manager of all time; his sudden death in 1934 left the football world devastated.*
◄ *Huddersfield Town FC, team of 1921–22. Herbert Chapman is seated at the far left of the front row.*

1939-45: THE SECOND WORLD WAR

Second time around

Football showed it had learned the lessons of the First World War when it was again thrown into confusion in 1939. War was declared in September that year, but rather than struggle on in the face of mounting public disdain, the game sensibly decided to fit itself around the hostilities and emerged with a great deal of credit for doing so.

1939-40 WINNERS

South A	▶ Arsenal
South B	▶ QPR
South C	▶ Tottenham
South D	▶ Crystal Palace
South West	▶ Plymouth
Midlands	▶ Wolves
East Midlands	▶ Chesterfield
West	▶ Stoke
North West	▶ Bury
North East	▶ Huddersfield
League Cup	▶ West Ham

Confusion reigns

Attendances were hit almost immediately after the outbreak of war, and there was little point in continuing a normal League programme. Play was suspended altogether at first, because the Government banned large groups of people meeting in public places, and many clubs decided to shut down completely to allow players and fans to concentrate on military service. The rest of the sides were organized into

▲ *Matches were banned at the start of the Second World War, the government feared an outbreak of unruly games, such as took place before footballing conventions were established.*

1940-41 WINNERS

North	▶	**Preston**
South	▶	**Crystal Palace**
London Cup	▶	**Reading**
West Regional Cup	▶	**Bristol City**
League Cup	▶	**Preston**

regional leagues, with few surprise winners – Arsenal, Wolves and Huddersfield were all champions and the practice continued for the duration of the war. A national League Cup was held in 1940 and won by West Ham United.

Englishmen abroad

There was plenty of football to be played for those professionals who fought abroad, although several hundred never returned. Stan Cullis, Tommy Lawton and Joe Mercer were among those who represented the Army in foreign fields, in particular France, even at the height of the hostilities. In the African regiments they even organized makeshift Leagues for the huge numbers of keen footballers who wanted to compete.

The guest system

Back home, what football survived was always entertaining but rarely skilful. Winston Churchill, unlike the political leaders of the 1910s, saw the game as important in lifting public morale and gave it his personal blessing. But clubs were lucky if they could field the same team for two matches running, such was the chaos of the system. All teams were allowed to field guest players, and international stars were very much in demand, often appearing for dozens of clubs in the same season.

◄ *Tommy Lawton – a footballing legend.*

▲ *After an initial suspension, football was encouraged during the war as an important way of boosting public morale.*

1941-42 WINNERS

North	▶ Blackpool
South	▶ Leicester
League Championship	▶ Manchester United
League Cup	▶ Wolves
London League	▶ Arsenal
London Cup	▶ Brentford

Packing a punch

Liverpool even signed the world heavyweight boxing champion Joe Louis in 1944, but he never made an appearance for them and it proved more a publicity stunt than a serious venture. More often than not, the guests who appeared were the result of desperation: there were no professionals left, on Government insistence.

couple of their reserve team, while several soldiers from the crowd made up the numbers but proved to be fairly hopeless and the goalkeeper arrived with only moments to spare. The makeshift side were no match for their fully-prepared hosts and lost 18-0, a record for any match played between League sides.

Shot to glory

Aldershot were the side who benefited most from the war. With an air force and army base in the town, soldiers and servicemen stopping over were only too happy to guest

Brighton on the rocks

Brighton suffered particularly badly; on Christmas morning 1940 they were desperately short of players for a game at Norwich and had to find six men at short notice. Their opponents provided a

1942-43 WINNERS

North	▶ Blackpool
North (Second Championship)	▶ Liverpool
South	▶ Arsenal
West	▶ Lovell's Athletic
League North Cup	▶ Blackpool
League South Cup	▶ Arsenal
League West Cup	▶ Swansea

for them in the Southern Championship, and this often meant they had some of the biggest names in English football playing for them. Tommy Lawton was a regular, as well as being one of the biggest scorers in the wartime game with 200 goals over five seasons, and internationals Stan Cullis and Jimmy Hagan wore the Hampshire club's colours alongside him.

1943-44 WINNERS

North	▶	**Blackpool**
North (Second Championship)	▶	**Bath**
South	▶	**Tottenham**
West	▶	**Lovell's Athletic**
League North Cup	▶	**Aston Villa**
League South Cup	▶	**Charlton**
League West Cup	▶	**Bath**

Glory for England

Neither did England stop their international programme during the war. Although matches were restricted to British opposition, England were dominant throughout the period and their finest hour came against Scotland at Maine Road in 1943. With the likes of Stanley Matthews, Dennis Compton and Raich Carter lining up, England won 8-0 in a brilliant performance and Lawton grabbed four of the goals.

Stan switches sides

There were other memorable victories. Against Wales later that year, England allowed Stan Mortensen to appear as a substitute for the opposition but still blitzed them 8-3. Scotland were defeated 6-3 thanks to another Lawton hat-trick in 1944, and England won three-quarters of their derby games during the war. Churchill himself turned up for a 1941 international and was introduced to the players before kick-off.

◀ *Blackpool's Stanley Mortensen in action.*

1944-45 WINNERS

North	►	**Huddersfield**
North (Second Championship)	►	**Derby**
South	►	**Tottenham**
West	►	**Cardiff**
League North Cup	►	**Bolton**
League South Cup	►	**Chelsea**
League West Cup	►	**Bath**

Pooling the cash

The pools were discontinued during the war, as all forms of gambling were outlawed and mail was restricted, but the companies got round this by donating large chunks of their profits to charity and joining forces to produce one unifying coupon and share postage costs.

Football had played a very important role in the country's well-being and morale by the time the war ended in 1945, a fact Churchill readily acknowledged. The entertainment it provided, both for spectators at home and the thousands of servicemen abroad who listened to their favourite teams playing on the BBC World Service, won the game a lot of popularity and goodwill which led to an attendance boom soon after peace was established.

Grounds for complaint

Sadly, the grounds themselves were less fortunate in the hostilities. Many were bombed, most famously Old Trafford, which had to be closed for repair for much of the 1945-46 season. Arsenal had to share with their rivals Tottenham due to bomb damage, as London clubs such as Millwall and West Ham were targeted by German planes. Plymouth and Swindon, two West Country clubs, also found themselves bombed out, and even Wembley was hit, although little damage was done.

Derby's days

Peace was restored in time for the FA Cup to resume in 1945-46, although no full League programme could yet be held. Raich Carter's Derby County beat Charlton 4-1 in the

▼*An aerial view of Old Trafford as it appears today; it had to be extensively repaired after bomb damage in the Second World War.*

1945-46 WINNERS

North	▶ **Sheffield United**
South	▶ **Birmingham**
Third Division North (West)	▶ **Accrington**
Third Division North (East)	▶ **Rotherham**
Third Division South (North)	▶ **QPR**
Third Division South (South)	▶ **Crystal Palace**
League Third Division North Cup	▶ **Rotherham**
League Third Division South Cup	▶ **Bournemouth**
FA Cup	▶ **Derby**

Final, although the competition had already been marred by tragedy when a wall collapsed under spectator pressure at the Bolton-Stoke quarter-final at Burnden Park and 33 fans died.

There is, however, always a happy side to be found, and football undoubtedly grew in stature after the war ended. It even found its own German star – Bert Trautmann, a former Prisoner of War who stayed in England after 1945 and established himself as a firm favourite in goal for Manchester City for the next decade despite his nationality.

▶ *A collection of football memorabilia spanning the decades.*

1946-60: ENGLAND JOINS THE WORLD

A double-edged sword

The end of the war provoked two sets of drastically different consequences: on the one hand, the nation's mood was ebullient and upbeat, glad to be finally rid of the devastating ravages the conflicts of the previous six years had brought on. On the other hand, however, the country was, both financially and socially, in a state of disarray.

A cautious start

Nowhere was this contrast better illustrated than in football. For too long the nation had been deprived of its most popular sport, and the end of the war brought with it huge expectation about the game's return. The 1945-46 season had been a typically cautious affair, with regional leagues, two-legged FA Cup ties (Derby County beat Charlton to take that year's trophy) and a whole host of problems for the authorities.

Grounds for concern

Many clubs were returning to grounds ravaged by bombing raids, and many key players had been killed or injured during the war. Furthermore, the stars of 1939 were frequently past their best in 1945, and the obvious lack of youth development in the interim years left hundreds to make their full debuts within weeks of signing for their clubs. The standard of football had rarely been so low.

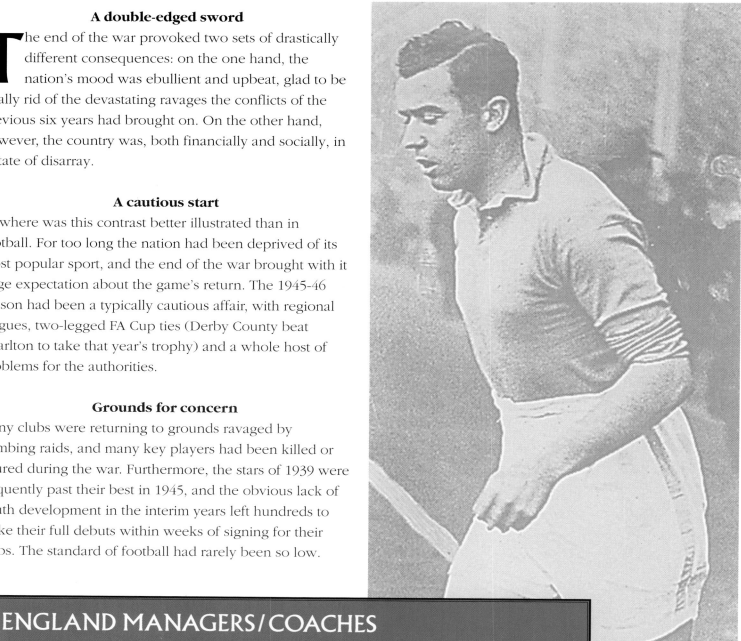

▶ *Sir Alf Ramsey, legendary England manager, photographed in 1967.*

ENGLAND MANAGERS/COACHES

	MATCHES	WON	DRAWN	LOST
Walter Winterbottom 1946 – 1962	139	78	33	28
Alf Ramsey 1963 – 1974	113	69	27	17
Joe Mercer (Caretaker) May 1974	7	3	3	1
Don Revie 1974 – 1977	29	14	8	7
Ron Greenwood 1977 – 1982	55	33	12	10
Bobby Robson 1982 – 1990	95	47	30	18
Graham Taylor 1990 – 1993	38	18	13	7
Terry Venables 1994 – 1996	33	11	11	11
Glenn Hoddle 1996 –	15	11	1	3

Tragedy strikes

The problems were highlighted to tragic effect at Burnden Park, Bolton, in March 1946, when 33 supporters were killed and over 500 injured after crash barriers collapsed during an FA Cup tie. The police had been unable to prevent thousands of extra fans spilling into the ground, which had been left in a particularly shabby state by the war. It prompted the authorities to find ways of improving grounds, staffing and organization as a matter of urgency.

Moscow calling

Yet there were positive sides to the drastic re-organization that was going on. For a footballing public desperately short of games to watch, the visit of Dynamo Moscow in 1945 was a godsend. The great Russian side were an unknown quantity, and were greeted with the usual sceptic mix of xenophobia and contempt, but they gave several British sides a major lesson in the progress being made by their European counterparts. Moscow drew with Chelsea and Rangers, edged ahead of Arsenal 4-3 in dense fog and walloped Cardiff 10-1 with their near-precise football. It was, in many ways, one of the most significant visits a foreign side were to make before the implementation of the European Cup.

◄ *Stanley Matthews in spectacular form for Blackpool.*

All sold out

The 1946-47 season kicked off with a full programme of matches at the end of August. Almost every ground in the entire Football League was sold out, even in the Third Division, as the public flocked to see what they had been missing (by 1948, a million people a weekend were paying to watch football, the highest level ever). As a goodwill gesture, clubs were still allowed to field guest players, which proved entertaining at least as clubs sought to find their feet once more.

> **IN THE 1948-49 SEASON, THE NUMBER OF SPECTATORS ATTENDING MATCHES ROSE TO 41,271,414.**

> **TOMMY LAWTON IS THE YOUNGEST SCORER FOR ENGLAND. HE WAS 19 YEARS, 6 DAYS WHEN HE SCORED A PENALTY AGAINST WALES ON 22 OCTOBER 1938.**

Pool of dreams

The season finished late, and Liverpool narrowly beat Stoke (who were without Stanley Matthews, a controversial departure to Blackpool) to the championship. Charlton avenged their previous defeat in the Cup Final by beating Burnley, but one of the biggest headline-makers of the season was Newcastle's Len Shackleton. The young forward, who had only just joined the club from Bradford, hit six goals on his debut in a 13-0 win against Newport County, a sensational start to what was to become a distinguished career.

Britain join up

There was promising news on the international front, where the British associations finally ended their argument with their continental counterparts and rejoined Fifa. The event was marked by a Britain v Rest of Europe game at Hampden Park, which the star-studded home side won 6-1. Though there was still stubborn resistance to the idea of building closer links with the rest of the world, it was slowly being worn away.

Busby's heyday

For Manchester United, the war could have been devastating. Instead, one man was to turn things around dramatically at Old Trafford – United were to become one of the country's most powerful clubs in the space of just over a decade. That man was Matt Busby. He was appointed, in February 1946, at one of the lowest ebbs in the club's proud history. Bomb damage to their ground

▲ *Danny Blanchflower, who won the Footballer of the Year award in 1958, pictured here in 1961, playing for Spurs.*

FOOTBALLER OF THE YEAR 1948-60

1948	▶	**Stanley Matthews (Blackpool)**
1949	▶	**Johnny Carey (Manchester United)**
1950	▶	**Joe Mercer (Arsenal)**
1951	▶	**Harry Johnston (Blackpool)**
1952	▶	**Billy Wright (Wolves)**
1953	▶	**Nat Lofthouse (Bolton)**
1954	▶	**Tom Finney (Preston)**
1955	▶	**Don Revie (Manchester City)**
1956	▶	**Bert Trautmann (Manchester City)**
1957	▶	**Tom Finney (Preston)**
1958	▶	**Danny Blanchflower (Tottenham)**
1959	▶	**Syd Owen (Luton)**
1960	▶	**Bill Slater (Wolves)**

forced them to share Maine Road with bitter rivals
Manchester City, and results on the pitch were disastrous.
Busby, however, was a man with a plan.

▼ *The England team of 1987 showing off their new kit –
a world away from the kit worn by the team of 1958.*

WORLD CUP SQUAD, SWEDEN – 1958

POSITION	NAME	CLUB	AGE	CAPS	GOALS
Goalkeepers	Eddie Hopkinson	Bolton	22	6	0
	Colin McDonald	Burnley	27	1	0
Full-backs	Tommy Banks	Bolton	28	1	0
	Don Howe	West Brom	22	7	0
	Peter Sillett	Chelsea	25	3	0
Centre halves	Maurice Norman	Tottenham	24	0	0
	Billy Wright (c)	Wolves	34	91	3
Wing-halves	Eddie Clamp	Wolves	24	1	0
	Ronnie Clayton	Blackburn	23	20	0
	Bill Slater	Wolves	31	6	0
Wingers	Alan A'Court	Liverpool	23	1	1
	Peter Brabrook	Chelsea	20	0	0
	Bryan Douglas	Blackburn	23	7	1
	Tom Finney	Preston	36	73	28
Centre forwards	Derek Kevan	West Brom	23	7	4
	Bobby Smith	Tottenham	25	0	0
Inside forwards	Peter Broadbent	Wolves	25	0	0
	Bobby Charlton	Manchester Utd	20	3	3
	Johnny Haynes	Fulham	23	20	8
	Bobby Robson	West Brom	25	2	2

EDDIE HOPKINSON, PETER SILLETT, MAURICE NORMAN, BOBBY SMITH AND BOBBY
CHARLTON DID NOT PLAY.

The plan works

That plan reached fruition in 1947-48, when Busby's young side of cheap buys and youth team players beat a Blackpool side containing Matthews and the great Stan Mortensen to the FA Cup. Sheer will and determination to win took the Manchester side from behind to a 4-2 victory. They took the third title in their history in 1951-52, as Busby's shrewd tactical changes and brilliant 'kidology' saw off a determined challenge from Arsenal. It was a well-deserved win, and confirmed Busby as one of the most capable managers anywhere in the world at that time.

Pompey chime

The war was kind on Portsmouth, too. So many servicemen had ended up in the coastal town after the war had ended that they had their pick of some of the finest talents in the land. The unfashionable side surprised many by winning the title in 1949 and could have won the

▲ *Terry Venables proudly sporting an England shirt, one of several former players turned manager.*

▶ *Ron Atkinson, ex-Aston Villa and Oxford player, photographed shortly after becoming manager of Sheffield Wednesday.*

Double, losing in the semi-finals of the FA Cup. There was another major Cup shock that year, as non-League Yeovil disposed of giants Sunderland 2-1. Yeovil's pitch, which it is claimed sloped from one end to the other, was to be the venue for many a giant-killing over the years; however, when the Somerset side went to Manchester United in the fifth round, they were comprehensively crushed 8-0.

CAREERS AFTER FOOTBALL – FOOTBALL MANAGEMENT (PLAYING CAREERS IN BRACKETS)

Billy Bingham
(Sunderland, Luton, Everton, Port Vale 1950-64)

Bobby Robson
(Fulham, West Brom 1950-66)

John Bond
(West Ham, Torquay 1951-68)

Don Howe
(West Brom, Arsenal 1952-66)

Brian Clough
(Middlesbrough, Sunderland, 1955-64)

John Barnwell
(Arsenal, Notts Forest, Sheffield Utd, 1956-70)

Ron Atkinson
(Aston Villa, Oxford 1956-71)

Terry Venables
(Chelsea, Spurs, QPR, Crystal Palace 1959-74)

Billy Bremner
(Leeds, Hull, Doncaster 1959-81) – now deceased

Will he manage?

England entered the World Cup for the first time in 1950, and though they returned home none the wiser following a humiliating defeat against the United States, there were important changes taking place within the international set-up. Walter Winterbottom, who had previously been the national side's chief coach, was made team manager in 1946 after a pair of disappointing post-war results. He was the first man to fill the role that has now become one of the most important in the English game.

> ANDY AWFORD IS THE YOUNGEST PLAYER TO APPEAR IN A SENIOR MATCH. HE WAS JUST 15 YEARS, 88 DAYS OLD WHEN HE CAME ON AS A SECOND-HALF SUBSTITUTE FOR WORCESTER CITY AGAINST BOREHAMWOOD IN AN FA CUP THIRD-ROUND QUALIFYING TIE ON 10 OCTOBER 1987.

> The 83,260 fans who packed into Maine Road on 17 January 1948 set the all-time attendance record for a League match as Manchester United took on Arsenal in Division One.

Important changes

A disciplined, thoughtful man with plenty of ideas, Winterbottom had enjoyed a long career with Man United and Chelsea before entering coaching. He will be remembered mainly for the changes he made to the national coaching set-up and the infrastructure of the England team; the actual role of the manager in the 1940s was very different to that in the 1990s. The England boss then had a relatively small input on actual team selection, and was accountable to a committee for his every decision. It was another 20 years before England bosses could claim to have achieved anything approaching autonomy.

▶ *Walter Winterbottom, the coach of the England team who was appointed manager in 1946.*

> LUTON TOWN'S JOE PAYNE PRODUCED THE BEST INDIVIDUAL GOAL-SCORING PERFORMANCE: HE BAGGED 10 GOALS ON HIS DEBUT IN A 12-0 VICTORY OVER BRISTOL ROVERS IN DIVISION THREE SOUTH ON 13 APRIL 1936.

Double figures

Winterbottom's impact was immediate; England thrashed Portugal 10-0 on an end-of-season tour, with Stan Mortensen hitting the back of the net four times on his debut. Results slowly but surely began to turn around, and the team was playing with a greater fluency than for many a year, dispelling the doubts of many within the game that an England manager was a bad idea. In May 1948, England marched into Turin and beat the Italians 4-0 in a confident display characterized by two Tom Finney strikes and a brilliant Mortensen goal.

King Nat

The 1950-51 season saw a minor slump in the national team's fortunes as they were held to a draw at home by the unfancied Yugoslavs before losing the International Championship with a 3-2 defeat against Scotland. But, a year later, England held Austria, rated the best side in Europe, to a draw at Wembley before beating them 3-2 with a brilliant performance in Vienna. Nat Lofthouse scored the winner, but collided with the Austrian goalkeeper in the process and was carried off the pitch unconscious.

By the seaside

Back home, Portsmouth won their second title in a row in 1950, but it was one of the closest ever finishes to a championship race and the South Coast side were never again to win such an honour. Arsenal were the Cup winners, and they did not have to leave London in their entire campaign. Liverpool were the beaten finalists; the face of modern football was beginning to take shape.

LEAGUE FOOTBALL RESUMED ON 31 AUGUST 1946 AFTER A SEVEN YEAR BREAK. IT WAS THE START OF A BOOM PERIOD FOR THE SPORT AS A WAR-WEARY NATION LOOKED TO ESCAPE FROM THE GLOOM AND DESPAIR OF THE CONFLICT. 35,604,606 FANS FLOCKED TO MATCHES IN THE FIRST SEASON.

▼ *The England squad that beat Italy 4-0 in 1948; the team were cheered by the Italians after an incredible victory.*

ONE OF FOOTBALL'S SHORTEST-
SERVING MANAGERS WAS BILL
LAMBTON – HE WAS IN CHARGE OF
SCUNTHORPE UNITED FOR JUST
THREE DAYS IN APRIL 1959.

▲ *Tom Finney of Preston North End, in his national team's shirt.*

Pay for play

With the huge increase in attendances and the vast profits being reported by clubs right across the board, it was only natural that the financial benefits should be passed on to the players. A minimum wage was still some way away, despite the best efforts of the Players' Union, but significant progress was made on the wages front in the early 1950s. From a post-war level of £9 per week the maximum wage rose to some £20 in 1958, although many of the best players received more through bonuses, signing-on fees and other examples of rule-bending.

Push and run

The players' surge in fortune provided a boost in morale and the benefits were soon felt on the pitch. Spurs manager Arthur Rowe revolutionized tactical thinking as he took his side to the Championship in 1950-51. His system was dubbed 'push and run' and involved short passes between players and plenty of movement of the ball; sometimes every member of the team would get a touch before a goal was scored. It was a philosophy that was to serve Tottenham well, particularly during the 1960s.

Newcastle were also in vogue at the time and took the FA Cup twice in a row. In 1951, the great Jackie Milburn scored two exquisite goals to dispose of Blackpool, and the following year they beat an injury-ravaged Arsenal, who played most of the match with just 10 men,

with a goal in the dying minutes. The 1953 Final is best known for Stanley Matthews' superb performance for Blackpool, as they beat Bolton to secure the great man his first medal, in a year which saw Arsenal sneak the title again.

▶▼ *W. Perry scoring Blackpool's winning goal against Bolton Wanderers in the 1953 FA Cup Final, Wembley.*

▼ *Jackie Milburn, England and Newcastle centre forward.*

LEAGUE HOOLIGANISM

IN MARCH 1985 THEN-PRIME MINISTER MARGARET THATCHER SET UP A GOVERNMENT TASK-FORCE AFTER SEEING TELEVISION PICTURES OF MILLWALL FANS CONFRONTING MOUNTED POLICE ON LUTON'S KENILWORTH ROAD PITCH. MORE THAN £25,000 DAMAGE WAS CAUSED AND THERE WERE DOZENS OF ARRESTS.

GEORGE HILSDON ANNOUNCED HIS ARRIVAL IN LEAGUE FOOTBALL BY SCORING FIVE IN HIS DEBUT MATCH: CHELSEA'S 9-2 SECOND DIVISION VICTORY OVER GLOSSOP ON 1 SEPTEMBER 1906.

Wolves at the door

But there was no doubting the best team of the decade: Wolverhampton Wanderers. The Midlanders won their first title in 1954 and repeated the honour another two times before the 1950s were out. Managed by former player Stan Cullis, a strict disciplinarian who favoured simple tactics over the complexity of many rivals, the team was a simple one and devoid of stars. Billy Wright, the first man to win 100 caps for England, was the defensive rock around which the whole side was built, and he remains an often-overlooked part of the game at that time. Wright was an unflappably cool man and a fearsome tackler; few defenders since have matched his level of achievement.

Spartak are stuffed

The pinnacle of Wolves' decade, however, was their series of 1954-55 floodlit challenge matches against European teams. Spartak Moscow had already beaten Arsenal at Highbury when they arrived at Molineux, but they were destroyed 4-0. Next up were Honved, with the legendary Ferenc Puskas in their side; Wolves beat them 3-2 and made headlines across Europe. It was a significant moment for the British game.

▶ *England's Billy Wright is chaired off the pitch after playing his 100th international.*

▼ *Wolverhampton Wanderers' past glory: their victorious FA Cup Final match against Everton in 1893, when Wolves won 1-0.*

A magical display

The Honved result was all the more remarkable because, just a season earlier, Wembley had witnessed one of its most thrilling matches when the Hungarian national side visited London for a friendly with England. Hungary were Olympic champions and a brilliantly talented team featuring Puskas, Bozsik and Hidegutki, but English arrogance demanded they be sent packing. Instead, the 'Mighty Magyars' took England apart 6-3, handing them their first ever home defeat by a non-British side. Thousands marvelled at the Hungarians' breathtaking play, and overnight attitudes were changing towards Europe.

United into Europe

It was Manchester United who dragged the British game kicking and screaming into European competition. They won the 1955-56 title by a record 11 points from Wolves and were invited to join the inaugural European Cup, a competition for champions across the continent. The Football League were bitterly opposed to their involvement, fearing the Cup would distract teams from domestic tasks and possibly lead to them eventually pulling out altogether; but they could not stop United.

◀ *Matt Busby (in dark glasses) and his Manchester United team of 1959 arriving at London airport – their first team flight since the Munich disaster.*

DENIS LAW HAS SCORED THE MOST FA CUP GOALS OF ANY PLAYER: 41 FOR HUDDERSFIELD TOWN, MANCHESTER CITY AND MANCHESTER UNITED.

CHESTER CITY'S BILL PRENDERGAST SCORED 15 GOALS IN A RECORD 12 SUCCESSIVE GAMES IN THE 1938-39 SEASON.

Recovering from tragedy

Matt Busby's side beat Belgian team Anderlecht 12-0 over two legs in their first European matches, and went all the way to the semi-finals before they eventually succumbed to the great Real Madrid team. Since then, European competition has livened up the British game no end. The 1958 Munich tragedy set United's cause back a good five years, but other teams kept the baton going for them in those terrible times; Wolves won the League in 1958 and 1959, and Bolton beat a makeshift United to the Cup.

England make progress

England reached the quarter-finals of the 1954 World Cup, where they eventually lost to Uruguay, but were shaken by the loss of their vital Man United players by the time 1958 came around and finished second in their group before losing 1-0 to the USSR in a qualification play-off. The football world was shocked by the Munich disaster that decimated that great side of Edwards, Pegg, Byrne and co., and much of the excitement that had built up through the 1950s quickly petered out. That the game recovered, and United themselves recovered, is a credit to football's ability to keep on going through the greatest of adversities.

INDIVIDUAL TRAGEDIES

Sim Raleigh died in hospital after suffering a clash of heads while playing for Gillingham at home to Brighton in Division Three South on 1 December 1934.

Tinsley Lindley scored in nine consecutive England internationals between March 1886 and March 1888. The Cambridge University player scored in matches against Ireland, Wales and Scotland.

▶ *Matt Busby leading the Busby Babes onto the pitch at Wembley, for the 1957 FA Cup Final against Aston Villa.*

The smallest crowd to watch England in action occurred when 15,628 watched them play Chile at Wembley on 23 May 1989. The poor attendance was blamed on a tube strike.

One of League football's worst home runs took place between November 1958 and October 1959: Portsmouth drew two and lost 14 matches at their Fratton Park home.

CAREERS AFTER FOOTBALL – FOOTBALL MANAGEMENT (PLAYING CAREERS IN BRACKETS)

Sir Matt Busby (Manchester City, Liverpool 1928-39) – now deceased

Bill Shankly (Carlisle, Preston 1932-48)

Joe Mercer (Everton, Arsenal 1932-53)

Johnny Carey (Manchester Utd 1936-53)

Bill Nicholson (Tottenham 1938-54)

Bob Paisley (Liverpool 1946-53)

Sir Alf Ramsey (Southampton, Tottenham, 1946-54)

Don Revie (Leicester, Hull, Manchester City, Sunderland, Leeds 1946-61)

Tommy Docherty (Celtic, Preston, Arsenal, Chelsea 1948-61)

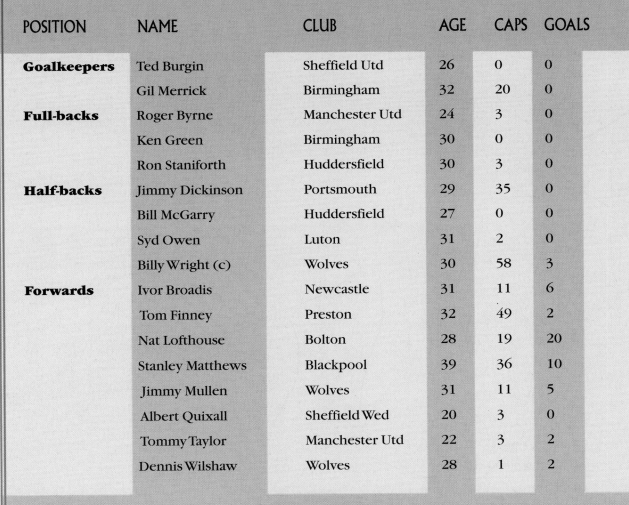

WORLD CUP SQUAD, SWEDEN – 1954

POSITION	NAME	CLUB	AGE	CAPS	GOALS
Goalkeepers	Ted Burgin	Sheffield Utd	26	0	0
	Gil Merrick	Birmingham	32	20	0
Full-backs	Roger Byrne	Manchester Utd	24	3	0
	Ken Green	Birmingham	30	0	0
	Ron Staniforth	Huddersfield	30	3	0
Half-backs	Jimmy Dickinson	Portsmouth	29	35	0
	Bill McGarry	Huddersfield	27	0	0
	Syd Owen	Luton	31	2	0
	Billy Wright (c)	Wolves	30	58	3
Forwards	Ivor Broadis	Newcastle	31	11	6
	Tom Finney	Preston	32	49	2
	Nat Lofthouse	Bolton	28	19	20
	Stanley Matthews	Blackpool	39	36	10
	Jimmy Mullen	Wolves	31	11	5
	Albert Quixall	Sheffield Wed	20	3	0
	Tommy Taylor	Manchester Utd	22	3	2
	Dennis Wilshaw	Wolves	28	1	2

TED BURGIN, KEN GREEN AND ALBERT QUIXALL DID NOT PLAY.

THE MUNICH DISASTER

Flight into tragedy

Flight 609 finally left Munich Airport at 15.03 on 3 February 1958 – its third and final attempt at take-off. Snow and engine problems had grounded the plane on two previous occasions, and the squad of footballers, journalists and Manchester United staff on board were growing restless. The charter flight had barely made it into the air when the engines failed again and it crashed to the ice-covered runway below, skidding through a fence and across a road before finally coming to a halt. The plane was wrecked and a generation of young talent was decimated.

▲ *For many, the last view of the doomed Manchester United team, leaving Manchester airport on their way to Belgrade.*

European glory

United had only stopped in Germany to refuel on their way back from Belgrade. They had defeated champions Red Star 5-4 on aggregate with a performance critics were near unanimous in describing as their finest for many years. The previous night had been spent in joyous but typically cautious celebration under the careful guidance of Matt Busby, the manager who had fashioned a home-grown squad into the 'Busby Babes' – a tag he hated. He preferred to think of them as a footballing Harlem Globetrotters; one day, he predicted, they would be too good for competitive

> **INDIVIDUAL TRAGEDIES**
>
> **Peter Houseman, an FA Cup winner with Chelsea in 1970, died in a car crash seven years later at the age of 32.**

matches. Seven of the Babes perished in Munich: Roger Byrne, Tommy Taylor, Eddie Colman, Mark Jones, Geoff Bent and the prodigious David Pegg were all killed instantly, while Duncan Edwards – without doubt the outstanding footballer of his generation – died two weeks later in hospital, aged 21. His final words – uttered to coach Jimmy Murphy – were: 'What time's kick-off on Saturday?'

Shattering consequences

Busby himself – like the city which came to a standstill on hearing the news – never fully recovered from that evening's events, and was unable to discuss what happened for several years. But even if there were to be no more Babes, he was still able to fashion a side which once again conquered Europe and dominated the domestic competitions. Both the great man and his adopted homeland were able to move on but never to forget.

> **INDIVIDUAL TRAGEDIES**
>
> **Sunderland's 23-year-old goalkeeper James Thorpe died in a diabetic coma in hospital three days after being injured during a First Division match against Chelsea at Roker Park on 1 February 1936.**

Final recovery

United played the next three months with a makeshift team, comprising Munich survivors like Bobby Charlton and hastily made new signings. To their huge credit they made it to the Cup Final and Busby returned from hospital to inspire his team. United lost 2-0, but it was the start of a long road back to recovery for one of Britain's proudest clubs.

▶ *The memorial plaque to those killed at Munich. It is placed above the entrance to Old Trafford.*

TOMMY LAWTON: A MODERN HERO

A wartime great

The war spoiled the careers of many potential footballing greats, and Tommy Lawton was no exception. Had the hostilities not intervened, Lawton could have made twice the number of international appearances he did and enjoyed the peak of his career in the top flight. As it was, he still puts together a very strong case for the title of Greatest English Centre Forward of All Time.

Lawton was not just a goalscorer, he was a versatile player who was lethal with the ball either at his feet or in the air, possessing fantastic awareness and a near-perfect temperament. He was a star in the making right from the beginning: in three seasons of Schoolboy soccer, he scored an incredible 500 goals and could have chosen to join any club in the land when he turned 16 in 1935. He opted for Burnley, and scored a memorable hat-trick against Spurs aged just 17.

Goodison glory

Everton poached the young Lawton for a huge £6,500 shortly afterwards, and he landed them the 1939 Championship with an average of a goal a game, making his England debut in the same year. Lawton played football wherever he could during the war – including a spell with Scottish side Morton while he was across the border for his honeymoon – and by 1946 Chelsea were prepared to part with over £11,000 for his services.

A sensational move

He lasted just one season at Stamford Bridge, before creating a sensation when he moved to Notts County, then in the Third Division. County shelled out a record £20,000 for his services, but it was money well spent. Crowds flocked to see Lawton at Meadow Lane and broke the club's attendance record several times, while the side made it to the Second Division with his goals. Lawton also became the first ever Third Division England international during his time with County.

▲ *Tommy Lawton and his new son: Thomas James Hugh Lawton, born in 1956.*

ENGLAND'S TOP MARKSMEN

	Goals	Games	Period
Bobby Charlton	49	106	1958-70
Gary Lineker	48	80	1984-92
Jimmy Greaves	44	57	1959-67
Tom Finney	30	76	1946-58
Nat Lofthouse	30	33	1950-58
Vivian Woodward	29	23	1903-11
Steve Bloomer	28	23	1895-07
David Platt	27	62	1989-96
Bryan Robson	26	90	1979-91
Geoff Hurst	24	49	1966-72
Stan Mortensen	23	25	1947-53
Tommy Lawton	22	3	1938-48
Mike Channon	21	46	1972-77
Kevin Keegan	21	63	1972-82
Martin Peters	20	67	1966-74

▲ *Tommy Lawton in action attacking Everton's goal during a match at Highbury.*

The veteran goalscorer

Even when he turned 33, Lawton's enthusiasm for the game remained undimmed, and he turned up at Brentford for a few months in the Second Division. Arsenal then shocked the game again by taking him to Highbury to add experience to their squad, and he repaid them with some superb performances. Lawton eventually retired in 1956 to embark on a disappointing spell in management, but he could never leave the game behind and sat on the first ever Pools Panel in the 1960s. Even as an elderly man, Lawton could still influence the outcome of matches.

JAMES PRINSEP WAS THE YOUNGEST ENGLAND INTERNATIONAL. HE MADE HIS DEBUT AGED 17 YEARS, 252 DAYS AGAINST SCOTLAND ON 5 APRIL 1879.

ENGLAND'S FIRST WORLD CUP

England's debut

There had already been three World Cup Finals tournaments by the time a disappointing 13 nations gathered in Brazil for the 1950 Finals. England, however, were taking part for the first time: and by the end of the whole affair they probably wished they'd never turned up in the first place.

A team of legends

The English team contained some of the greatest players of the era – captained by the Wolves great Billy Wright, and featuring the talents of future manager Alf Ramsey and the legendary Tom Finney. They were seeded among the top four and were expected to sail through their group games to make the final 'pool', a group which would play-off for the title of world champions. England's opening match saw them dispose of Chile 2-0 with goals from Stan Mortensen and Will Mannion, and the omens looked good.

> BRYAN ROBSON SCORED THE QUICKEST EVER ENGLAND GOAL, 27 SECONDS INTO THE WORLD CUP MATCH AGAINST FRANCE IN BILBAO, SPAIN ON 16 JUNE 1982.

▲ *Billy Wright, England captain for the country's first World Cup tournament, sporting his international shirt and cap.*

The US upset

And then the USA came along. The part-timers had already given Spain a minor scare, but nothing could prepare the world for their game against England. Wright's men kept the Americans pinned into their own half for most of the opening period, but then on 37 minutes Larry Gaetjens rose to head past Bert Williams and they never relinquished their lead. The US had won 1-0 and the greatest shock in English international history was complete. The world's press went wild, while the domestic papers proclaimed the result 'humiliating'.

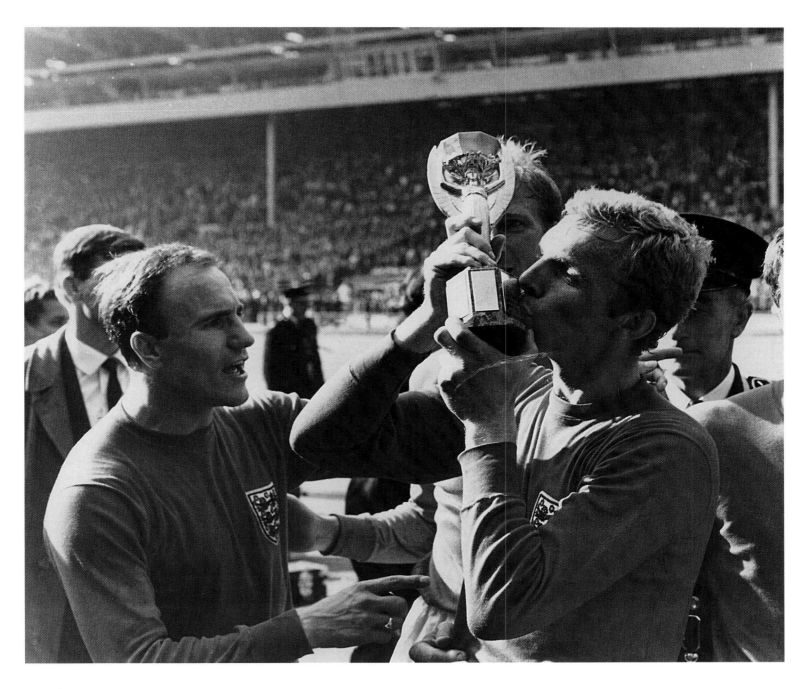

▲ *Bobby Moore kisses the Jules Rimet trophy after England's 1966 World Cup victory.*

No way past Spain

England could still have made it if they had beaten Spain in their final group game, but when Jackie Milburn's goal was disallowed on 14 minutes their spirit was broken and they went on to lose 1-0; an inglorious exit from what should have been an important chance to show the rest of the world what the nation that popularized the game could do. The team left Brazil immediately and didn't hang around for the rest of the tournament. The American defeat is still recalled with horror today.

Brazil slip up

Almost 200,000 turned out for what was effectively the final between Brazil and Uruguay. The Brazilians included the young Pele in their squad but were unable to break

down a resolute Uruguayan defence and lost 1-0. The football superpowers of future years had been well and truly humbled; for England in particular it was a bitter pill to swallow, but an important lesson to learn.

INTERNATIONAL HOOLIGANISM

Fences went up around the Wembley pitch after Scotland fans spilled on to the pitch following a 2-1 victory over England in June 1977. The crossbar was broken and damage worth £150,000 was caused as hundreds of Scots raced on to the surface at the final whistle.

SIR MATT BUSBY: THE GREATEST

A Glasgow boy

The north-east of Glasgow is famed for its mining communities and its staunchly working-class population. It has another claim to fame: three of Britain's greatest club managers – Jock Stein, Bill Shankly and Matt Busby – were all born and grew up there. And it was Busby who was the most celebrated and successful of the trio.

Manchester's new hero

Rejected by both Glasgow giants during adolescence, Busby got his footballing break in Manchester and enjoyed a distinguished career for City from 1928 to 1936, when he moved to Liverpool until the end of the war. In 1945 he was the controversial choice to become Manchester United's new manager on just £15 per week. It proved an inspired decision; the club had long been starved of

success, but in 1946-67 Busby took them to second in the League with a mixture of good signings, promising youngsters and unparalleled motivational skills.

The Busby Babes

In 1948 he steered United to a 4-2 FA Cup Final win over Stanley Matthews' Blackpool with a team increasingly dominated by some fine young charges – 'The Busby Babes'. They took the League in 1952, by four points, from Spurs and won it again in 1956. The following year saw United semi-finalists in the first European Cup; a truly historic achievement. The side oozed quality in every department and, moreover, a genuine sense of togetherness few have been able to match.

▼ Ten years after the tragedy of Munich, Sir Matt Busby can smile again – holding the European Cup with George Best (centre) and Pat Crerand.

INDIVIDUAL TRAGEDIES

John White, the Scottish international inside forward who starred in Tottenham's 1961 League and Cup Double was killed when he was struck by lightning while playing golf on 21 July 1964. He was 27.

Recovering from tragedy

Even the Munich air disaster of 1958 could not stop Busby or his team. The great man came perilously close to death in the crash that claimed some of his brightest talents, but he bravely returned for his team's Cup Final appearance and rebuilt the side around the survivors and a new batch of kids. The crash very nearly put him off the game for life, and it took huge courage to return to Old Trafford afterwards, but it was only Busby's presence that kept the club together and allowed them to become the huge force they are today.

▲ *Kevin Keegan, seen here playing for England against Bulgaria in 1979, is one of the élite – he has made it to top-flight management after a distinguished playing career.*

CAREERS AFTER FOOTBALL, FOOTBALL MANAGEMENT (PLAYING CAREERS IN BRACKETS)

George Graham (Aston Villa, Chelsea, Arsenal, Manchester Utd, Portsmouth, Crystal Palace 1962-77)

Howard Kendall (Preston, Everton, Birmingham, Stoke, Blackburn, Everton 1962-81)

Alan Ball (Blackpool, Everton, Arsenal, Southampton, Bristol Rovers, 1962-82)

Graham Taylor (Grimsby, Lincoln 1963-72)

Bobby Gould (Coventry, Arsenal, Wolves, West Brom, Bristol City, West Ham, Bristol Rovers, Hereford 1963-79)

Billy Bonds (Charlton, West Ham 1964-87)

Harry Redknapp (West Ham, Bournemouth, Brentford 1965-82)

Kenny Dalglish (Celtic, Liverpool 1967-89)

Kevin Keegan (Scunthorpe, Liverpool, Hamburg, Southampton, Newcastle 1968-83)

Roy Evans (Liverpool 1969-73)

The greatest

After a decade of the most thrilling domestic football this country has seen, United finally took Europe's top prize – Busby's ultimate aim in football. Busby continued to advise United bosses until well into his 70s and remained a legend for future generations of supporters until his death in 1994. It was Shankly who was to provide his most fitting epitaph: 'He is without doubt the greatest manager that ever lived.'

STANLEY MATTHEWS: WIZARD ON THE WING

▲ *Stanley Matthews in action, playing his first match for Stoke City after his return in 1961.*

A modest hero

Matthews' skills on the wing were legendary and marked him out as the world's most outstanding player for a good 20 years; he was capable of not just beating, but humiliating, any defender who stood in his way, but was not a showman. His every manoeuvre was geared towards firing his side to victory. And in a glorious 35-year career, he invariably did. Furthermore, he was unfailingly modest, once claiming: 'I can't take people going on about how good I was. You just do your best, don't you?'

Loyal and special

The 'Wizard' was doing his best from his first day as a professional. Born in Hanley in 1915, he signed for local side Stoke as a 15-year-old on a wage of just a pound a week and made his full debut a little over two years later. His excellence marked him out at an early age, and in his first 17-year spell with the Potteries club made well over 200 appearances, establishing them as an important, if unfashionable force. It would have been easy to have signed for a more successful club, yet loyalty was one of Matthews' strongest assets.

A rock of ages

It seems incredible today that anyone, even the most talented of players, could continue to perform in the First Division past their 50th birthday, particularly in an attacking role. Stanley Matthews did more than just play, however, he remained, until his very last match for Stoke in 1965, the most talented footballer England has produced.

> Ronnie Dix was aged just 15 years and 180 days when he scored for Bristol Rovers against Norwich in Division Three South on 3 March 1928.

▶ *A distinguished Sir Stanley Matthews, photographed in 1998.*

The team player

He made his England debut within two years of his First Division debut, scoring against Wales, and went on to win 84 caps for his country. Yet it was on the domestic front where Matthews was to make his name, and his 1947 move to Blackpool finally gave him the chance to win some of the game's biggest honours. His Blackpool career took him to the brink of the League title and reached an exhilarating peak with the 1953 FA Cup Final. Matthews' performance in that game was to lead to its being dubbed 'The Matthews Final'. He set up a brilliant winner to give the side a 4-3 victory over Bolton, yet it was his friend and team-mate Stan Mortensen whose hat-trick was equally vital to the eventual result. Matthews never forgot he was a team player and when asked how to stay at the top once answered: 'By being eager to learn all the time, by being a good club man, by undertaking constant and regular private training and by keeping your feet on the ground.'

CBEs

Bobby Charlton (Manchester United, England)
Denis Compton (Arsenal, England)
Stanley Matthews (Stoke City, Blackpool, England)
Bobby Robson (England manager)
Billy Wright (Wolves, England)

Forever a legend

Stoke's favourite son returned home in 1961, aged 46, and played four more years for the club. Age made his appearances less regular but no less accomplished, and his final game against Fulham in 1965 was a celebration of his notable achievements. Matthews retained a fond place in the hearts of all who saw him play; his knighthood shortly after his retirement was a fitting reward for one of England's most famed and admired sportsmen.

1960-70: FOOTBALL FOR FUN?

A decade of change

The Sixties saw huge changes to football and to British life as a whole, which was turned upside down. It was the decade of pop music, beatnik literature, campus protests and free love, and the national game was there in the thick of things all the way through. Above all, the Sixties were a showcase of footballing talent and the emergence of the new order.

Going abroad

Given this, it is tempting to ponder why several of Britain's brightest stars were tempted abroad as the decade began. The advent of European competition had seen the building of ever closer links with the Continent, but it was still a shock to patriotic supporters when their heroes abandoned England. Money was certainly a factor; Italian clubs in particular had really begun to take off, and could afford to match and often better the Home Nations for wages and bonuses, with no limits on payments. Also, there was the romanticism of a new challenge abroad and the chance to capitalize on the new training methods and tactics employed there. But not all the exiles enjoyed a happy holiday.

The Gentle Giant

John Charles began the mini-exodus in 1957. A championship winner with Leeds and a bruising yet deceptively skilful forward, he caused quite a stir after moving to Juventus, with accusations of treachery from many commentators. Yet Charles came to be idolized in Italy, winning three Serie A titles in five years out there, and even going back for a second spell with Roma in 1962 after briefly returning to Leeds. Juventus fans dubbed him 'The Gentle Giant'.

Others were not as talented or as fortunate as Charles, however. Scotsman Joe Baker disappeared without trace after signing for Torino in 1960, while Gerry Hitchens of Chelsea, who joined Inter Milan for £80,000, is best known for his part in a major drugs scandal in Italy, after it was claimed he had tested positive for banned stimulants in 1961. The charge was never proven, but it took the transfer of two of the game's biggest names, Jimmy Greaves and Dennis Law, to give the whole Italian adventure credibility.

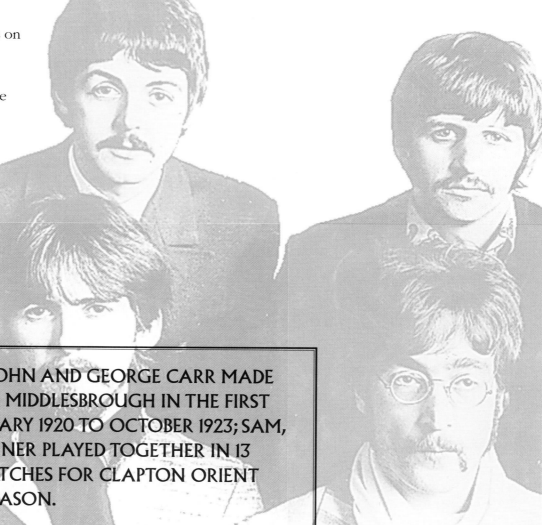

BROTHERS WILLIAM, JOHN AND GEORGE CARR MADE 24 APPEARANCES FOR MIDDLESBROUGH IN THE FIRST DIVISION FROM JANUARY 1920 TO OCTOBER 1923; SAM, JAMES AND JACK TONNER PLAYED TOGETHER IN 13 SECOND DIVISION MATCHES FOR CLAPTON ORIENT DURING THE 1919-20 SEASON.

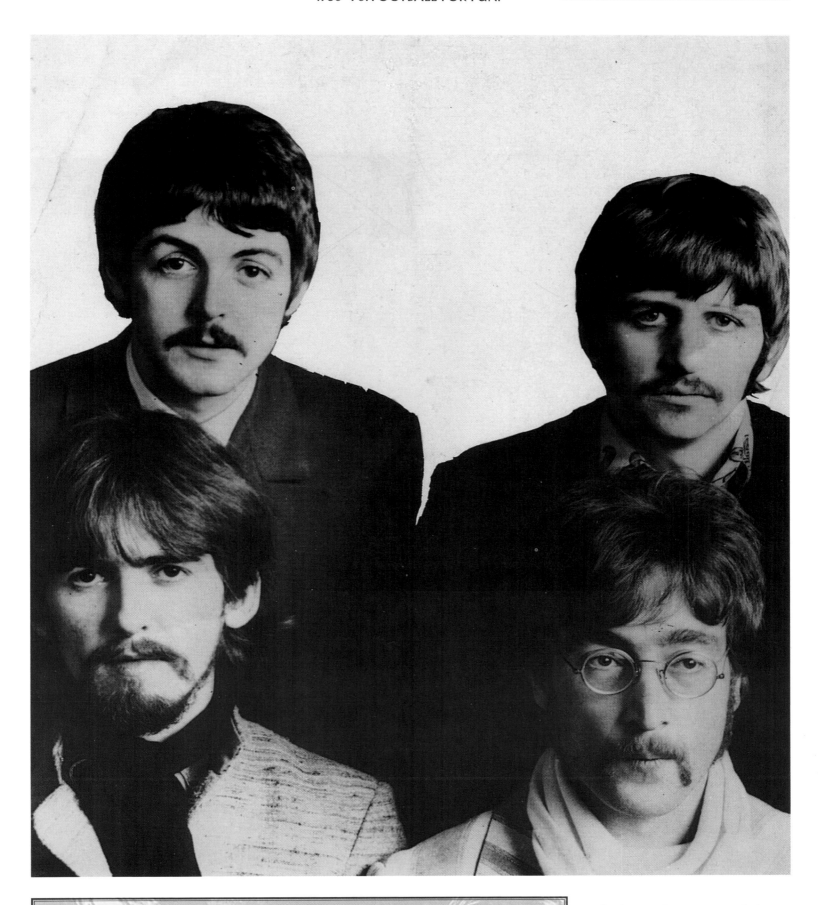

▲ *The Beatles were a symbol of everything that changed in British life in the 1960s.*

THE LEAGUE CUP AT WEMBLEY

1967 ▶ **Queens Park Rangers 3 v 2 West Bromwich Albion**

1968 ▶ **Leeds United 1 v 0 Arsenal**

1969 ▶ **Swindon 3 v 1 Arsenal**

1970 ▶ **Manchester City 2 v 1 West Bromwich Albion**

Exiles are axed

Even more dramatically, four big names – including Neil Franklin of Stoke and England and Charlie Mitten, Manchester United's rebel penalty king – were lured to Bogota of Colombia by the promise of huge wages and a lavish lifestyle. Unsurprisingly, they failed to settle and when Franklin returned home he was suspended for a year for breaking his contract. Mitten never played top-flight football again.

Bill Nick – future champion

Another significant milestone had also taken place before the start of the decade. Tottenham appointed Bill Nicholson as their manager in 1959; it proved to be an act of genius. Nicholson certainly knew the territory, having spent his entire playing career at the club, and had later become coach to the innovative Arthur Rowe. A gruff Yorkshireman famed for his tough disciplinary stance, he gave Busby and Sir Alf Ramsey a real run for their money in the 'Best Manager of the 1960s' stakes and was hailed on retirement as one of the all-time greats, revered by his players and never crossed.

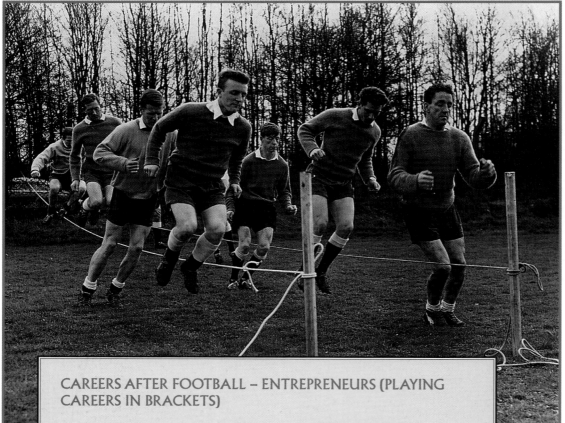

◄ *Tottenham Hotspur getting in training for their Cup Tie match with Sunderland in 1961.*

Milan maestro?

Jimmy Greaves was being touted as one of the best natural goalscorers for decades when AC Milan paid Chelsea £80,000 for his services in 1960. He was unsure about moving abroad, but respected Charles's successful example and was made such a flattering financial offer he could not realistically refuse. Yet Greaves could not cope with the Italian lifestyle or his coach and played just 15 games in Milan before heading home to join Spurs. He was particularly aggrieved at Milan's insistence he did not play for England while on their books. At White Hart Lane he became a legend, breaking scoring records, capturing Championships and establishing himself as a regular fixture for England before illness and a battle with alcoholism curtailed his career later in the decade. Spurs had paid £99,999 for him, as they did not want to burden him with being the first £100,000 player.

CAREERS AFTER FOOTBALL – ENTREPRENEURS (PLAYING CAREERS IN BRACKETS)

Francis Lee (Bolton, Manchester City, Derby, 1960-75) –
Racehorse owner/trainer and re-cycled paper business founder
Ron Harris (Chelsea, Brentford 1961-83) –
Owns holiday and fishing complex
Dennis Viollet (Manchester Utd, Stoke 1962-66) –
Runs soccer camps in US
Frank Casper (Rotherham, Burnley 1962-75) –
Runs own clothing shop
David Sadler (Manchester Utd, Preston 1963-76) –
Corporate hospitality company
Dennis Tueart (Sunderland, Manchester City, Stoke, Burnley 1968-83) –
Corporate promotions firm
Craig Johnston (Middlesbrough, Liverpool 1977-87) –
Football boot designer
Ricardo Villa (Tottenham 1978-82) –
Owns 740-acre ranch in Argentina

▲ *Dennis Law* (left) *and Bobby Charlton at Manchester United in 1962.*

The Lawman

Dennis Law was little happier in Italy, after Torino took him abroad in 1961 for a six-figure sum. His spell in Italy was undistinguished, and returning home was the most sensible move he ever made: Manchester United boss Matt Busby took him to Old Trafford, and he forged a career as part of a devastating forward line with George Best and Bobby Charlton. Ironically, he was voted European Footballer of the Year two years later.

FIVE CLUBS HAVE WON EVERY HOME MATCH IN A SEASON

Liverpool won 14 in 1893-1894.

Second Division Bury won 15 in 1894-1895.

Sheffield Wednesday won 17 in 1900-1901.

Birmingham won 17 in 1902-1903.

Brentford won 21 in 1929-1930.

A bright start

Nicholson perfected Rowe's push and run principles and shaped a close-knit side of exceptional ball skills and no-nonsense tackling. He won his first match in charge by an incredible 10-4 against Everton and encouraged lively, attacking football throughout his reign. He was aided by some of the most gifted players of the era, not least the visionary wing-half Danny Blanchflower, the Belfast lad who led Spurs on the pitch for the best part of a decade. It was Blanchflower who remained Nicholson's rock when things went badly, and he also came up with the 'Glory Game' tag made famous by Hunter Davies' book of the same name.

The Ghost stars

The other components in that great side were no less impressive; the steel and strength of the legendary Dave Mackay in the centre of things, the speedy Cliff Jones on the wing and playmaker John White, nicknamed 'The Ghost' for his stealth. Nicholson had not yet signed Jimmy Greaves to put the fear of God into defences; he was merely the icing on the cake, and in the meantime the goals rained in from all parts of the field, particularly Bobby Smith and Les Allen.

▼ *Danny Blanchflower leading Tottenham Hotspur out on to the pitch in February 1961.*

Seeing Double

The 1960-61 season will go down as the greatest in Tottenham's history. Quite simply, they dominated every competition they entered and were peerless in the First Division despite having one of the smallest squads of any club. Their first 11 matches were straight victories, a new record. They took the championship by some eight points; the outcome was never in any doubt. Amazingly, Spurs were also on course for the Cup Final, which, if they won, would have landed Nicholson the Double. No team had achieved it in the 20th century, and many suggested it was impossible with the constraints of schedules and the increased competitiveness of the English game.

FOOTBALLERS WHO HAVE BEEN KNIGHTED

Sheffield Wednesday's Charles Clegg, who played once for England, was knighted in 1927. He was President of the Football Association at the time.

Stanley Matthews was knighted in 1965. He is England's oldest international and played his last match for Stoke City against Fulham aged 50 years, 5 days on 6 February 1965.

England manager Alf Ramsey was knighted in 1967 after leading the country to our only World Cup triumph.

Matt Busby was knighted in 1968 after surviving the Munich air crash and rebuilding his Manchester United team to become League Championship and European Cup winners.

Former 'Busby babe' Bobby Charlton, a Munich survivor and World Cup winner in 1966, was honoured in 1994.

Eventually, it was only little Leicester City who stood between the North London giants and the greatest achievement in club football. Ravaged by injury and the aftermath of a demanding campaign, Tottenham were far from their best and were pinned back for much of the game. It was Smith who finally unlocked the Leicester defence to set his side on their way, and Dyson's second goal killed the match and allowed Blanchflower the honour of receiving the Cup.

MANCHESTER UNITED'S GARY AND PHILIP NEVILLE BECAME ONLY THE SECOND PAIR OF BROTHERS TO PLAY FOR ENGLAND IN MODERN TIMES WHEN THEY PLAYED AGAINST CHINA IN BEIJING ON 23 MAY 1997.

◄ *The Neville brothers holding the Carling Premiership trophy for Manchester United, 11 May 1997.*

Into Europe

Spurs made a very good attempt at repeating the trick in 1961-62, but were unable to gel in the League and were distracted by their first ever European campaign. They made the semi-finals of the European Cup, but found the Portuguese giants Benfica a little too hot to handle. 3-1 down from the first leg and soon trailing 4-1 in the second at White Hart Lane, they still managed to rally round and come within a goal of levelling the tie on aggregate, but the sell-out crowd was to be disappointed. It was left to the Cup to provide Nicholson with his consolation prize,

as Greaves, Smith and a late Blanchflower penalty helped them beat Burnley 3-1 in the Final.

A wage dispute

If football was to become ever more proficient, however, it needed to be reflected in players' pay packets. The Corinthian spirit dictated that wages should be capped to prevent players' egos being inflated by the trappings of success, but it was widely felt within the game that this was an arcane practice and that those who succeeded at the highest level should take their fair share of the spoils.

OBEs

Gordon Banks
(Chesterfield, Leicester City, Stoke City, England)

Jack Charlton
(Leeds United, England)

Brian Clough
(Manager Derby County, Brighton, Leeds United, Nottingham Forest)

George Eastham
(Ards, Newcastle United, Arsenal, Stoke City, England)

Tom Finney
(Preston, England)

Emlyn Hughes
(Blackpool, Liverpool, Wolverhampton Wanderers, Rotherham United, Hull City, Swansea City, England)

Pat Jennings
(Newry Town, Watford, Tottenham Hotspur, Arsenal, Northern Ireland)

Kevin Keegan
(Scunthorpe United, Liverpool, SV Hamburg, Southampton, Newcastle United, England)

Gary Lineker
(Leicester City, Everton, Barcelona, Tottenham Hotspur, England)

Joe Mercer
(Everton, Arsenal, England)

Bobby Moore
(West Ham, Fulham, England)

Bryan Robson
(West Bromwich Albion, Manchester United, Middlesbrough, England)

Bill Shankly
(Liverpool manager)

Emlyn Hughes, OBE, working up a sweat ▲ for Liverpool, 1973.

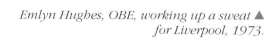

▲ *Jack Charlton, OBE, photographed in 1996 at the launch of his autobiography.*

The process of change began with the appointment in 1957 of Jimmy Hill as chairman of the Players' Union, which was quickly renamed the Professional Footballers' Association.

Hill saves the day

Hill was charismatic, intelligent and well-liked within the game, and he was perfectly positioned to win players some important concessions. In 1960, he led a series of negotiations with the Football League to settle the main issues; the abolition of a maximum wage, the end of the practice of tying star players to long contracts (although to describe them as 'slaves' was a little over the top) and the right to a slice of all transfer fees. If clubs could pay hundreds of thousands for players, Hill and his colleagues argued, why should the players not be entitled to part of it?

A strike looms

The discussions between the PFA and the League were lengthy and heated, but Hill refused to back down and won support for the idea of an all-out strike in January 1961. The League backed down and agreed to revise contracts, and in June that year they abolished the maximum wage. The floodgates were opened for the best players to earn a fortune for their talents, and Hill's success was a double-edged sword for football as a whole. Wages rose throughout the game, but it led to many smaller clubs going out of business.

▲ *Gary Lineker outside Buckingham Palace after receiving his OBE.*

▲ *Jimmy Hill on his way to the meeting with League chiefs in 1960. Hill's contribution to footballers' rights was hugely important in the 1960s.*

Restraint of trade

There was one final twist to come, in 1963, when George Eastham – a centre forward who had temporarily quit the game after Newcastle refused to release him, took his old club to court to settle the issue once and for all. The judge ruled that the system of retaining registrations once a contract had ended was an 'unreasonable restraint of trade'; from then on, players could be transferred at their own request and not merely at their clubs' whims.

Trouncing the Scots

The upward surge of the times certainly filtered through to the England team. In April 1961, the national side took on Scotland at Wembley in what was expected to be a relatively close affair – a decider to the International Championship. Scotland fielded almost their first choice side, including Law, McKay and Liverpool's Ian St John, but they were trounced 9-3 in a remarkable display of attacking power. Jimmy Greaves got a hat-trick, and Bobby Smith and Johnny Haynes each scored twice. England went on to thrash Mexico 8-0; they were beginning to learn the lessons international isolation had failed to teach them.

THE YOUNGEST EVER LEAGUE PLAYERS MADE THEIR DEBUTS AT THE AGE OF 15 YEARS, 158 DAYS. ALBERT GELDARD SET THE MARK FOR BRADFORD CITY AGAINST MILLWALL ON 16 SEPTEMBER 1929. KEN ROBERTS WAS EXACTLY THE SAME AGE WHEN HE APPEARED FOR WREXHAM AGAINST BRADFORD CITY ON 1 SEPTEMBER 1951.

Big guns fail to fire

A new competition was introduced in 1960: the League Cup. It failed to make an impact at first, however, due to the refusal of larger clubs to field full-strength teams. They were incensed by the further clogging of an already-crowded fixture list, and did not see the point of the competition, which was open to all Football League teams. It is a debate that still rages in the 1990s: sides already in contention for two or three main trophies are unwilling to risk injuries or fatigue to key players in what is perceived as the 'poor man's FA Cup'. It was only the introduction of a European place for the winners that really stirred interest in the League Cup.

▶ *Jimmy Greaves* (left) *talking to his new manager, Billy Nicholson, after a controversial signing from Milan, 1961.*

PETERBOROUGH UNITED SMASHED IN 134 GOALS IN 46 FOURTH DIVISION GAMES IN THE 1960-61 SEASON.

CAREERS AFTER FOOTBALL – ENTREPRENEURS (PLAYING CAREERS IN BRACKETS):

TED DITCHBURN
(Tottenham 1946-58) –
set up sports, toy and game shops
plus printing business (now retired)

TOM FINNEY
(Preston 1946-59) –
Founded plumbing, heating and electrical firm

JOHN CHARLES
(Leeds, Cardiff (1948-65) –
Children's shop

BOBBY CHARLTON
(Manchester Utd, Preston 1956-74) –
Founder of sports school

COLIN BARLOW
(Manchester City, Oldham, Doncaster 1957-64) –
Own international import/export company

GORDON BANKS
(Chesterfield, Leicester, Stoke 1958-72) –
Sports Promotion

JEFF ASTLE
(Notts County, West Brom 1959-73) –
Runs industrial cleaning firm

Humble beginnings

Aston Villa beat Rotherham United in that first two-legged final, but the country's five top teams declined to take part. It was not until 1967, and the first one-leg Wembley final, that the competition really came alive. Third Division QPR outclassed holders West Brom 3-2 in a dramatic game of twists and turns, but were unable to compete in the Fairs Cup because they were not in the top flight. Swindon's 1969 victory over high-flying Arsenal was another high point, as winger Don Rogers' two goals crushed the Gunners.

▶ *Gordon Banks, photographed in 1997,
31 years after he was England's World Cup hero.*

Unlikely champions

Spurs' inability to retain the League title in 1962, the year after their Double win, left the door open for new champions to emerge. They were certainly an unlikely set of heroes: Ipswich Town, under the tutorship of Alf Ramsey. Ipswich had never been in the top flight before, and were widely expected to sink straight back to the Second Division, but Ramsey used this to his advantage. He took his collection of cheap signings and young players, who he had taken from the bottom of the Third Division to the First in just a few years, to believe in themselves and believe they could beat anyone on their day.

Team of grit and graft

The side had no stars, and Ramsey brought in only one new player that season. But his side were loyal and his tactical system, a hybrid of 4-4-2, outfoxed many classier opponents. They accrued only 56 points over the course of the season, but it was enough to give them the title. Over the next two decades, Ipswich were to become perennial underdogs and underachievers; for Ramsey, there were even greater things to come.

Chile too spicy

Given the brilliant performances England had delivered over the previous couple of years, the World Cup Finals of 1962, held in the unusual venue of Chile, were something of an anticlimax. Walter Winterbottom's team struggled through to the quarter-finals, with one win, one draw and one defeat, although they did manage to beat Argentina

3-1 in the process; Jimmy Greaves, new boy Alan Peacock and Bobby Charlton scoring the goals. When England were paired with Brazil in the quarter-finals, the writing was on the wall.

Brazil put on a marvellous display, without the injured Pele, and were always going to be the winners. Gerry Hitchens scored to keep his side in the match, but a glorious long-range effort from Garrincha sent England on their way. There were some promising moments for England, but also a lot of lessons still to be learned.

► Thirty-five years on from Walter Winterbottom, England manager Glenn Hoddle leads his team against Italy.

FOOTBALLER OF THE YEAR

1961 ► **Danny Blanchflower (Tottenham)**

1962 ► **Jimmy Adamson (Burnley)**

1963 ► **Stanley Matthews (Stoke)**

1964 ► **Bobby Moore (West Ham)**

1965 ► **Bobby Collins (Leeds)**

1966 ► **Bobby Charlton (Manchester United)**

1967 ► **Jack Charlton (Leeds)**

1968 ► **George Best (Manchester United)**

1969 ► **Shared – Tony Book (Manchester City) & Dave Mackay (Derby)**

1970 ► **Billy Bremner (Leeds)**

WORLD CUP SQUAD, CHILE – 1962

MANAGER: WALTER WINTERBOTTOM

POSITION	NAME	CLUB	AGE	CAPS	GOALS
Goalkeepers	Alan Hodgkinson	Sheffield Utd	25	5	0
	Ron Springett	Sheffield Wed	26	21	0
Full-backs	Jimmy Armfield	Blackpool	26	25	0
	Don Howe	West Brom	26	23	0
	Ray Wilson	Huddersfield	27	11	0
	Ron Flowers	Wolves	27	32	7
	Maurice Norman	Tottenham	28	1	0
	Peter Swan	Sheffield Wed	25	19	0
Midfield	Stan Anderson	Sunderland	28	2	0
	George Eastham	Arsenal	25	0	0
	Johnny Haynes (c)	Fulham	27	52	18
	Bobby Moore	West Ham	21	1	0
	Bobby Robson	West Brom	28	2	0
Forwards	Bobby Charlton	Manchester Utd	24	35	24
	John Connelly	Burnley	3	8	3
	Bryan Douglas	Blackburn	27	29	8
	Jimmy Greaves	Tottenham	22	18	19
	Gerry Hitchens	Internazionale	24	5	3
	Roger Hunt	Liverpool	23	1	1
	Alan Peacock	Middlesbrough	24	0	0

ALAN HODGKINSON, DON HOWE, PETER SWAN, STAN ANDERSON, GEORGE EASTHAM, BOBBY ROBSON, JOHN CONNELLY AND ROGER HUNT DID NOT PLAY.

Walter walks

The Football Association responded to public disquiet at England's inability to tame the world by sacking Winterbottom and replacing him, somewhat surprisingly, with Ipswich boss Alf Ramsey, who had won many plaudits for his achievements with the Suffolk side. For the first time, the manager was given autonomy in team selection and took on the role full-time. The FA already knew they had won the right to host the next World Cup and needed a strong side to prevent a major embarrassment. Ramsey's first game in charge ended a dismal 5-2 to France, and a number of similar early defeats did not bode well. But by the autumn of 1963, England had re-discovered their golden touch and hammered Switzerland 8-1, among others. 'We will win the World Cup in 1966,' claimed Ramsey. Words which were to prove prophetic.

MANAGER OF THE YEAR

1966 ▶ **Jock Stein (Celtic)**

1967 ▶ **Jock Stein (Celtic)**

1968 ▶ **Matt Busby (Manchester United)**

1969 ▶ **Don Revie (Leeds)**

1970 ▶ **Don Revie (Leeds)**

The big freeze

The 1962-63 season was, in more ways than one, the winter of that decade. From Christmas to March, it became impossible to complete a full League programme as the country was lashed by snowstorms and freak weather conditions, and the season had to be extended well into May to clear the backlog. Clubs tried all manner of bizarre innovations, from flame-throwers to hot-air tents, to shift the snow and ice, but to no avail. The pools companies overcame the problems of postponed matches and returned stakes by introducing the Pools Panel that season. A group of former professionals and experts, they met whenever a significant number of matches had been called off and decided which teams would have won had the games been played.

Bonus for Blues

Everton used their vast squad to overcome the backlog problems and take the title that season, while Manchester United continued their recovery from the Munich disaster by condemning Man City to Second Division football and taking the Cup with a 3-1 victory over Leicester. Dennis Law, back from his spell with Torino, scored the opener and set up the other two; alongside Bobby Charlton he was nursing one of the most exciting partnerships in the game. Players like those two and, later, George Best, made United one of the most fashionable and successful teams of the decade. And where were Spurs? Their League and Cup ambitions took a back seat as they became the first English side to win a European trophy, thrashing Atletico Madrid 5-1 in Rotterdam to take the Cup Winners' Cup. Dyson and Greaves were the Spurs heroes, but the glory of a wonderful, if delayed, season was overshadowed next year by another shocking scandal.

LES ALLEN BEGAN THE TREND OF PLAYER-MANAGERS WHEN HE WAS APPOINTED TO THE DUAL ROLE AT QUEENS PARK RANGERS FOR THE 1968-69 SEASON.

▲ *George Best – excellence in its prime.*

Shock, horror

April 1964 saw the breaking of a story in *The People* which claimed three Sheffield Wednesday players, two of them England internationals, had conspired to throw a match against Ipswich in 1962. The paper said they had won money by betting against their team; within a few weeks, a match-fixing ring spanning all four divisions had been uncovered and shame had once again been brought on football. Many of the betting coups were linked to ex-player Jimmy Gauld who masterminded the scheme, but it was the players who were to suffer: around a dozen were banned for life, including Wednesday's Tony Kay and Peter Swan. Gauld was sent to jail for four years. Just as in 1915, the game's profile in the eyes of the public was diminished by the actions of a few.

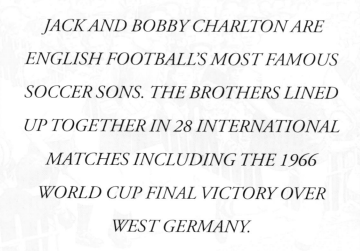

JACK AND BOBBY CHARLTON ARE ENGLISH FOOTBALL'S MOST FAMOUS SOCCER SONS. THE BROTHERS LINED UP TOGETHER IN 28 INTERNATIONAL MATCHES INCLUDING THE 1966 WORLD CUP FINAL VICTORY OVER WEST GERMANY.

United in victory

Manchester United pipped Leeds to the 1965 title, their first since Munich, and Liverpool gained their first ever FA Cup against the same team. Meanwhile, West Ham lifted the European Cup Winners' Cup at Wembley thanks to two goals from new winger Alan Sealey, beating Munich 1860 2-0. England skipper Bobby Moore was hailed as the hero for his superb defensive performance. Liverpool went one better in 1966, running away with the First Division with the likes of Ian St John, England striker Roger Hunt

▲ *Jack and Bobby Charlton played together for England in the 1966 World Cup squad.*

and Ian Callaghan their stars. Bill Shankly had begun the succession of great Liverpool managers by establishing a super squad that was regularly scaring opponents out of the game.

Simply the Best

Liverpool, however, couldn't land themselves a European trophy that year. There were to be no honours for English teams, but Man United did manage to record perhaps the greatest British victory of the decade in 1966 when they visited the great Benfica, who had dominated the European Cup since 1961. Benfica were already 3-2 up from the first leg of the quarter-final, but within 10 minutes of the second leg starting, George Best had begun work. He put the visitors 2-0 ahead with two dazzling goals, and they went on to win by an incredible 5-1; having done the hard work and been mobbed at the final whistle by amazed spectators, United then crashed to Partizan Belgrade in the semi-finals.

◄ *Sir Bobby Charlton, one of soccer's most famous brothers, photographed in 1998.*

THE LEAGUE CUP

1961 ◄ Aston Villa 3 v 2 Rotherham United on aggregate (0-2a, 3-0h)

1962 ◄ Norwich City 4 v 0 Rochdale (3-0a, 1-0h)

1963 ◄ Birmingham City 3 v 1 Aston Villa (3-1h, 0-0a)

1964 ◄ Leicester City 4 v 3 Stoke City (1-1a, 3-2h)

1965 ◄ Chelsea 3 v 2 Leicester City (3-2h, 0-0a)

1966 ◄ West Bromwich Albion 5 v 3 West Ham United (1-2a, 4-1h)

World champions

George Best was the toast of Europe, but by the start of the 1966-67 season it was the England team who were the hottest properties in the game. The World Cup win raised the spirits of a nation and gave the English game the confidence it needed to make the late 1960s and 1970s a heyday on the pitch.

Strangely, though, none of the winning team had great seasons immediately afterwards. Scotland even came to Wembley in April 1967 and won 3-2, while Spurs, whose main England star Jimmy Greaves had a poor tournament, beat Chelsea in the Cup Final and Man United landed themselves the title again.

Off he goes

England entered the 1968 European Championships as red-hot favourites having qualified from the Home International Championship. They eased their way past Spain in the quarter-finals, but what should have been a comfortable semi-final with Yugoslavia turned sour following the dismissal of Alan Mullery, the first time an England international had been sent off in competition. The Eastern Europeans won 1-0, before losing to Italy in the Final.

Benfica humbled

It was left to Man United, therefore, to keep the English flag flying abroad. They achieved this with a resounding 4-1 extra-time victory against Benfica, with Charlton, Best and 19-year-old Brian Kidd the heroes. For Matt Busby, it was a glorious and deeply significant trophy, and he retired happy in January 1969. Most importantly, a British club had once again proved they could beat the best the continent could offer.

Super City

Manchester City shocked the established order by taking the 1968 League title under Joe

Mercer and Malcolm Allison, with the astute signings of Francis Lee, Colon Bell and Mike Summerbee the key to their success. Leeds were the form side of 1968-69, losing only twice in the entire season to set a new record for defensive frugality. Johnny Giles and Billy Bremner powered Don Revie's side to the title; for both sides, success was to be sparse over the 20 years that followed. Newcastle, similar underachievers, took the Fairs Cup against Ujpest Dozsa.

Arise Sir Alf

Fittingly, the decade ended with its outstanding men being not players but managers. Alf Ramsey, mastermind of England's World Cup success, and the great Manchester United boss Matt Busby were both knighted for services to the game. And what a service they provided.

THE BIGGEST OFFICIAL ATTENDANCE FOR A MATCH IN BRITAIN IS THE 149,547 WHO WATCHED ENGLAND PLAY SCOTLAND AT HAMPDEN PARK, GLASGOW ON 17 APRIL 1937.

▼*Jimmy Armfield with his Player of the Year award from Blackpool Football Club, 1966.*

WORLD CUP SQUAD, ENGLAND – 1966

MANAGER: ALF RAMSEY

POSITION	NAME	CLUB	AGE	CAPS	GOALS
Goalkeepers	Gordon Banks	Leicester	28	27	0
	Peter Bonetti	Chelsea	24	1	0
	Ron Springett	Sheffield Wed	30	33	0
Full-backs	Jimmy Armfield	Blackpool	30	43	0
	Gerry Byrne	Liverpool	28	2	0
	George Cohen	Fulham	26	24	0
	Ray Wilson	Everton	31	45	0
Centre-backs	Jack Charlton	Leeds	30	16	2
	Ron Flowers	Wolves	31	49	10
	Norman Hunter	Leeds	22	4	0
	Bobby Moore (c)	West Ham	25	41	2
Midfield	Alan Ball	Blackpool	21	10	1
	Bobby Charlton	Manchester Utd	28	68	38
	George Eastham	Arsenal	29	19	2
	Martin Peters	West Ham	22	3	1
	Norbert Stiles	Manchester Utd	24	14	1
Forwards	Ian Callaghan	Liverpool	24	1	0
	John Connelly	Manchester Utd	27	19	7
	Jimmy Greaves	Tottenham	26	51	43
	Roger Hunt	Liverpool	27	13	12
	Geoff Hurst	West Ham	24	5	1
	Terry Paine	Southampton	27	18	7

PETER BONETTI, RON SPRINGETT, JIMMY ARMFIELD, GERRY BYRNE,
RON FLOWERS, NORMAN HUNTER AND GEORGE EASTHAM DID NOT PLAY.

▲ *Geoff Hurst in training for England's match against Russia, 1967.*

1966 – ENGLAND'S FINEST HOUR

Still the underdogs

England may have been the hosts, but on their dismal showings in previous World Cups nobody seriously expected them to win the 1966 tournament. Brazil had more stars, the Germans were more ruthless and the Russians more tactically aware. Furthermore, Alf Ramsey was hardly the most high-profile choice for manager; how wrong the doubters were to be proved.

Wembley winners

All England's group matches were played at Wembley, and they made an inauspicious start with a dour goalless draw against Uruguay before powering past Mexico and France with 2-0 wins. Ramsey ignored FA Council advice over team selection (they wanted him to drop Nobby Stiles) and set the side up with a quarter-final against Argentina. Brazil, meanwhile, finished only in Group Three and the 'little fish' of North Korea shocked Italy by qualifying from Group Four at their expense. They were unfortunate to lose 5-3 to Portugal in the next round.

Argentina self-destruct

It was the Argentina match that really captured the public's imagination and gave them a taster of what was to come. The South Americans were an aggressive team, bordering on violent, but England rose to the challenge admirably and after captain Antonio Rattin was sent off for dissent, Geoff Hurst headed home the only goal of the game. Bobby

ENGLAND V GERMANY

The first game between the two countries was staged on 10 May 1930 in Berlin. A thrilling match ended as a 3-3 draw. Since then they have met on 18 occasions. Only three have been in competitive fixtures – the 1966 World Cup Final, a goalless World Cup round-two match in 1982 and the nail-biting European Championship semi-final shoot out won by the Germans in 1996.

▲ *Bobby Moore held aloft by his jubilant England team after defeating West Germany 4-2.*

ENGLAND'S FULL RECORD AGAINST WEST GERMANY					
Played	Won	Lost	Draw	For	Against
18	9	7	2	35	21

Charlton was the semi-final hero as Portugal were defeated 2-1, with Stiles marking the great Eusebio out of the game. England were in the Final, and the country was swept with football fever like never before.

A nation waits

Wembley, 30 July 1966, was the setting for the game against West Germany, and England ground to a standstill as millions gathered to watch the match. The home side went behind after just 13 minutes, but rallied round thanks to a Geoff Hurst header. Hurst had been a controversial choice after Jimmy Greaves was dropped, yet he was to prove a hero. When West Ham team-mate Martin Peters put England 2-1 ahead with 11 minutes to go, they looked safe, but Germany equalized under controversial circumstances and forced half-an-hour's extra time.

It is now!

What followed was to become one of the most contentious incidents in the history of the game, as Hurst's 100th-minute shot rebounded off the underside of the bar and dropped on the line. The Russian Linesman, consulted by the referee, awarded the goal, which modern technology says should not have been allowed to stand. Germany pressed forward desperately, but with seconds left England counter-attacked and Hurst was left with a clear run on goal to score a fourth. 'Some people are on the pitch,' TV commentator Kenneth Wolstenhome told the country, 'they think it's all over.... It is now!' Bobby Moore lifted the trophy, a nation celebrated and English football was put firmly on the world map.

▼ *Geoff Hurst (number 10) heading England to victory at Wembley.*

THE BOYS OF 66

A great team

That there was no one outstanding star of the 1966 World Cup is a testament to the way Alf Ramsey moulded his team to traditional English strengths; he had no time for individuals, only those who worked solely for the common good. Where the Brazilians and Argentinians got their tactics and strategy wrong, England's brilliant preparation helped them overcome teams with far more talented performers.

Banks of England

They owed a lot to the safe pair of hands Gordon Banks possessed. He was beaten only three times in the whole tournament, twice in the final, and inspired confidence through the whole team. The twin towers of Jack Charlton and Bobby Moore dominated the England back-line and they complemented each other perfectly; Charlton's height was a brilliant asset in attack or defence, while Moore's timely tackles thwarted many an attacker. George Cohen and Ray Wilson, the two half-backs, were the least-known of the team and never enjoyed the same public adulation as the others in future years, yet they too played an important rôle in the victory.

ENGLAND V WEST GERMANY 1930-65

Friendly – Olympic Stadium Berlin, 10 May 1930.
West Germany 3 (R Hoffman 3)
England 3 (Bradford 2, Jack)

Friendly – White Hart Lane, 4 December 1935.
England 3 (Camsell 2, Bastin)
West Germany 0

Friendly – Olympic Stadium Berlin, 14 May 1938.
West Germany 3 (Gellesch, Gauchel, Pesser)
England 6 (Robinson 2, Matthews, Broome, Goulden, Bastin)

Friendly – Wembley Stadium, 1 December 1954.
England 3 (Bentley, Allen, Shackleton)
West Germany 1 (Beck)

Friendly – Olympic Stadium, Berlin, 26 May 1956.
West Germany 1 (Walter)
England 3 (Edwards, Grainger, Haynes)

Friendly – Stadtisches Stadium, Nuremberg, 12 May 1965.
West Germany 0
England 1 (Paine)

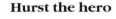
◄ The heroes of a nation – England's World Cup squad of 1966.

The iron men

For steel, England turned to the midfield pairing of Alan Ball and Nobby Stiles. The gap-toothed Stile, of Manchester United, would remorselessly hound opponents into submission with his fearsome tackling, while Ball fetched and carried to the attackers and helped set up that famous third goal in the Final.

The four amigos

Yet it was the front line who were to have the biggest impact on the outcome of the World Cup. Four distinct individuals who formed a brilliant combination of styles and skills; from Bobby Charlton, brother of Jack and classic English centre forward, to the pacy skills of Liverpool youngster Roger Hunt. West Ham pair Martin Peters and Geoff Hurst provided the meat in the sandwich, although either might not have made the Final had Jimmy Greaves not been dropped for lack of form.

Hurst the hero

Eventually, the hero of the hour was Hurst. Amazingly, he was making only his

ENGLAND V WEST GERMANY 1966-78

FRIENDLY – WEMBLEY, 23 FEBRUARY 1966
ENGLAND 1 (STILES)
WEST GERMANY 0

WORLD CUP FINAL – WEMBLEY, 30 JULY 1966
ENGLAND 4 (HURST 3, PETERS)
WEST GERMANY 2 (HALLER, WEBER)

FRIENDLY – NIEDERSACHSEN STADIUM, HANOVER, 1 JUNE 1968.
WEST GERMANY 1 (BECKENBAUER)
ENGLAND 0

FRIENDLY – WEMBLEY, 12 MARCH 1975.
ENGLAND 2 (BELL, MACDONALD)
WEST GERMANY 0

FRIENDLY – OLYMPIC STADIUM, MUNICH, 22 FEBRUARY 1978.
WEST GERMANY 2 (WORM, BONHOF)
ENGLAND 1 (PEARSON)

eighth international appearance in the Final, but Alf Ramsey knew all about his eye for a chance and made sure balls were fed into the spaces he thrived on. His hat-trick goal against West Germany was typical of his pacy, direct style – with typical modesty, he refused to take the acclaim for England's victory, It was, he said, a team performance. He was right.

▲ The most coveted football trophy in the world.

BOBBY MOORE – THE EMPEROR

◄ Alf Ramsey's 'right-hand man' in his footballing prime.

ENGLAND'S MOST-CAPPED PLAYERS

125	◄	Peter Shilton
108	◄	Bobby Moore
106	◄	Bobby Charlton
105	◄	Billy Wright

An all-time great

There should be a law against him,' the great Jock Stein once said of Bobby Moore. 'He knows what's happening 20 minutes before anybody else.' Indeed, it was his vision and foresight, when coupled with an incredible ability to tackle cleanly and effectively that made Moore the greatest defender England has ever seen, and a born leader on the pitch. He became England's youngest ever captain in 1963 and won 108 caps for his country. If the 1966 World Cup finals (where he lifted the Cup in front of a packed Wembley) were a high, however, 1970 was a low – Moore was arrested in Bogota, Colombia, on suspicion of theft.

The fabricated charges were dropped, however, and he went on to have a superb tournament including a tackle on Pele that earned the greatest of plaudits from the world's most spectacular player.

CAREERS AFTER FOOTBALL – SALESMEN

Jack Sewell (Notts County, Sheffield Wed, Aston Villa, Hull 1946-60) – Cars (now retired)
Ronnie Clayton (Blackburn 1950-68) – Tyre company (now retired)
Martin Peters (West Ham, Tottenham, Norwich, Sheffield Utd 1961-80) – Car insurance
Allan Clarke (Walsall, Fulham, Leicester, Leeds Utd, Barnsley 1963-79) – Ventilating firm

A Hammer through and through

Moore was born in Essex in 1941 and joined his local side and boyhood idols West Ham United relatively late. He had not been spotted as early as many peers, but made up for lost ground as the Hammers turned from also-rans to front-runners, winning the FA Cup and European Cup Winners' Cup. Moore was the centre of it all, tall and dignified at the back and a fine example to his younger colleagues.

Quick thinking

He succeeded because he read the game so quickly, and was always one step ahead of play. He could tackle with either foot and a slight lack of pace proved no hindrance with his superior thinking. Furthermore, he was never once sent off and always retained a cool head on the pitch. His mistakes over the years can be counted on the fingers of one hand.

From Park to Cottage

He finally left Upton Park in 1974, but rather than hang up his boots he joined Fulham and steered them to the FA Cup Final. After retirement, he enjoyed a brief spell as manager of Southend but quickly decided it was not for him and embarked on a career in print and television. He died in 1993, aged just 52, and the greatest names in the history of the game came out for his funeral – a fitting tribute to a great player.

'He was the heartbeat of the team in 1966,' said Alf Ramsey. 'He was my right-hand man, my lieutenant on the field, a cool, calculating footballer I could trust with my life.'

►Bobby Moore playing for England.

GEORGE BEST – THE BELFAST BOY

A unique talent

Did George Best fulfil his true potential or was his career a waste? It's the question that has proved the most contentious talking point in modern football, and the debate continues today. Best was arguably more naturally gifted than any other British player, and ranks alongside some of the world's greats, yet he quit the game aged just 26.

Best was born in Belfast in 1941 and turned professional with Manchester United, who spotted his talents in Northern Ireland. He reached national stardom in United's European Cup tussle with Benfica in 1966, and two years later was an instrumental force in their lifting the trophy again. He was supremely talented, and able to keep the ball at his feet for as long as he needed to, coasting round defenders and carving the opposition into pieces.

Booze talking

Yet Best's problems off the pitch arguably ruined his potential on it. He was treated for alcoholism after quitting the game, and while still playing led a hectic life of fast cars, women and champagne which affected his performances and, perhaps unfairly, led to his being labelled as flash and uncommitted. Benfica fans dubbed him 'El Beatle' for his popular haircut.

▲ *The icon of a footballing generation.*

MANCHESTER UNITED FOOTBALLER OF THE YEAR WINNERS

1949 Johnny Carey
1966 Bobby Charlton
1968 George Best
1996 Eric Cantona

Despite this, he still managed to land two championships, the European Footballer of the Year award and the European Cup. In 1970 he scored six in one match against Northampton, a dazzling display on his return from suspension. He never performed in the World Cup Finals, as Northern Ireland didn't ever qualify.

▲ *The Best in action, just two years before his premature retirement.*

Premature retirement

Best announced his retirement in 1972, tired of the constant attention and death threats he had received. He came back, both with United and a whole host of other clubs including Stockport, Fulham, Hibernian, several American sides and even non-League Dunstable Town, then managed by ex team-mate Barry Fry, but by the 1980s he had been reduced to a novelty act and it took him another 10 years to quit alcohol.

That even Matt Busby failed to tame Best shows just how maverick a talent his was. Had he continued in the game, it is tempting to speculate just what he might have achieved in his mature years; instead, as Manchester United fans will admit, it was enough just to have seen him play in the first place.

> THE QUICKEST DISMISSAL IN A LEAGUE FIXTURE WAS SUFFERED BY CREWE KEEPER MARK SMITH. HE GOT HIS MARCHING ORDERS AFTER JUST 19 SECONDS OF A THIRD DIVISION FIXTURE AT DARLINGTON ON 12 MARCH 1994.
>
> THE FASTEST FA CUP DISMISSAL WAS SWINDON'S IAN CULVERHOUSE WHO LASTED JUST 52 SECONDS OF A CUP-TIE AT EVERTON ON 5 JANUARY 1997.

1970-80: TAKING ON THE WORLD

It's all gone wrong

The 1970 World Cup Finals seemed a poisoned chalice for England before a ball had even been kicked in anger. The side, who went to Mexico as world champions for the first time in history, were embroiled in scandal while still making their way to Central America and, in retrospect, never recovered from the psychological effects of their ordeal.

Stop, thief!

England had stopped over in Bogota a few days before the tournament began, when the news broke that skipper Bobby Moore had been arrested for stealing an expensive bracelet from a gift shop and was being kept in custody. For players and fans alike – accustomed to Moore's role as the rock of the team and a squeaky-clean ambassador for the game – it was an astounding development, and quickly turned into a major international incident.

False accusations

Only after days of waiting and wondering, as a court case began against the England skipper, did it emerge that Moore had been the victim of an

▲ *Bobby Moore in his time with Fulham FC.*

LIVERPOOL PRODUCED THE LONGEST EVER UNBEATEN HOME RUN – 85 MATCHES BETWEEN JANUARY 1978 AND JANUARY 1981. IT COMPRISED 63 LEAGUE GAMES, NINE LEAGUE CUP, SEVEN EUROPEAN CUP, AND SIX FA CUP TIES.

elaborate sting perpetrated by the shop's owners, who were later themselves charged. England arrived in the searing heat of Mexico tired and drained – hardly the ideal preparation for what was to prove one of the most skilful and closely contested Finals tournaments of all time.

Brazil's challenge

England saw off Romania in their opening game, but were quickly thrown into the lions' den as they lined up for the second of their

THE LEAGUE CUP 1971-80 (AT WEMBLEY)

1971 ▶	**Tottenham Hotspur 1 v 0 Norwich City**
1972 ▶	**Stoke City 2 v 1 Chelsea**
1973 ▶	**Tottenham Hotspur 1 v 0 Norwich City**
1974 ▶	**Wolverhampton Wanderers 2 v 1 Manchester City**
1975 ▶	**Aston Villa 1 v 0 Norwich City**
1976 ▶	**Manchester City 2 v 1 Newcastle United**
1977 ▶	**Aston Villa 3 v 2 Everton (after 0-0 and 1-1 draws)**
1978 ▶	**Nottingham Forest 1 v 0 Liverpool (after 0-0 draw)**
1979 ▶	**Nottingham Forest 3 v 2 Southampton**
1980 ▶	**Wolverhampton Wanderers 1 v 0 Nottingham Forest**

▲ *The exhilarated face of football.*

group matches – against the mighty Brazil. They fought like tigers and outplayed the eventual champions for large periods of the game, but still conspired to lose 1-0. Despite this, the game threw up two of the most memorable pieces of skill England internationals have ever produced.

Save of the century

The first arrived on 10 minutes, when Pele powered a header towards the corner of the goal and turned, ready to celebrate the opening strike of the game. Gordon Banks, however, had other ideas and flew across his line, seemingly defying both speed and gravity to scoop the ball away. It was immediately dubbed the 'save of the century' and stands as a highpoint in the great goalkeeper's career.

Moore, please

And then, as Brazil pushed forward in the second half with Pele ever more menacing, Moore bade his time patiently before diving in on the yellow-shirted superstar to produce a magnificent, clean tackle and come away with the ball. The two men embraced on the final whistle; Brazil had won the game, but England had won the argument.

Boom time

If the nation was disappointed at not retaining the Jules Rimet Trophy, it was not reflected on the pitch. Everton had taken the 1969-70 League, Chelsea the FA Cup and Arsenal the Fairs Cup, but the following season will stand as one of the most thrilling and unexpected of the century.

Double delights

It was the year Arsenal did the Double, exactly 10 years after their north London rivals Spurs and a fitting riposte to those who had begun to doubt whether the Gunners would ever once again become a major force in the game. They took the title by the narrowest of margins, ironically at White Hart Lane, when a 1-0 win against Tottenham saw off Leeds' spirited challenge.

Crawford's brace

That left them with just the Cup to win. The competition had already proved an erratic one, when Third Division Colchester humbled Leeds 3-2 in a fifth round tie at Layer Road. Former England cap Ray Crawford scored two of the crucial goals for the ageing Essex side, a result which sent shock waves across the country. Everton thrashed Colchester 5-0 in the quarter-final, but Arsenal knew they would have a far more difficult time of it when they met Liverpool at Wembley.

Away from home

Arsenal had been handed an away draw in every round of the competition that year, and it looked as though they would fail at the final hurdle when Steve Heighway put the Merseysiders ahead in extra-time. But the Gunners drew level, and their boys' own hero Charlie George sealed it with a perfect finish late-on. It was a hard-fought and well-deserved victory for a diverse team: George's flair entertained the fans, while George Graham and Ray Kennedy grafted in midfield, and Bob Wilson, owner of one of the safest pairs of hands in the game, was an inspiration between the sticks.

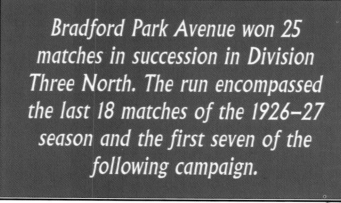

FOOTBALLER OF THE YEAR

1971	▶	Frank McLintock (Arsenal)
1972	▶	Gordon Banks (Stoke)
1973	▶	Pat Jennings (Tottenham)
1974	▶	Ian Callaghan (Liverpool)
1975	▶	Alan Mullery (Fulham)
1976	▶	Kevin Keegan (Liverpool)
1977	▶	Emlyn Hughes (Liverpool)
1978	▶	Kenny Burns (Notts Forest)
1979	▶	Kenny Dalglish (Liverpool)
1980	▶	Terry McDermott (Liverpool)

Bradford Park Avenue won 25 matches in succession in Division Three North. The run encompassed the last 18 matches of the 1926–27 season and the first seven of the following campaign.

▲ *England striker Trevor Francis demonstrating why he was Britain's first million-pound footballer.*

Radford reigns

There was another Cup shock in January 1972, and it was to prove one of the most memorable and enduring ever. Hereford, then a non-League side, held Newcastle to a 2-2 draw at St James' Park before taking them back to Edgar Street and winning 2-0. It was Ronnie Radford who scored the decisive opening goal, as he lashed the ball in from 30 yards through a mudbath of a midfield. The strike was quickly followed by a pitch invasion of Parka-sporting supporters. 'Somebody shouted "my ball, Ronnie" but it just sat up, waiting to be hit,' Radford later recalled.

Super Leeds

Leeds went on to win the 100th Cup when an Allan Clarke goal separated them from Arsenal, Derby surprising many by winning the League by the narrowest of margins and Spurs taking the UEFA Cup (formerly the Fairs Cup) in an all-English final with Wolves. It was the first time the competition had been played under its new name, and it was to prove a rich vein of trophy success for British clubs over the next few years.

▶ *Sir Alf Ramsey, an inspiration to all who played for him.*

FA CUP FINAL ROYAL GUESTS

1951	▶	King George VI, Queen Elizabeth, Duke of Gloucester, Prince William, Princess Mary
1953	▶	Queen Elizabeth II
1954	▶	Queen Mother, Princess Margaret
1955	▶	Princess Mary, Duke of Edinburgh
1956	▶	Queen Elizabeth II
1957	▶	Queen Elizabeth II and Duke of Edinburgh
1958	▶	Queen Elizabeth II and Duke of Edinburgh
1959	▶	Queen Elizabeth II and Duke of Edinburgh
1960	▶	Duke of Gloucester

controversial figures of the decade. Having guided Derby to the title, he walked out in 1973, furious at being asked to tone down some of his more colourful outbursts to the press.

Sadly, that dominance did not extend to the 1972 European Championships, where England's progress was halted in the quarter-finals by a German side out for revenge after their 1966 defeat. The Germans won 2-1, and Alf Ramsey suddenly found himself facing a mounting barrage of criticism for his selections and tactics.

Refs get tough

In the first of many such interferences over the years, in 1972 referees were ordered to clamp down on a number of offences, including tackling from behind – which was to carry a mandatory red card. Refs, however, became confused at their new guidelines and sendings-off and bookings soared over the course of the season, until the FA stepped in to give further powers of discretion to officials.

All of this only served to enrage Brian Clough, Derby County supremo and one of the most highly-regarded young managers in the game. Clough was successful and eccentric, and one of the most colourful and

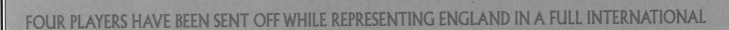

FOUR PLAYERS HAVE BEEN SENT OFF WHILE REPRESENTING ENGLAND IN A FULL INTERNATIONAL

Alan Mullery in a European Championship match against Yugoslavia on 5 June 1968.

Alan Ball in a World Cup qualifier against Poland on 6 June 1973.

Trevor Cherry in a friendly against Argentina on 15 June 1977.

Ray Wilkins in a Mexico World Cup first-round match against Morocco on 6 June 1986.

Eccentric genius

A promising young striker whose career had been curtailed through injury but who had already won two caps for England, Clough was never far from controversy but was also blessed with a fine football brain and a good eye for a player. He walked straight out of Derby and into a job with Brighton (then of the Third Division) followed as ever by his assistant Peter Taylor. He lasted under a year.

WEST BROMWICH ALBION'S DEREK CLARKE BECAME THE FIRST SUBSTITUTE IN 1968 WHEN HE REPLACED JOHN KAYE IN THE BAGGIES 1-0 WIN OVER EVERTON.

The 44 days

Leeds were Clough's next port of call, and they put up with him for just 44 days before player dissatisfaction cut short his Elland Road stay. Fortunately for Clough, Nottingham Forest were in the market for a manager at the time, and over the next 15 years he became a legend at the City Ground. Clough would answer to no one and, if he sometimes appeared desperately eccentric, it was often part of an intricate psychological web he wove.

◀ *Brian Clough at Middlesbrough, before injury put paid to his dreams of continuing his footballing career.*

MANAGER OF THE YEAR

Year		Manager (Club)
1971	▶	Bertie Mee (Arsenal)
1972	▶	Don Revie (Leeds)
1973	▶	Bill Shankly (Liverpool)
1974	▶	Jack Charlton (Middlesbrough)
1975	▶	Ron Saunders (Aston Villa)
1976	▶	Bob Paisley (Liverpool)
1977	▶	Bob Paisley (Liverpool)
1978	▶	Brian Clough (Nottingham Forest)
1979	▶	Bob Paisley (Liverpool)
1980	▶	Bob Paisley (Liverpool)

'Supreme dictator'

Over the years, Clough-related folklore was lapped up by a public and press fascinated by a man who seemed to have little control over what he was doing but still managed to turn out successful attacking teams on a consistent basis. Clough quizzed his first-team players over whether or not they ate vegetables, made the eating of Kit-Kats on the team bus compulsory, proclaimed himself 'supreme dictator' of the English game and thought nothing of criticizing his stars in public. Unsurprisingly, he was continually passed over for the England job despite widespread support – who knows what would have happened had he taken the international hot seat?

Scots are sunk

England responded to their European Championship disappointments with a 5-0 victory over Scotland at Hampden Park in 1972. As Bobby Moore celebrated his 100th cap, Allan Clarke (2), Martin Chivers and Mick Channon (2) piled on the misery for the beleaguered Scots and greatly lifted the pressure building around Ramsey – for a short while, at least.

Shankly the saviour

Liverpool, meanwhile, were beginning their stranglehold on the domestic competitions. It was the culmination of the club's rebirth under Bill Shankly, following a barren spell at the turn of the decade – having won the title in both 1964 and 1966, Shankly announced his intention to build an even better side, 'so they'll have to send a team from Mars to beat us'.

With Kevin Keegan the biggest star and Ray Clemence the League's safest pair of hands, the Anfield club boasted quality in abundance at either end of the field. In between the pair was an exciting mixture of talented youngsters and hard-grafting older players who, as a unit, were a formidable sight. The jewel in the crown, however, was Shankly himself; a hard disciplinarian with an incredible knowledge of and hunger for, the game.

Modest expectations

Shankly refused to talk up his side's title aspirations at the start of the season, but it quickly became clear that Liverpool were streets ahead of the rest. Arsenal kept up the chase most of the way but could not break their opponents'

▲ *Bill Shankly – the man who pulled Liverpool out of the wilderness and left the competition standing.*

▶*Kevin Keegan, one of Liverpool's most famous players of all time.*

stranglehold and missed out by three points. Liverpool exceeded even their own expectations by adding the UEFA Cup to their spoils, seeing off Borussia Moenchengladbach 3-2 on aggregate thanks to a Clemence penalty save.

Heighway to joy

The next year they swept all before them in the Cup, crushing Newcastle 3-0 in a glittering Wembley final thanks to two Keegan goals and one from Steve Heighway. So it was something of a shock when Shankly announced his resignation immediately

PLAYER OF THE YEAR (SELECTED FROM VOTES CAST BY FELLOW PROFESSIONALS)

1974	▶	**Norman Hunter (Leeds)**
1975	▶	**Colin Todd (Derby)**
1976	▶	**Pat Jennings (Tottenham)**
1977	▶	**Andy Gray (Aston Villa)**
1978	▶	**Peter Shilton (Notts Forest)**
1979	▶	**Liam Brady (Arsenal)**
1980	▶	**Terry McDermott (Liverpool)**

afterwards, citing the pressures of top-flight management as his reason. Fortunately, Liverpool had a ready-made replacement in Shankly's right-hand man Bob Paisley.

Paisley takes over

Paisley, like his predecessor, was Liverpool through and through. He had been at the club in one capacity or another since the Second World War, and relished the challenge of finally taking the top job. He went on to outdo Shankly in terms of trophies; it was another triumph for the 'Boot Room' which made Anfield respected and feared throughout the game. The club bred a succession of coaches, bosses and senior players behind the scenes (hence the 'Boot Room' tag, a reference to the venue for the inner sanctum's regular meetings) and achieved fluidity and consistency by insisting on appointing from within.

It took 29 matches for Leeds United to lose a League match during the 1973-74 season. In that time they won 19 and drew 10. Liverpool matched them in the 1987-88 season, winning 22 and drawing seven.

Bruges bruised

Paisley saw an almost immediate reward when Liverpool scooped the title in 1976, and added the UEFA Cup again following a tense final with Belguim's Club Bruges. It seemed the quality – among both players and coaching staff – just kept rolling off the production line.

There was still time for the smaller clubs to shine, however. Sunderland were unlikely FA Cup winners in 1973, outshining a Leeds team a division above them and at the peak of their powers. Ian Porterfield's goal separated the sides, but the Wearsiders owed much to the heroics of goalkeeper Jim Montgomery.

No tears for the clown

It was another charismatic goalkeeper who was to spoil things for England later that year. Jan Tomaszewski of Poland had been labelled a 'clown' before his country visited Wembley in a World Cup qualifier, but a string of saves belied the cruel tag and restricted the hosts to a 1-1 draw which ended their chances of making the Finals in Germany. At the end of the 1973-74 season, Sir Alf Ramsey paid the ultimate price when he was sacked over the non-qualification. It may well have been that the euphoria of 1966 and the failure to match it in subsequent years made his position untenable.

Don graduates

The FA appointed Joe Mercer as coach while they searched for a replacement. They found him in the shape of Don Revie, whose Leeds side had been one of the best club sides of the era. They had won the 1974 Championship with room to spare and remained

FA CUP HOOLIGANISM

Crystal Palace fan Paul Nixon died after falling into the path of a coach during a brawl between Palace supporters and rivals from Manchester United before the 1995 FA Cup semi-final.

THE WORST DAY FOR DISMISSALS IN FOOTBALLING HISTORY WAS 20 NOVEMBER 1982. 15 PLAYERS WERE DISMISSED: THREE IN LEAGUE MATCHES AND 12 IN THE FA CUP FIRST ROUND.

consistent while those around them floundered. Revie's international reign was to prove a mixed one; England recorded some notable victories when they were on song, but failed to impose themselves on the world stage or make the quarter-finals of the European Championship.

One Law for them

Manchester United were also in the doldrums. A new generation of superstars had failed to emerge from Old Trafford following the 1968 European Cup success, and by 1974 the club were battling an unthinkable relegation to the Second Division. They needed to beat Manchester rivals City to stand any chance of staying up, but former United legend Dennis Law ended his former club's hopes with a back-heeled winner late in the game. A pitch invasion ensued which forced the referee to abandon proceedings early, but it was already too late for United.

◄ ▼ *Old Trafford as it looked in 1971.*

▲ *Billy Bremner and Kevin Keegan after being sent off for fighting on the pitch.*

Off they go

The 1974-75 season gave few initial causes for cheer. The Charity Shield, the traditional pre-season curtain-raiser between League Champions and Cup winners, descended into controversy after Liverpool's Kevin Keegan and Billy Bremner of Leeds were both sent off for fighting at Wembley. Both tore off their shirts as they left the field and were banned for six weeks as a result. It was a poor start to the season, and things got worse when Bill Nicholson quit as Spurs boss due to a 'lack of respect' and 'greed' from modern players.

Mackay to the rescue

It was one of Nicholson's old charges, Dave Mackay, who rewrote the bad headlines. He took over Brian Clough's mantle at Derby and steered the club to a second Championship in a title race that could have gone any one of five ways with just a few weeks to go. Mackay proved as tough and determined a manager as he had a player.

Stoke upsets United

Those other over-achieving underdogs, Southampton, upset the apple cart in 1976. They lined up to face newly-promoted Manchester United in the Cup Final additionally fired up by disparaging comments from United boss Tommy Docherty regarding their relative prowess. Docherty was left feeling humbled when Lawrie McMenemy's team took the lead through Bobby Stokes and never relinquished it.

MBEs

IVOR ALLCHURCH *(SWANSEA CITY, NEWCASTLE UNITED, CARDIFF CITY, WALES)*

PETER BEARDSLEY *(CARLISLE UNITED, MANCHESTER UNITED, NEWCASTLE UNITED, LIVERPOOL, EVERTON, BOLTON, ENGLAND)*

BILLY BINGHAM *(NORTHERN IRELAND MANAGER)*

BILLY BONDS *(CHARLTON ATHLETIC, WEST HAM UNITED)*

TREVOR BROOKING *(WEST HAM, ENGLAND)*

IAN CALLAGHAN *(LIVERPOOL, SWANSEA CITY, ENGLAND)*

RAY CLEMENCE *(SCUNTHORPE UNITED, LIVERPOOL, TOTTENHAM HOTSPUR, ENGLAND)*

Doc packs it in

Docherty was to quit Old Trafford a year later, after an affair with physio's wife Mary Brown hit the tabloids. Many felt such private matters should not be allowed to interfere with footballing decisions, but the board felt they had no option. 'I have been punished for falling in love,' claimed the colourful boss, who was replaced by Dave Sexton. It was ironic that United had only just landed themselves the 1977 FA Cup at the time, beating hot favourites Liverpool 2-1, Jimmy Greenhoff's winner denying the Reds a crack at the Double, after they had already won the League.

Eastern promise

England, meanwhile, were all but out of the running for a 1978 World Cup Finals place, and it was no surprise when manager Don Revie announced his decision to quit the job. What was surprising, however, was that he already had another role lined up in the Middle East, a turn of events that eventually took him to court against the FA, who were furious.

CAREERS AFTER FOOTBALL – COMMENTATORS/JOURNALISTS (PLAYING CAREERS IN BRACKETS)

▶ **ANDY GRAY**
(DUNDEE UTD, ASTON VILLA, WOLVES, EVERTON, NOTTS COUNTY, WEST BROM 1973-88)

▶ **ALLAN HANSEN**
(PARTICK THISTLE, LIVERPOOL 1973-89)

▶ **MARK LAWRENSON**
(PRESTON, BRIGHTON, LIVERPOOL 1974-87)

▶ **DAVID FAIRCLOUGH**
(LIVERPOOL, NORWICH, OLDHAM, TRANMERE, WIGAN 1975-90)

▶ **ALAN BRAZIL**
(IPSWICH, TOTTENHAM, MANCHESTER UTD, COVENTRY, QPR, 1977-86)

▶ **TERRY BUTCHER**
(IPSWICH, COVENTRY 1977-90)

▶ **GARY LINEKER**
(LEICESTER, EVERTON, TOTTENHAM 1988-93)

▲ *Ron Greenwood, photographed in 1982, five years after taking charge of the national squad.*

Suffolk success

It was a future England manager, Bobby Robson, who was doing the talking on the domestic scene in 1978. Just like Alf Ramsey before him, Robson took Ipswich to FA Cup glory (they beat Arsenal 1-0 to that year's final) and into Europe without spending excessive amounts of money. John Wark, Paul Mariner, Alan Brazil and Cup hero Roger Osborne were effective unknowns for the Suffolk side who lost out in the quarter-finals of the Cup Winners' Cup to Barcelona the following year.

Clough's revenge

If Clough was bitter at missing out on the top job, he got his revenge in the best manner possible, leading Forest to the Championship in their first season back in top flight in 1978. New goalkeeper Peter Shilton was missing by the time the side lined up for the League Cup Final, but

No job for Clough

The question of who should replace Revie was a vexed one; the press plumped for Brian Clough, but the FA were never likely to sanction it. The Forest supremo did turn up for an interview and made no secret of his desire to have a go at managing England, but he was considered too radical a choice and the authorities appointed West Ham boss Ron Greenwood instead.

NEWPORT COUNTY WENT 25 MATCHES WITHOUT A WIN AT THE START OF THE 1970-71 SEASON. THEY DREW FOUR AND LOST 21 FOURTH DIVISION GAMES.

▼

MANCHESTER UNITED MADE THE WORST EVER START WHEN THEY SUFFERED 12 STRAIGHT DEFEATS IN DIVISION ONE IN THE 1930-31 CAMPAIGN.

▲ *Argentinian player Oswaldo Ardiles meets the fans at his new club, 1978.*

inexperienced 18-year-old deputy Chris Woods stepped into the breach and kept Liverpool at bay as his side won 1-0. The Merseysiders got their glory with a 1-0 European Cup Final win against Bruges.

Record breakers

In 1979, Liverpool were at their most rampant. They won the title with a record number of points and in double-quick time, conceding the lowest number of goals ever in the First Division in the process – a mere 16. Arsenal were Cup winners in extra-time against Man United, and Malmo became Forest's latest victims – they surrendered the European Cup to a solitary goal.

NOTTINGHAM FOREST WERE UNDEFEATED FOR 42 MATCHES. IT INCLUDED 26 GAMES AT THE END OF SEASON 1977-78 AND THE FIRST 16 OF SEASON 1978-79. THEY WON 21 AND DREW 21. THE SEQUENCE CAME TO AN END WITH A 2-0 DEFEAT AT LIVERPOOL.

Villa in the South

It was money that dominated the end of the 1970s. The ethos of the new Tory government seemed to have filtered down to football, with dramatic results. Spurs reaped immediate rewards when they poached two of Argentina's World Cup-winning stars, Ricky Villa and Ossie Ardiles, for a combined £700,000 in 1978. The transfers were a shock, as Tottenham had only just been promoted back to the First Division and Argentinians were in huge demand across the world. The pair were heroes at White Hart Lane and helped the club to a mid-table position in their first season, as well as adding a touch of South American skill to the English game.

Ossie rules

Ricky Villa, in particular, was a tricky forward with exquisite ball control, while Ardiles was an intelligent passer of the ball and a hard-working and popular midfielder. Their signings, however, overshadowed the more important progress of black players in the game at the time; Viv Anderson became the first black England cap, while many others – from Laurie Cunningham to Luther Blissett – were challenging traditional taboos and establishing themselves in the English game.

▲ *Trevor Brooking at the launch of his autobiography in 1981.*

CAREERS AFTER FOOTBALL – COMMENTATORS/JOURNALISTS
(playing careers in brackets)

Eammon Dunphy ▶ *(Manchester Utd, York, Millwall, Charlton, Reading 1962-76)*
Bob Wilson ▶ *(Arsenal 1963-73)*
Trevor Brooking ▶ *(West Ham 1967-83)*
Clive Allen ▶ *(QPR, Crystal Palace, Spurs, Manchester City, Chelsea, West Ham, Millwall, England 1978-94)*
Steve Archibald ▶ *(Clyde, Aberdeen, Tottenham, Blackburn, Reading, Scotland 1974-91)*
Gary Bailey ▶ *(Manchester Utd, England 1978-86)*

game were shocked that traditional Saturday night highlights were to be lost from the 'Beeb' and tried to have the deal reversed – eventually it was agreed that the two operators would alternate coverage season-by-season.

England prospered, and handed Ron Greenwood an important lifeline in his new role as manager, by qualifying for the 1980 European Championships. They dismissed Northern Ireland, Bulgaria and Eire in their qualifying group and held out against Denmark – an important step to avenging the disappointments of failing to make the past two World Cup Finals.

One in a million

The money merry-go-round finally hit new heights in February 1979, when Trevor Francis became the first ever £1 million transfer as he joined Brian Clough's Nottingham Forest from Birmingham City. Clough wanted the young striker, who had been highly rated since bursting on to the scene as a 16-year-old and was already an England international, to help his side retain the title, while Birmingham badly needed cash to stave off relegation. The fee doubled the previous record, which had itself been set only a couple of months beforehand.

'Snatch of the Day'

Off the pitch, TV company ITV pulled off the 'Snatch of the Day' when they secured Football League TV rights for the 1979-80 season ahead of the BBC. Many within the

Francis pays his dues

There was uproar when the Francis move was announced, but Clough dismissed the indignation. It was a milestone transfer, albeit one that would have arrived eventually anyway, but not since Alf Commons £1,000 move had any player sparked so much controversy. Francis, however, just got on with the job in hand, and on his European debut in that year's European Cup Final against Malmo scored the only goal. It may not have been worth £1 million, but it went some way to repaying a slice of that fee.

▲ *Steve Daley* (centre) *puts his signature to a contract worth £1,460,500.*

ENGLAND WORLD CUP SQUAD, MEXICO – 1970
MANAGER: ALF RAMSEY

POSITION	NAME	CLUB	AGE	CAPS	GOALS
Goalkeepers	Gordon Banks	Stoke	32	59	0
	Peter Bonetti	Chelsea	28	6	0
	Alex Stepney	Manchester Utd	25	1	0
Full-backs	Terry Cooper	Leeds	24	8	0
	Emlyn Hughes	Liverpool	22	6	0
	Keith Newton	Everton	28	24	0
	Tommy Wright	Everton	25	9	0
Centre-backs	Jack Charlton	Leeds	34	34	6
	Norman Hunter	Leeds	26	13	1
	Brian Labone	Everton	30	23	0
	Bobby Moore (c)	West Ham	29	80	2
Midfield	Alan Ball	Everton	25	41	7
	Colin Bell	Manchester City	24	11	2
	Bobby Charlton	Manchester Utd	32	102	49
	Alan Mullery	Tottenham	28	27	0
	Martin Peters	Tottenham	26	38	14
	Norbert Stiles	Manchester Utd	28	28	1
Forwards	Jeff Astle	West Brom	28	3	0
	Allan Clarke	Leeds	23	0	0
	Geoff Hurst	West Ham	28	38	20
	Francis Lee	Manchester City	26	14	6
	Peter Osgood	Chelsea	23	1	0

Alex Stepney, Emlyn Hughes, Jack Charlton and Norbert Stiles did not play.

THE DECADE OF HOOLIGANISM

Getting worse

As the make-up of the average football crowd changed during the 1970s, so did concern about their behaviour. Problems with hooliganism increased from a small trickle of minor incidents to a crescendo of violence as the decade progressed.

Leeds go loopy

The problems first hit the headlines in 1971, when a disputed West Bromwich Albion goal against Leeds Elland Road sparked a full-scale riot as fans surged on to the pitch to confront the referee, Ray Tinkler. Players were forced to

protect the official as the game was held up for over five minutes; incredibly, both Leeds manager Don Revie and his chairman Percy Woodward refused to condemn the incident, and claimed they could understand the supporters' reaction.

Mad in Manchester

There was more to come; the 1974 Manchester derby, which saw United relegated, ended in a massive pitch invasion and subsequent abandonment. Spurs fans were involved in angry scuffles with police and Dutch fans as their side lost the UEFA Cup Final to Feyenoord and riot police were called in to deal with rampaging Leeds fans during the European Cup Final of the next season. By

▼ *Police attempt to stop trouble from Millwall fans at the 1978 FA Cup Final.*

now, England had a reputation throughout Europe for causing trouble that would prove difficult to shake.

Scotland on the rampage

The situation reached a nadir after a fiery England-Scotland clash in 1977, when visiting fans celebrated capturing the International Championship by ripping out goal nets and carving up the Wembley turf. Hooliganism had become a recurring national problem, but solutions were thin on the ground. As the average age of fans got younger and younger, things only got worse. Chelsea fans wrecked a train following a game in Luton, and mass city-centre riots became a regular feature of a Saturday afternoon. The name of the game was being tarnished, and the consequences were to make the late 1970s and 1980s a low point in football's history.

▲ *A Scotland fan on top of one of Wembley's goals after England's 1977 match against Scotland.*

LEAGUE HOOLIGANISM

In January 1998, Linesman Edward Martin was beaten unconscious by a Sheffield United follower who attacked him during a First Division match against Portsmouth at Fratton Park.

Lock 'em up

Several clubs introduced fences to 'cage' fans and prevent them spilling on to the pitch, while several footballing figures demanded the return of the birch to deal with persistent troublemakers. A more logical solution was the introduction of an ID card scheme, which has never been adopted; British Rail delivered their own verdict on the game by refusing to run football trains from 1975 unless clubs paid for the damage. Things were going to get worse before they could get better.

In February 1995 England's friendly international with the Republic of Ireland at Landsdowne Road, Dublin was called off early in the first half as England supporters threw seats and lumps of wood at rival fans. It was the first time an England international had been abandoned because of crowd violence. The official inquiry into the violence discovered the trouble had been orchestrated by fans using mobile phones.

KEVIN KEEGAN:
AN ENGLISH SUPERSTAR

Dedicated Follower of Fashion

If there was one man who was the archetypal 1970s footballer it was Kevin Keegan. Stocky, speedy, always well-dressed and always sporting the trademark bubble perm of the times, Keegan looked the part and played his heart out on the pitch to become one of the era's best-loved and most celebrated players.

his persona that quickly endeared him. His success abroad – as well as his numerous triumphant 'homecomings' – made him a thoroughly modern player with a knack for being in the right place at the right time: 'He is the most modern of modern footballers,' claimed Ron Greenwood of his favourite player.

▲ *Kevin Keegan playing for England against Belgium, 1 June 1980.*

The human touch

There were other important factors in his success; his sending-off in the 1974 Charity Shield at Wembley was a moment of hot-headedness, but displayed a human side to

CAREERS AFTER FOOTBALL –
FOOTBALL MANAGEMENT
(PLAYING CAREERS IN BRACKETS)

Graeme Souness (Tottenham, Middlesbrough, Liverpool (1970-83)

Trevor Francis (Birmingham, Notts Forest, Manchester City, QPR, Sheffield Wed 1970-91)

Steve Coppell (Tranmere, Manchester Utd 1973-82)

Bryan Robson (West Brom, Manchester Utd, Middlesbrough 1974-96)

Glenn Hoddle (Tottenham, Swindon, Chelsea 1975-95)

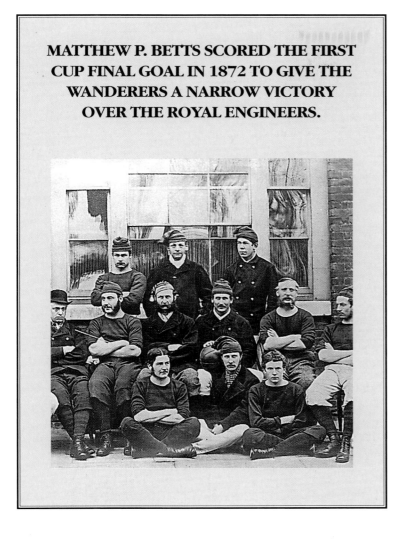

MATTHEW P. BETTS SCORED THE FIRST CUP FINAL GOAL IN 1872 TO GIVE THE WANDERERS A NARROW VICTORY OVER THE ROYAL ENGINEERS.

Shankly's big signing

Keegan was a natural goalscorer and an electric forward with a deft touch and undeniable pace. He began his career at Scunthorpe, but was quickly spotted by Bill Shankly, who took him to Liverpool for £33,000. At Anfield, he won three League Championships and the European Cup and was the most popular player in an ever-popular team. When he left for Hamburg, fans were distraught, but he made a success of his career in Germany and raised his profile on the Continent.

Back to Southampton

With England, Keegan never settled and injury hampered his only World Cup Finals appearance in 1982. Bobby Robson dropped him when he was appointed shortly afterwards, but Keegan continued to exert a magical influence on the domestic game. He sprung a shock by joining First Division minnows Southampton in 1980 but quickly proved he had lost none of his sparkle, and ended his career playing some of the best football of his life in Newcastle.

Keegan the manager

It was with Newcastle that he returned to the game in 1992, this time as manager, and fashioned a team in his own image; the Magpies attacked relentlessly, spent money like it was going out of fashion but still could not win a trophy. The fans, though, could forgive Keegan anything, and did. It would be an irony, but definitely not an impossibility, for him to manage England before his managerial career is over – and few would have deserved the honour more.

◄ Keegan the manager urging on his team, 1997.

KENNY DALGLISH: IDOL OF ANFIELD

Great Scot

From William Webb Ellis back in the nineteenth century, to Alex Ferguson's dominant Manchester United team of the 1990s, Scotsmen have been among the leading figures in the English game. Kenny Dalglish stands out among such distinguished company as perhaps the greatest Scottish influence on football; as player, manager and icon.

King Kenny

Dalglish learned the game with Celtic, helping them to the Double in 1972 and winning over 100 caps for his country. When Kevin Keegan left Liverpool for Hamburg in 1977, Bob Paisley already knew the man he considered his natural replacement, even though many considered Keegan a one-off. Dalglish signed that summer and went on to dwarf even Keegan's achievements for the club. The fans nicknamed him 'King Kenny'; it seems the only appropriate moniker for him.

The quiet man

Dalglish is famed for being a 'man of few words' off the pitch, but on it he was eloquent and intelligent. He had ball skills reminiscent of the world's greats, but could score too, particularly in important situations, and never allowed his ego to overshadow the knowledge that he was a team player. Liverpool chairman John Smith described him as the best signing the club had made for a century.

FA CUP FINAL ROYAL GUESTS	
1971	Duke and Duchess of Kent
1972	Queen Elizabeth II and Duke of Edinburgh, Duke and Duchess of Kent
1973	Duke of Kent
1974	Princess Anne, Duke of Kent
1975	Duke and Duchess of Kent
1976	Queen Elizabeth II and Duke of Edinburgh
1977	Duke and Duchess of Kent
1978	Princess Alexandra
1979	Prince of Wales
1980	Duke and Duchess of Kent

From player to boss

Dalglish was at the centre of everything as the Merseyside club took every major trophy going through the late 1970s and early 1980s, and then stepped into the breach when Joe Fagan stepped down as manager in 1985, becoming the first player-boss of a major British club. He led by example, continuing to find the net whenever the need arose and fashioning a side to take the Double in 1986.

A resounding success

By the time he retired, Liverpool were once again the biggest club in the game and Dalglish had presided over one of the most fruitful periods in their history. They had won the title an incredible nine times in 14 years, as well as tasting European glory and Cup success, setting

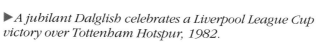

▶ A jubilant Dalglish celebrates a Liverpool League Cup victory over Tottenham Hotspur, 1982.

▲ *Kenny as player-manager for Liverpool in 1987.*

goalscoring and defensive records in the process. After a brief spell outside the game he lead Blackburn to a surprise Championship in 1995 and is now manager at Newcastle. Those who write him off have forgotten the key facet to Dalglish's play and management; he always rises to the occasion.

MANAGER OF THE YEAR

1990	Kenny Dalglish (Liverpool)
1991	George Graham (Arsenal)
1992	Howard Wilkinson (Leeds)
1993	Alex Ferguson (Manchester United)
1994	Alex Ferguson (Manchester United)
1995	Kenny Dalglish (Blackburn)
1996	Alex Ferguson (Manchester United)
1997	Alex Ferguson (Manchester United)

BRYAN ROBSON: CAPTAIN MARVEL

The rock of United

Some players are fleetingly skilful, others are solid and reliable. Bryan Robson – veteran of over 600 games for Manchester United and winner of 89 England caps – was purely and simply unbreakable.

Captain Marvel

Robson earned the 'Captain Marvel' tag that became as recognizable as his own name for his constant and unstinting devotion to the cause, his tireless midfield graft for club and country and his shining example to younger players during a 25-year career at the highest levels. He was a complete and flawless performer; a near-perfect

▲ *Bryan Robson takes centre stage at Old Trafford to lift the FA Carling Premiership trophy, 8 May 1994.*

CAREERS AFTER FOOTBALL – ENTREPRENEURS (PLAYING CAREERS IN BRACKETS)

David Herd (Stockport, Arsenal, Manchester Utd, Stoke, 1950-69) – Garage business

Johnny Haynes (Fulham 1952-69) – Dry cleaning business

David Whelan (Blackburn, Crewe 1956-65) – Set up JJB Sports shop chain

George Cohen (Fulham 1956-68) – Property developer

George Eastham (Newcastle, Arsenal, Stoke, 1956-73) – Sportswear business

Roger Hunt (Liverpool, Bolton 1959-71) – Haulage business

Geoff Hurst (West Ham, Stoke, West Brom 1959-75) – Managing director of car warranties firm

Frank McLintock (Leicester, Arsenal, QPR, 1959-76) – Owns shop chain; also a football agent

Mike Summerbee (Swindon, Manchester City, Burnley, Blackpool, Stockport 1959-79) – Shirt-making business for celebrities

tackler, an intelligent passer of the ball and a scorer of consistently crucial goals. When these factors came together in just one man, the English public took him to their hearts.

Fans' favourite

Robson was a fans' favourite because he was willing to give everything for the cause. It was a quality that marked him out for greatness during the 1970s, as he began his career with WBA and progressed to captain the club. Ron Atkinson was determined to take the young maestro to Old Trafford, and landed him for a then-record £1.5 million fee, despite the insistence of West Brom's chairman that he would be sold 'over my dead body'.

United's hero

With United, Robson progressed quickly and captained the side as they began their renaissance from First Division strugglers to the reclaiming of their crown at the top of the football tree. He remained a constant, settling influence in a turbulent decade for the club and blossomed further when Alex Ferguson took over at Old Trafford. Fergie's tutorship has enabled Robson to take over the reigns at Middlesbrough and continue to lead by example from the dugout.

Ruined by injury

England perhaps never saw the best of their Captain Marvel, as the injuries that blighted his career sent him home early from both the 1986 and 1990 World Cups. But in 1982, he had scored the fastest World Cup Finals goal of all-time when he netted against France in just 27 seconds. He will be best remembered as a legend at Old Trafford – and as a unique and incredible talent few have ever come close to matching.

▲ *Keeping the ball up for Manchester United, 1994.*

MANCHESTER UNITED BOAST THE BIGGEST PREMIER LEAGUE WIN, 9-0 V IPSWICH ON 4 MARCH 1995.

1980-90: DECADE OF DISASTER

▲ *Unaware of the decade ahead, Trevor Francis (left) bonds with John Bond in 1981.*

Getting worse

It took just a few years for the good work of the previous century to be undone. The 1980s will go down in history as the English game's blackest hour, a desperate decade marred by tragedy and major worries over the way football was heading. Not only did the three biggest disasters seen in this country take place in the space of five years, but over-commercialization, rising ticket prices, hooliganism and a European ban made for a bleak time.

Shame of the game

For a while, it became almost embarrassing to admit to being a football supporter, as the

Government and the press lambasted the game and the fans. While football in Italy, Spain and Germany was flourishing, the country that spawned it seemed to have been left behind.

Millionaires club

There were important clues at the beginning of the decade as to where the game was going. Trevor Francis's £1 million move was judged a success, as he inspired Brian Clough's Nottingham Forest to some of their best ever football before joining Manchester City for £1.2 million. By the time he retired in the early 1990s he had won 52 caps for England and boasted an enviable strike rate in the First Division.

But Francis's milestone transfer opened the floodgates, and there followed a succession of £1 million-plus moves that ranged from the unlikely to the completely baffling. Malcolm Allison, Man City manager in 1979-80, spent money like there was no tomorrow, but quickly found he was unable to buy success.

City on the spend

Allison, a flamboyant, cigar-smoking playboy who went on to manage over a dozen clubs, splashed out £1,437,500 on Steve Daley of Wolves, but the player could not reproduce his previous form at Maine Road and was sold within a few months. Then came Kevin Reeves, who had one England cap to his name, at a cost of £1.25 million from Norwich. Again, the signing did not live up to expectations but still outlived Allison at City; he left after 12 games of the season, to be replaced by the equally cash-happy John Bond.

INDIVIDUAL TRAGEDIES

THERE HAVE BEEN SEVERAL CASES OF PLAYERS DYING DURING A GAME. BURY RIGHT-BACK SAM WYNNE DIED IN THE DRESSING ROOM AFTER COLLAPSING FIVE MINUTES BEFORE HALF-TIME IN A FIRST DIVISION MATCH AT SHEFFIELD UNITED ON 30 APRIL 1927.

THE LEAGUE CUP AT WEMBLEY

1981 ▶ **Liverpool 2 v 1 West Ham United (after 1-1 draw)**

MILK CUP:
1982 ▶ **Liverpool 3 v 1 Tottenham Hotspur**
1983 ▶ **Liverpool 2 v 1 Manchester United**
1984 ▶ **Liverpool 1 v 0 Everton (after 0-0 draw)**
1985 ▶ **Norwich City 1 v 0 Sunderland**
1986 ▶ **Oxford United 3 v 0 Queens Park Rangers**

Fash rides in

Brian Clough at Forest was also getting in on the act. He broke the seven-figure barrier for Norwich's centre forward Justin Fashanu, but the player struggled to find the net and his spell at the City Ground was marked by a series of bitter clashes between him and Clough. Fashanu (who admitted in 1989 that he was homosexual – the first footballer to do so) didn't stay with any club longer than six months after leaving Forest. It was his brother John who was to become the more famous of the two, winning the FA Cup with Wimbledon and appearing for England.

Tricky Trevor

Often it was the clubs who spent only modest amounts and nurtured their youth teams as well as their first teams, who saw the most success. West Ham avoided the transfer merry-go-round of the early 1980s, but still took the 1980 FA Cup thanks to a header from Trevor Brooking, who spent his entire playing career at Upton Park and later went on to become a successful TV commentator.

Shilts the saviour

As Liverpool won the League with a game in hand that year, and Arsenal missed out on the Cup Winners' Cup in a penalty shoot-out, Nottingham Forest retained the European Cup against Kevin Keegan's Hamburg. John Robertson scored their goal, while Peter Shilton – whose place in the team had

been in doubt through injury – performed several spectacular saves at the other end.

Agony abroad

The 1980 European Championship saw further shame heaped on English supporters, as a lacklustre tournament for the England team – who failed to get past the group stage after only drawing with Belgium – descended into a series of running battles between drunken fans and police. The FA were later fined for the incidents. The aftermath of the violence, coupled with political problems among the Home Nations, caused the Home International Championship to be abolished the following year – despite widespread public support, it has never been revived.

In April 1971 Leeds United fans invaded the Elland Road pitch and a Linesman was knocked out after West Bromwich Albion took a controversial 2-0 lead in a crucial First Division game.

Villa break the mould

Aston Villa managed to interrupt Liverpool's seemingly unhaltable progress by taking the title in 1981, but it was a one-off victory. The Reds were more interested in the European Cup, which they won by beating Real Madrid 1-0 in Paris. Meanwhile, Spurs' astute capture of Ardiles and Villa bore fruition when they beat Manchester City to the FA Cup. Keith Burkinshaw's side needed a replay and were still level at 2-2 with just a few minutes left, but Ricky Villa danced his way round half the City defence to score one of the best Cup Final goals ever and seal the win.

▲ *John Barnes, Liverpool and England star, was voted Footballer of the Year in 1988.*

▶ *A hero's welcome for Trevor Brooking after scoring two goals against Hungary, 1981.*

FOOTBALLER OF THE YEAR – WINNERS

1981	▶	**Frans Thijssen (Ipswich)**
1982	▶	**Steve Perryman (Tottenham)**
1983	▶	**Kenny Dalglish (Liverpool)**
1984	▶	**Ian Rush (Liverpool)**
1985	▶	**Neville Southall (Everton)**
1986	▶	**Gary Lineker (Everton)**
1987	▶	**Clive Allen (Tottenham)**
1988	▶	**John Barnes (Liverpool)**
1989	▶	**Steve Nicol (Liverpool) – special award to Liverpool players for compassion to victims of Hillsborough tragedy.**
1990	▶	**John Barnes (Liverpool)**

Ossie's dreams shattered

Things turned sour for the Argentinian pair a year later, when Spurs won the FA Cup again by beating QPR. The Falklands War had just begun, and the club decided they could not play either Villa or Ardiles in the Final for fear of causing international embarrassment. Both players left the club that summer, although Ardiles returned to White Hart Lane when the hostilities were over.

Ipswich into Europe

Ipswich gave warning in 1981 of just what could be achieved without spending millions. Bobby Robson's boys were unlucky to miss out on the two domestic trophies, but made amends in the Uefa Cup, where they came from behind to beat Dutch side AZ 67 Alkmaar 5-4 on aggregate.

Tribute to Shankly

It was a new-look Liverpool side that took the field at the start of the 1981-82 season, but they continued the fine traditions of their predecessors as the League introduced the three points for a win system for the first time. The new innovation encouraged more attacking play and was deemed an instant success; it suited Bob Paisley's side down to the ground. They remained unbeaten in their last 16 games, and their title win was a fitting tribute to Bill Shankly, who died that year.

Nigel off the bench

In Europe Aston Villa followed up their Championship success of the previous year by taking the European Cup in unusual circumstances. Keeper Jimmy Rimmer went off injured after just eight minutes against the mighty Bayern Munich, and Nigel Spink – who had played just one first team game for the club – replaced him and kept a brilliant clean sheet as Tony Morley's goal divided the sides.

◄ *Ossie Ardiles and Ricky Villa of Spurs – their contracts were forcibly terminated by the Falklands War in 1982.*

No joy in Spain

England should therefore have been fairly optimistic going into the 1982 World Cup Finals in Spain, but the tournament was to prove a disappointment for them yet again. Both the first and second rounds were played as group stages, feeding into the semi-finals, and Ron Greenwood's side looked impressive in beating France, Czechoslovakia and Kuwait in their opening games. However, being grouped with West Germany and Spain proved the death of England, and when they could only manage an unconvincing goaless draw with the Germans in the last game they were eliminated unbeaten.

◄ *Bob Paisley led Liverpool to many a victory and won the Manager of the Year award twice.*
◄▼*Kenny Dalglish was also Manager of the Year twice.*

MANAGER OF THE YEAR

1981	►	**Ron Saunders (Aston Villa)**
1982	►	**Bob Paisley (Liverpool)**
1983	►	**Bob Paisley (Liverpool)**
1984	►	**Joe Fagan (Liverpool)**
1985	►	**Howard Kendall (Everton)**
1986	►	**Kenny Dalglish (Liverpool)**
1987	►	**Howard Kendall (Everton)**
1988	►	**Kenny Dalglish (Liverpool)**
1989	►	**George Graham (Arsenal)**

Greenwood retires

The result sounded the death knell for Greenwood, who retired shortly afterwards. His replacement proved a popular choice, if not a big name at the time – Bobby Robson who, like Sir Alf Ramsey, had taken little Ipswich to considerable success at home and in Europe. Robson proved a popular boss, and though he could not put silverware in the FA's trophy cabinet, he did drag the national side into the modern era by greatly improving the English infrastructure and development of young players.

Barnes beats Brazil

Robson also gave England one of their greatest ever games, when the national side beat Brazil 2-0 on a South American tour in 1984. John Barnes' second goal was good enough to have been scored by a Brazilian, as he coasted through the defence single-handedly finishing stylishly.

Sadly, England did not qualify for that year's European Championships in France, a major disappointment.

Fagan steps in

There were changes at Liverpool, too, as the 1982-83 season ended. Bob Paisley stepped down after nine glorious years and handed over the reigns to Joe Fagan, a fellow product of Liverpool's 'Boot Room' and a former player. Anfield, celebrating another title triumph, was shocked. Liverpool had seen

STOKE CITY FOUND THE NET ON ONLY 24 OCCASIONS IN 42 FIRST DIVISION MATCHES DURING THE 1984-1985 CAMPAIGN.

off a plucky challenge from Graham Taylor's underdogs Watford, who later sold their star player John Barnes to Liverpool and seemed on course for further domination under Paisley – but there was no need to worry.

Smith must score...

Manchester United, who finished third in the Championship, found themselves facing relegated Brighton in the Cup Final, and received a shock when they were held 2-2. The south-coast side could even have won it in the dying moments, when Gordon Smith squandered a glorious chance, prompting the oft-repeated phrase 'And Smith must score...' from the television commentary of the match. United won the replay 4-0.

Maxwell buys 'em up

Football, however, was beginning to mount the slippery slope to oblivion – and newspaper baron Robert Maxwell saw the chance to make some quick profits for a minimal outlay. The Mirror Group owner saved Oxford from bankruptcy by buying them in 1982, but caused controversy when he also purchased southern rivals Reading a year later and announced plans to merge the two clubs and form the Thames Valley Royals.

◀ *Robert Maxwell* (left) *and American businessman Alan Davis signing a sponsorship deal for Oxford United, Maxwell's new team.*

WORLD CUP SQUAD, MEXICO – 1986

MANAGER: BOBBY ROBSON

POSITION	NAME	CLUB	AGE	CAPS	GOALS
Goalkeepers	Gary Bailey	Manchester Utd	27	2	0
	Peter Shilton	Southampton	36	79	0
	Chris Woods	Norwich	26	3	0
Full-backs	Viv Anderson	Arsenal	29	20	1
	M Gary Stevens	Everton	23	8	0
	Kenny Sansom	Arsenal	27	63	1
Centre-backs	Terry Butcher	Ipswich	27	38	3
	Terry Fenwick	QPR	26	14	0
	Alvin Martin	West Ham	27	14	0
	Gary A Stevens	Tottenham	24	4	0
Midfield	Glenn Hoddle	Tottenham	28	31	8
	Steve Hodge	Aston Villa	23	2	0
	Peter Reid	Everton	29	5	0
	Bryan Robson (c)	Manchester Utd	29	50	17
	Trevor Steven	Everton	22	9	3
	Ray Wilkins	AC Milan	29	78	3
Forwards	John Barnes	Watford	22	25	3
	Peter Beardsley	Newcastle	25	3	0
	Kerry Dixon	Chelsea	24	5	4
	Mark Hateley	AC Milan	24	16	6
	Gary Lineker	Everton	25	12	6
	Chris Waddle	Tottenham	25	14	2

GARY BAILEY, CHRIS WOODS AND VIV ANDERSON DID NOT PLAY.

The fat controller

Maxwell was eventually outvoted but remained undeterred. He tried to buy Manchester United, but refused to meet the eventual asking price, and then made his son chairman of Derby, his third club. By now, the Football League were becoming worried at one man having so much power over so many clubs, and when he tried to buy Watford in 1987 they stepped in to stop him. Maxwell was furious and quickly ended his involvement in the game – no bad thing, as he had achieved little with his existing three clubs and left all three struggling to recover from debt.

Liverpool go trophy crazy

Liverpool cruised to the title again in 1984, rarely troubled and with Ian Rush scoring 32 League goals. They also added the League Cup to their impressive haul, and won the Uefa Cup against Roma on a tense night in the Olympic Stadium. Alan Kennedy scored the final spot-kick in a dramatic penalty shoot-out to complete a remarkable first season in charge for Joe Fagan.

Second best Blues

Spare a thought, though, for Everton. Howard Kendall had created a majestic side at Goodison Park and, had Liverpool not been so dominant at the time, they might have outdone their fellow Merseysiders in the honours stakes. Everton beat Watford 2-0 to the 1984 FA Cup, and in the likes of Neville Southall, Andy Gray, Gary Lineker, Kevin Ratcliffe and Peter Reid they had world-class players who gelled to form a slick side.

LITTLEWOODS CUP

1987	◄	**Arsenal 2 v 1 Liverpool**
1988	◄	**Luton Town 3 v 2 Arsenal**
1989	◄	**Nottingham Forest 3 v 1 Luton Town**
1990	◄	**Nottingham Forest 1 v 0 Oldham Athletic**

▼ *A victorious Everton, after trouncing Watford 2-0 in the 1984 FA Cup Final. It was their first major trophy in 14 years.*

PLAYER OF THE YEAR (SELECTED FROM VOTES CAST BY FELLOW PROFESSIONALS)

1981 ◄ **John Wark (Ipswich)**
1982 ◄ **Kevin Keegan (Southampton)**
1983 ◄ **Kenny Dalglish (Liverpool)**
1984 ◄ **Ian Rush (Liverpool)**
1985 ◄ **Peter Reid (Everton)**
1986 ◄ **Gary Lineker (Everton)**
1987 ◄ **Clive Allen (Tottenham)**
1988 ◄ **John Barnes (Liverpool)**
1989 ◄ **Mark Hughes (Manchester United)**
1990 ◄ **David Platt (Aston Villa)**

Tragedy steps in

Football, however, became something of a secondary consideration after two horrific tragedies befell the game. On 11 May 1985, Bradford City should have been celebrating promotion during their match with Lincoln City. Instead, their Valley Parade stadium was turned into an inferno and 56 people were killed when a huge fire broke out in the main stand. Hundreds more suffered burns as a result of the fire, which is thought to have been caused by a dropped match or cigarette igniting rubbish underneath the stand. The disaster reminded the public just how run-down and neglected so many lower division grounds had become.

Everton go top

Everton gained the upper hand in their rivalry with Liverpool during the 1984-85 season, where they finally won the League with some style. They might have made it a Double, but their FA Cup Final with Manchester United was historic for all the wrong reasons – United's Kevin Moran became the first man to be sent off in the match, when he was dismissed for a tackle on Reid. However, Norman Whiteside won the match for United and became the youngest Cup Final goalscorer at the same time.

Three brothers, Southampton's Danny, Rodney and Ray Wallace, made 25 First Division appearances for the Saints between October 1988 and September 1989.

Another disaster

The game suffered another blow just over two weeks later, when a wall collapsed at the European Cup Final between Liverpool and Juventus at the Heysel Stadium in Brussels. The two sets of fans had been fighting in the stands, and 40 people, mostly Italians, were killed. Liverpool supporters were deemed the responsible parties, and Uefa took a strong line against what it saw as just the latest example of English hooliganism.

Walter Tait of Burnley scored the first League hat-trick in only its second week of existence, as his side beat Bolton Wanderers 4-3 on 15 September 1888.

England is banned

English clubs were to be banned from Europe indefinitely, and Liverpool would be banned for another three years after the rest of the clubs had returned. The ban was devastating – it set the English game back a good 10 years, as tactics and talent lagged behind the rest of the Continent. There was a widespread sense of shame and revulsion at the state of the game and its fans, and at the severe punishment handed out. Some 26 Liverpool fans were later charged with manslaughter for their part in the Heysel Stadium tragedy, and the European ban remained in force until after the 1990 World Cup.

Game on the slide

The ban was not the only problem facing the game at the time. Attendances were falling all across the Leagues as genuine fans stayed away through fear of intimidation or hooliganism. Grounds fell into disrepair as many lower division clubs feared for their very survival. Wolves, the proud side of the 1950s, were close to bankruptcy at the wrong end of the Fourth Division, and many others came close to being wound up, including Bristol City and Middlesbrough. The nation profile of the game had never been lower, and it seemed the hooligans had won the battle. Their deplorable behaviour abroad, particularly with the national side, only exacerbated the problem, as did a series of ugly incidents on the pitch including a £3,000 fine for Arsenal's Paul Davis after he broke an opponent's jaw with a punch.

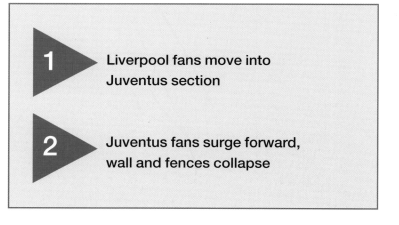

1 Liverpool fans move into Juventus section

2 Juventus fans surge forward, wall and fences collapse

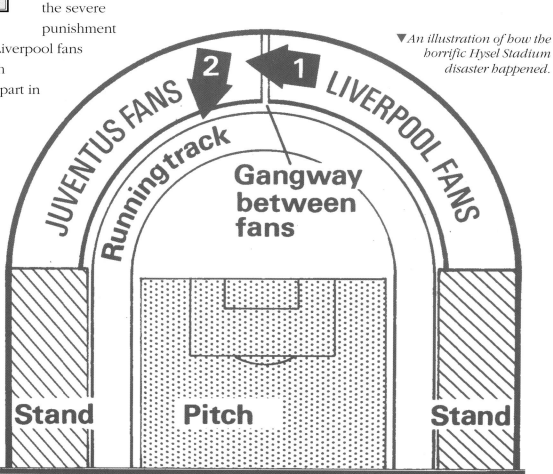

▼*An illustration of how the horrific Hysel Stadium disaster happened.*

JUVENTUS FANS · Running track · LIVERPOOL FANS

Gangway between fans

Stand · Pitch · Stand

Playing on plastic

Several clubs tried gimmicks or marketing campaigns to bring the fans back. QPR announced their intention to fit a plastic pitch in 1981 and did so a year later, but the idea did not catch on. Visiting clubs complained about the bounce of the pitch, which Rangers themselves seemed to have difficulty mastering – Preston, Oldham and Luton also flirted with the idea a few years later, but quickly abandoned it. Luton also tried banning away fans to drive away trouble, but the move sparked uproar. Later, talk of mergers between QPR and Fulham and Wimbledon and Crystal Palace led to widespread protests but proved fruitless.

▶ *Bryan Robson, part of the 1982 World Cup squad, seen here in action for Manchester United.*

WORLD CUP SQUAD, SPAIN – 1982
MANAGER: RON GREENWOOD

POSITION	NAME	CLUB	AGE	CAPS	GOALS
Goalkeepers	Ray Clemence	Tottenham	33	59	0
	Joe Corrigan	Manchester City	33	9	0
	Peter Shilton	Notts Forest	32	37	0
Full-backs	Viv Anderson	Notts Forest	25	10	0
	Mick Mills	Ipswich	33	37	0
	Phil Neal	Liverpool	31	37	3
	Kenny Sansom	Arsenal	23	23	0
Centre-backs	Terry Butcher	Ipswich	23	4	0
	Steve Foster	Brighton	24	2	0
	Phil Thompson	Liverpool	28	35	1
Midfield	Trevor Brooking	West Ham	33	46	5
	Steve Coppell	Manchester Utd	26	36	6
	Glenn Hoddle	Tottenham	24	11	4
	Terry McDermott	Liverpool	30	25	3
	Graham Rix	Arsenal	24	8	0
	Bryan Robson	Manchester Utd	25	19	3
	Ray Wilkins	Manchester Utd	25	47	3
Forwards	Trevor Francis	Manchester City	28	27	6
	Kevin Keegan	Liverpool	31	62	21
	Paul Mariner	Ipswich	29	21	10
	Peter Withe	Aston Villa	30	6	0
	Tony Woodcock	Notts Forest	26	22	7

RAY CLEMENCE, JOE CORRIGAN, VIV ANDERSON, TERRY MCDERMOTT AND PETER WITHE DID NOT PLAY.

Reds go rampant

Everton had led the title race for much of the 1985-86 season, but when they stuttered towards the end their great rivals nipped in with a typically accomplished run-in. It was a first trophy for new player-manager Kenny Dalglish, and there was quality throughout the side, from the extrovert goalkeeping antics of Bruce Grobbelaar, through the brilliant Alan Hansen and Mark Lawrenson in defence, Ronnie Whelan and Craig Johnston in midfield and Ian Rush and Dalglish up front.

Double delight

Dalglish turned the title triumph into the club's first ever Double when they beat Everton again, this time at Wembley in the Cup Final. Gary Lineker had given Everton the lead in an impressive first half, but Rush, Johnston and Dane Jan Molby proved too strong for them. They were a side in the great Double mould, and it seemed nobody would be able to stop them.

Lineker lights up

England's 1986 World Cup Finals performance in Mexico also provided some reason to be cheerful. A Lineker hat-trick against Poland took Bobby Robson's side through the first round, and he was to become the tournament's top scorer with six strikes. Lineker scored another two as minnows Paraguay were swept aside 3-0 to set up a quarter-final match with Argentina that was to become one of the most exciting and controversial games of the decade.

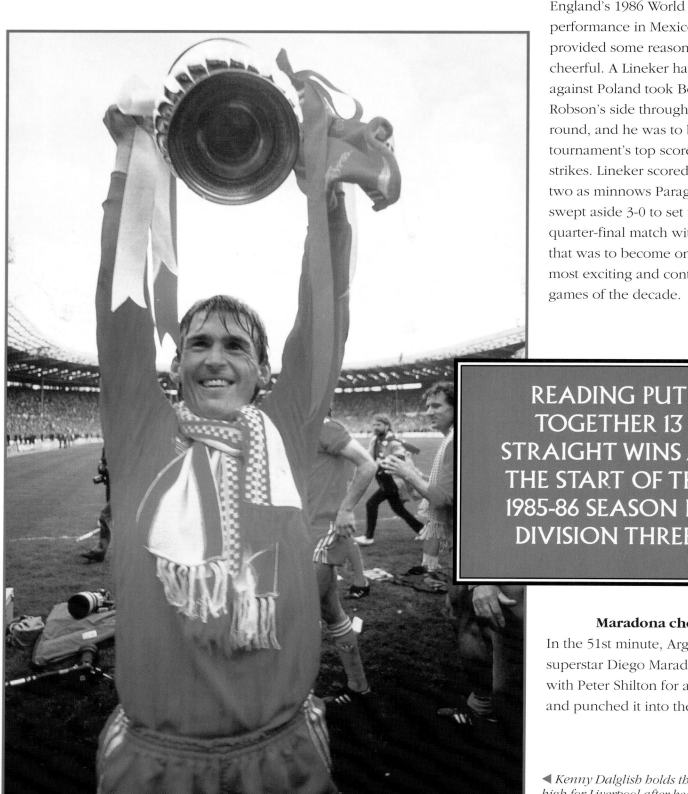

> READING PUT TOGETHER 13 STRAIGHT WINS AT THE START OF THE 1985-86 SEASON IN DIVISION THREE.

Maradona cheats

In the 51st minute, Argentinian superstar Diego Maradona rose with Peter Shilton for a high ball and punched it into the net above

◀ *Kenny Dalglish holds the FA Cup high for Liverpool after beating fellow Merseysiders, Everton, in 1986.*

INDIVIDUAL TRAGEDIES

York City striker David Longhurst, 25, died from a rare heart condition after collapsing during a Division Four match at home to Lincoln City on 8 September 1990.

the England goalkeeper. The referee allowed the goal to stand, but television replays later proved him wrong – it was a massive injustice that was to cost England dear, and Maradona later claimed the 'Hand of God' had scored the goal. He scored the second himself, though, mesmerizing the defence as he ran from the half-way line to score what is possibly the greatest goal ever; England rallied bravely and pulled one back through Lineker, but in the searing heat they were broken and went home empty-handed but not disgraced.

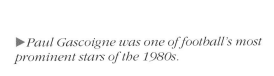

All change, please

There were two crucial managerial changes over the course of the 1986-87 season; Everton won the League following a titanic duel with Liverpool, and were then shocked when Howard Kendall left in May to take charge at Spanish side Athletic Bilbao. Over at Old Trafford, Alex Ferguson replaced Ron Atkinson in the hot-seat and began plotting Liverpool's downfall, a task that took some time to achieve. It was Coventry who usurped the bigger names to win the Cup, beating Spurs 3-2. The London side appointed Terry Venables as manager for the start of the next season, and he quickly signed a promising young midfielder by the name of Paul Gascoigne from Newcastle.

▶ *Paul Gascoigne was one of football's most prominent stars of the 1980s.*

Playing off

For the first time, the Football League introduced play-offs to increase end-of-season excitement and decide promotion and relegation issues. At first, teams at the bottom of a division would play teams at the top of the division below, but it was later decided that the play-offs should decide promotion only.

Back to normal

Liverpool resumed normal service in time for 1987-88, the year Wimbledon beat them to the Cup, thanks to a Lawrie Sanchez goal and a Dave Beasant penalty save. They took the League in emphatic fashion, losing only two matches all season and went for nine games without conceding a single goal. Only Everton prevented them going 30 games without defeat in a glorious campaign.

Embarrassing for England

There was nothing for English supporters to cheer during the 1988 European Championships, which Holland won 2-0. England were beaten by eventual finalists the USSR and the Dutch during the group stages, but their most

▼ *The twin tragedies of the 80s were sadly reminiscent of the Ibrox Stadium disaster at the turn of the century.*

LEAGUE HOOLIGANISM

IN 1985, A BOY DIED WHEN LEEDS'S FANS WENT ON THE RAMPAGE AT ST ANDREWS AS THEIR SIDE MET BIRMINGHAM CITY ON THE FINAL SATURDAY OF THE 1984-85 SEASON. THE YOUNGSTER WAS CRUSHED UNDER A WALL AND DOZENS OF OTHER FANS AND POLICE OFFICERS WERE INJURED. THE INCIDENT HAPPENED ON THE SAME DAY AS 55 PEOPLE PERISHED IN THE BRADFORD STADIUM FIRE.

Cambridge United endured 31 Second Division matches without a win during the 1983–1984 season. They lost 21 and drew 10 between 8 October and 23 April. They finished the season bottom of the table.

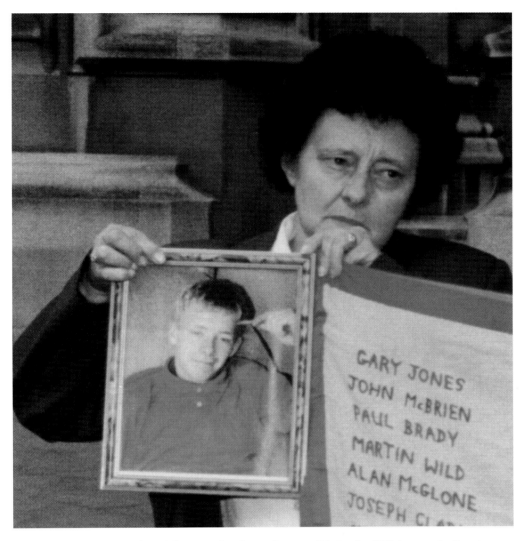

▲ *A poignant reminder of the senseless loss of young life in the Hillsborough disaster.*

put it afterwards: 'Football is irrelevant now.'

A terrible toll

The match taking place was the FA Cup semi-final between Liverpool and Nottingham Forest, the former leading the title race and chasing the Double. The match had got underway without trouble, but outside several hundred ticketless Liverpool fans were milling around. The gate to the Leppings Lane end of the ground was opened – whether by police or supporters is still unclear – and the crowd surged forward under the pressure of the new arrivals.

embarrassing moment came when Jack Charlton's Republic of Ireland side – the majority of whom would have been eligible to play for the English – beat them 1-0.

Football is irrelevant

If anyone thought the 1988-89 season would be any better, they were to be sadly mistaken, and the light gradually appearing at the end of the tunnel was fully extinguished by the end of the season. On 15 April 1989, football's worst-ever disaster took place at Sheffield Wednesday's Hillsborough stadium, and as Kenny Dalglish

Killed in the crush

Hundreds of fans were crushed against the fences at the edge of the pitch and the game was immediately abandoned. Ninety-six people died and the pictures of the disaster shocked the game around the world, prompting a period of national mourning and soul-searching as to how this tragedy could have been allowed to occur. Particularly harrowing was footage of fans using advertising boards as makeshift stretchers to ferry dead and injured supporters across the pitch, on to which thousands had spilled to escape the carnage. Both Dalglish and Forest manager Brian Clough were close to tears.

Liverpool take the Cup

It was fitting, then, that the FA Cup Final was an all-Merseyside affair. Liverpool had insisted the game go ahead, as the dead fans would have wished, and they beat Everton 3-2 thanks to two Rush goals. Liverpool lost the title to Arsenal in one of the most dramatic finishes to a season ever recorded; the Gunners needed a 2-0 victory at Anfield in the final match to steal the Championship, and

they sealed it in the final seconds of the match when Michael Thomas added to Alan Smith's earlier strike.

Taylor judges

Hillsborough, however, had overshadowed everything. The Government ordered a report into the state of football – Lord Justice Taylor, who carried it out, made a number of important recommendations to make the game safer, including the introduction of all-seater stadia being made compulsory and the removal of the fences which had killed so many that day.

Looking to the future

English football needed time to recover, and Hillsborough was its lowest ebb to date. The tragedy forced the game to look at itself and where it was going, and dragged it into the 1990s determined there should be no repeat of the tragedy. Things could get no worse than this.

▲ *A sad memorial message inscribed on the wall at Liverpool's Anfield ground.*

GARY JONES
JOHN McBRIEN
PAUL BRADY
MARTIN WILD
ALAN McGLONE
JOSEPH CLARKE
STEVEN COPOC
KESTER BALL
CARL BROWN

BARRY GLOVER
COLIN SEFTON
RICHARD JONES
TRACY COX
GRAHAM WRIGHT
DAVID MATHER
CARL HEWITT
NICHOLAS HEWITT
ERIC HUGHES

ANDREW BROOKES
PETER THOMPSON
JON-PAUL GILHOOLEY
KEVIN WILLIAMS
PETER McDONNELL
KEVIN TRAYNOR
CHRISTOPHER TRAYNOR
STUART THOMPSON
CHRISTOPHER DEVENSIDE

GERARD BARON
DERRICK GODWIN
PHILIP HAMMOND
ADAM SPEARRITT
DAVID THOMAS
BARRY BENNETT
ARTHUR HORROCKS

JAMES HENNESSEY
ROY HAMILTON
JAMES ASPINALL
DAVID BROWN
GARY CHURCH
PAUL MURRAY
CARL RIMMER
PAULA SMITH
HENRY ROGERS

NICHOLAS JOYNES
GORDON HORN
PAUL HEWITSON
JOHN ANDERSON
SARAH HICKS
VICTORIA HICKS
ANTHONY KELLY
LEE NICOL
PETER TOOTLE

DAVID HAWLEY
STEPHEN O'NEIL
CARL LEWIS
PAUL CARLILE
HENRY BURKE
PAUL CLARKE
DAVID BIRTLE
GARY COLLINS
SIMON BELL

HILLSBOROUGH
15. 4. 1989.

YOU'LL NEVER WALK ALONE

PATRICK THOMPSON
STEPHEN HARRISON
GARY HARRISON
JOSEPH McCARTHY
CHRISTOPHER EDWARDS
JAMES DELANEY
STEPHEN ROBINSON
FRANCIS McALLISTER
VINCENT FITZSIMMONS

DAVID RIMMER
COLIN ASHCROFT
IAN WHELAN
THOMAS HOWARD
THOMAS A. HOWARD
INGA SHAMSIDES
PETER HARRISON
COLIN WAFER

MARIE McCABE
BRIAN MATTHEWS
PETER BURKETT
KEITH McGRATH
CHRISTINE JONES
JOHN OWENS
ALAN JOHNSTON
ERIC HANKIN
KEVIN TYRRELL
IAN GLOVER

STEVEN FOX
RAYMOND CHAPMAN
MICHAEL KELLY
PHILIP STEELE
DAVID BENSON
GRAHAM ROBERTS
ROY PEMBERTON

▲ *Two members of the Hillsborough Family Support Group on their way to a meeting with Home Secretary Jack Straw. The banner bears the names of all who died that day.*

THE HOOLIGANS TAKE OVER

A growing concern

Those who hoped the hooligan problem of the 1970s would be eradicated in the stricter, more conservative 80s, were sadly mistaken. The rising tide of unemployment and social injustice seemed to spill over into football more and more as the decade progressed – with dramatic and tragic consequences. By now, there were large, well-organized gangs behind the trouble, and distinctive rivalries and agendas had taken over from the wanton wrecking sprees of the 1970s.

Millwall go mental

The situation reached a nadir in March 1985, when a nation watched their televisions with horror as Millwall fans ran riot at Luton in the FA Cup quarter-final. Play was delayed for almost half-an-hour, and the Kenilworth Road terraces were wrecked by the end of the game. The incident provoked an urgent inquiry from Margaret Thatcher's government, and an extreme reaction from Luton themselves.

Go away

David Evans, chairman of the Bedfordshire club, reacted to the ever-increasing hooligan problem by banning away fans from the ground and attempting to introduce an ID card scheme for all supporters. Unfortunately, they found the former to be unenforceable and the latter failed to win widespread support, with many fearful of the civil liberties aspects to such actions.

Shock treatment

At Chelsea, chairman Ken Bates had his own solution to the problem. He tried to install a huge electric fence similar to the one he used to protect cattle at his Buckinghamshire mansion, around the Stamford Bridge pitch. Again, the authorities took a dim view and the current was never switched on. These were extreme measures, but reflected the belief at the time that crowd disturbances were undoing all the good work of the previous century and would see the game consigned to history's dustbin if they were not stamped out.

▼ *The electric fence installed at Chelsea's Stamford Bridge by Ken Bates – a reaction to the appalling outbreaks of crowd violence throughout the 80s.*

▲ *Trouble in Dublin as England supporters throw part of a bench over the balcony, during the match between England and the Republic of Ireland.*

IN 1975 JUBILANT WEST HAM FANS SPILLED ON TO THE PITCH TO CELEBRATE THEIR SIDE'S 2-0 SUCCESS OVER FULHAM. PLAYERS WERE MOBBED BY DELIRIOUS SUPPORTERS. NO ONE WAS HURT.

Kiss and make up

In the end, it took investment in safer stadia and better stewarding and policing to eradicate the problem, but not before English clubs had endured a heartbreaking European ban and had been shunned by the rest of the Continent. The organized gangs who blighted the 1980s simply grew up and moved on, and for the next generation hooliganism was simply too risky a past-time. Perhaps the authorities should have followed Brian Clough's lead – after hauling two supporters off the pitch at the City Ground, he met up with them literally to kiss and make up at the next match. Diplomacy, however, seemed to hold little sway with most of the troublemakers.

MANCHESTER UNITED'S KEVIN MORAN WAS THE FIRST PLAYER EVER TO BE SENT OFF IN AN FA CUP FINAL WHEN HE WAS DISMISSED DURING HIS SIDE'S 1-0 VICTORY OVER EVERTON IN 1985.

WIMBLEDON: THE CRAZY GANG

Crazy days

The 1988 Cup Final was billed as a one-sided affair. Liverpool, League champions and dominant team of the age, were expected to crush little Wimbledon to pieces; perhaps, in retrospect, they were too complacent. By the end of the match, every football fan in the world knew of the boys from south London who had upset the apple cart – 'The Crazy Gang' had beaten Kenny Dalglish's men 1-0.

Giant-killers to giants

Wimbledon's rise through the ranks had been incredible. In the 1970s, they were not Cup winners but lowly giant-killers, beating Burnley and scaring Leeds in 1975, among others. They finally made it to the League when Workington resigned in 1978, and thereafter mounted the divisions one by one.

Route one football

Wimbledon won few friends among neutrals with their bruising, direct style, which relied on getting the ball to the forwards as quickly as possible, mainly with long balls straight up the middle of the park. Gary Lineker once famously claimed he would, 'rather watch them on Teletext', than in the flesh, but it was water off a duck's back for the Dons. They had fewer fans than any other top-flight team, and won few new converts.

The club allied their unique playing style to a series of pranks off the pitch. All new recruits would be stripped naked and left in the car park of a local supermarket, while on the eve of the Cup Final the squad went down the pub to relax. As they emerged from the tunnel at Wembley, the Wimbledon players began a loud chant which out-psyched Liverpool and made them nervous right from the start.

SHORTEST-SERVING MANAGERS

In May 1984 Crystal Palace announced Dave Bassett was taking over as manager. He never signed a contract, changed his mind four days later and stayed at Wimbledon.

▼ *Wimbledon's John Fashanu holds aloft the FA Cup in front of the town's cheering crowds.*

▲ *A 1916 illustration of the East Surrey regiment kicking footballs as they advance on the German trenches.*

Fash The Bash

The Crazy Gang thrived on its characters, from charismatic boss Dave Bassett to hard-man skipper and former hod-carrier Vinnie Jones. Balding striker Alan Cork held the club record for goalscoring, alongside strike partner John Fashanu, a gangling, physical frontman known as 'Fash The Bash,' and then there was Dave Beasant, the penalty-saving goalkeeper who did much to win his club the Cup.

One-offs?

Wimbledon's ascent to the aristocracy of English football has now been accepted; today, they are regular fixtures in the top flight and continue to survive on a mixture of low gates, little outlay and plenty of pluck. The question is: can any club ever do what they did again, or are the Crazy Gang truly unique?

Many of London and the South-East's footballing talent was called up to serve in the World Wars. On 1 July 1916, a battalion of Surrey soldiers played with four footballs as they advanced on Prussian Guards defending the Montauban Ridge during the Battle of the Somme. They kept playing despite coming under machine gun and mortar attack. Captain W. P. Nevill, who produced the balls, was killed in the action which ended with English troops capturing the ridge.

GLENN HODDLE:
THE CONTINENTAL TOUCH

▲ *Hoddle heads after the ball for Tottenham Hotspur in 1986.*

TOTTENHAM'S MOVE TO WHITE HART LANE
CAME ABOUT AFTER A DEAL WITH A BREWERY
WHO OWNED THE LAND – WITH AN EYE TO
THE MAIN CHANCE, THE BREWERS HOPED
THAT HUNDREDS OF FOOTBALL FANS WOULD
FLOCK TO THE LOCAL WHITE HART INN.

Just like Brazil

Tottenham Hotspur were 1-0 down with just 10 minutes to go in the 1981 Cup Final, when they were awarded a free-kick just outside the penalty area. Glenn Hoddle stood squarely behind the ball and lined up his shot; City scorer Tommy Hutchinson knew the Spurs midfielder could curl the ball like a Brazilian, and so positioned himself to the side of the wall to cover all eventualities.

The match-winner

Hoddle's kick curled all right – straight on to Hutchinson and then on into the net. The Tottenham maestro had done it again, spared his club's blushes and set them up to beat City in the replay. For Hoddle, however, it was just another day in the office.

Continental trickery

Hoddle possessed ball skills more typical of a European player than an Englishman. He could pass over 40 yards straight to a player's feet, place a free-kick wherever he chose or unlock the tightest of defences with his perfect control. While he may not have been the most complete player England has ever produced, he was one of the most pleasing.

Spurs superstar

He signed for Spurs as a youngster in 1975 and quickly made his way to the first team. By 1979 his skills had been recognized at international level, but Hoddle was accused of being inconsistent for England and he was dropped by both Ron Greenwood and Bobby Robson, to huge public

▲ *Manager Hoddle getting the England team in shape, 1996.*

TOTTENHAM HOTSPUR HAVE BEEN AT WHITE HART LANE SINCE 1899. WHEN THEY ARRIVED THE SITE WAS A DILAPIDATED GARDEN NURSERY. THEY DEVELOPED THE EXISTING STADIUM FOLLOWING THEIR ELECTION TO THE FOOTBALL LEAGUE IN 1908.

criticism. He still won over 50 caps. With Spurs, he remained the focal point of the team which took the FA Cup twice and enjoyed success in Europe.

Hoddle the manager

A born-again Christian, Hoddle took his skills to French club Monaco in 1987 and wowed the crowds with his Continental-style trickery. Injury ended his playing career prematurely, but not before he had led Swindon to promotion and won plaudits as Chelsea's player-manager from 1993 to 1996. When Terry Venables left the England team after Euro 96, the FA called in their adviser, Jimmy Armfield – the man who had found Venables. Hoddle was the obvious choice for the job. So far he has kept the team playing the characteristic good football he made his trademark on the pitch – while also grinding out the results he hopes will make him as successful a boss as he was a footballer.

AS ENGLAND BOSS, STRONG CHRISTIAN GLENN HODDLE MADE THE CONTROVERSIAL MOVE OF EMPLOYING A FAITH HEALER, TO HELP BOOST HIS TEAM'S CHANCE OF WINNING IN THE 1998 WORLD CUP IN FRANCE.

IAN RUSH –
GOALSCORER OF THE DECADE

A natural finisher

Anytime, anywhere and against anyone: Ian Rush cared little for reputations and paid only lip service to adversity. Quite simply, he could score goals in any situation and did so week in, week out in a brilliant career spanning hundreds of strikes and dozens of scoring records.

The Welsh wonder

Throughout the Eighties, Rush reigned, and it was with Liverpool that he did his damage. He had joined the Merseysiders from little Chester City in 1980 as a teenage rookie, a Welsh lad from the valleys with rough edges ready to be knocked into shape. At Anfield, Rush's goal sprees coincided with the team's utter dominance of the decade. Whether partnering the enigmatic John Barnes, the reliable Peter Beardsley or Kenny Dalglish himself, Rush's golden touch never left him.

▲ *Player-manager Kenny Dalglish* (left) *with double goalscorer Ian Rush after Liverpool beat Everton 3-1 in the 1986 FA Cup Final.*

> During their 1978-79 campaign, Liverpool produced the best ever defensive performance – conceding just 16 goals in 42 First Division games.

Liverpool's hero

With Liverpool, he became the top FA Cup Final goalscorer of all time as he helped his side to the 1986 Double, scoring twice against Everton, and to five League Championships. He also became the greatest Merseyside derby scorer of all time, overtaking Everton's Dixie Dean. Liverpool fans were stunned when Rush joined the Italian giants Juventus in 1986-87, but they needn't have worried – he was back in the fold a season later, having found the Continental game contrary to his direct style.

Rush turns supersub

The 1989 Cup Final was undoubtedly Rush's greatest moment. A Merseyside derby overshadowed by the earlier Hillsborough disaster, the Welshman started it on the bench as lookalike John Aldridge led the Liverpool attack. But as the teams went into extra-time, level at 1-1, Rush came into his own. Within four minutes of coming on he

put his side 2-1 ahead with a brilliant finish, and two minutes after Everton drew level again he headed a glorious winner to seal one of the club's most important and historic trophies ever. He wasn't left on the bench much after that.

> In 1890 William Townley scored the Final's first hat-trick as Blackburn Rovers thrashed Sheffield Wednesday 6-1.

Still scoring...

Ron Atkinson described Rush as being 'from another planet'. Such was his eye for a goal that he continued to find the net well into his 30s, although after leaving Liverpool to dismay from fans, he hit a rough patch with new club Leeds. He was reunited with Kenny Dalglish at Newcastle, and helped the club to the 1998 Cup Final. The best goalscorer of the latter part of the 20th century still has more goals to score yet.

▶*In 1986, human dynamo Rush became the highest FA Cup Final goalscorer of all time.*

THE 1990S: AS GOOD AS IT GETS

Where are we going?

English football began the decade in sombre mood, and more than a little confused. No one seemed to know quite where the game should go after the disasters of the previous few years and the gloom that had

The soaring cost

Of course, such a boom had its downside. Ticket prices rose considerably, and the ordinary working class fans felt they were being priced out of the game. Many resented the flotation of clubs on the Stock Market and the ever-increasing gap between highly paid players and directors and those who effectively pay their wages.

COCA-COLA CUP

1993	◄	**Arsenal 2 v 1 Sheffield Wednesday**
1994	◄	**Aston Villa 3 v 1 Manchester United**
1995	◄	**Liverpool 2 v 1 Bolton Wanderers**
1996	◄	**Aston Villa 3 v 0 Leeds United**
1997	◄	**Leicester City 1 v 0 Middlesbrough** (after 1-1 draw)
1998	◄	**Chelsea 2 v 0 Middlesbrough**

descended upon the national game. Within six years, however, football was back to its brilliant best and the shame and indignity of the past had been all but forgotten.

Taylor's new rules

The Taylor Report, though it had its critics, must take a lot of the credit for cleaning the game up. The introduction of all-seater stadia in the top flight did a lot to reassure the public over safety concerns, as did the removal of the fences blamed for Hillsborough, and as the game became more skilful with the introduction of exciting foreign stars and an improvement in the national team's fortunes, so the crowds came flocking back to such an extent that most Premier League grounds were sold out by the latter part of the 1990s. Police were given greater powers to improve safety.

► *Chelsea's best foreign import: Gianfranco Zola. He took his team to new heights in 1998 when he scored in the final of the European Cup Winners' Cup.*

Brawl over now

There were relatively few glimpses of the riches to come back in 1990. The season was characterized by a number of ugly on-pitch brawls, including the particularly notorious Arsenal-Norwich incident which resulted in fines totalling £70,000. Liverpool took the League for the third time in five seasons, nine points ahead of Graham Taylor's plucky long-ball merchants, Aston Villa, whose manager had repeated his achievements with Watford but was again denied by the big boys.

Takeover time

Manchester United had an unusual year, but were generally accepted to be moving towards becoming a major force once again. They were the subject of a takeover bid early in the season, when entrepreneur Michael Knighton offered to buy out chairman Martin Edwards' interest in the club. For a good two months, fans were unsure who was actually in charge, until it eventually emerged that Knighton had received insufficient backing and would not be going ahead.

The biggest recorded footballing crowd is the 199,850 fans who packed into the Maracana Stadium, Rio de Janeiro, Brazil, for the 1950 World Cup Final between Brazil and Uruguay on 16 July. They paid £125,000 in gate receipts.

▼*Manchester United's 'kids' with the 1997 Carling Premiership trophy: (l-r) Gary Neville, Ole Gunnar Solskjaer, David Beckham and Phil Neville.*

Wright on the night

The team was beginning to gel on the pitch, culminating in a Cup Final appearance in May against Crystal

Don't bet on it

At the other end of the scale, Swindon were denied promotion to the First Division when the FA charged them with

Palace who, fired by the irrepressible Ian Wright, had seen off Liverpool in a thrilling semi-final. Palace took United to a replay after a dramatic 3-3 draw, but Alex Ferguson's side triumphed after young defender Lee Martin proved an unlikely match-winner. For Martin, it was a career high point; he later moved to the Scottish First Division but was unable to settle at any club.

PICKERING'S BOBBY SCAIFE CAME UP AGAINST HIS 21-YEAR-OLD SON NICK PLAYING FOR BISHOP AUCKLAND IN THE FIRST QUALIFYING ROUND OF THE FA CUP IN SEPTEMBER 1996. YOUTH TRIUMPHED OVER AGE WITH BISHOP AUCKLAND WINNING 3-1.

making illegal payments to players and placing bets on the outcome of their own matches; it seemed the bad old days had far from disappeared.

Robson walks away

England went to the 1990 World Cup Finals in Italy knowing they would need a new manager at the end of the tournament. Bobby Robson had intended to keep his forthcoming departure to Dutch side PSV Eindhoven a secret until after the Finals, but it was leaked in the papers and he had no choice but to confirm it. In the end, Robson did a pretty good job of keeping the morale high, and both England's progress and their performance in Italia 90 was the most promising it had been since 1966.

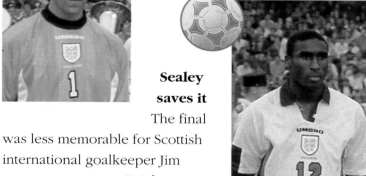

Sealey saves it

The final was less memorable for Scottish international goalkeeper Jim Leighton, who made a number of mistakes in the first match and was replaced by on-loan stand-in Les Sealey for the replay. Sealey generously gave Leighton his winners' medal after the match.

A tame start

There were doubts raised after the opening game, a 1-1 draw with the Republic of Ireland, but England managed to qualify for the second stage all the same by holding Egypt and Holland. They faced Belgium for a quarter-final place, and sealed the game in the final minute of extra-time, when Aston Villa midfielder David Platt volleyed home Paul Gascoigne's free-kick.

FA CUP FINAL ROYAL GUESTS

1991	●	replay Duke and Duchess of Kent
1992	●	Duke and Duchess of Kent
1993	●	Duke and Duchess of Kent
1993	●	replay Duchess of Kent
1994	●	Duchess of Kent
1995	●	Prince of Wales and Duke of Kent
1996	●	Duke and Duchess of Kent
1997	●	Duke and Duchess of Kent

▼*Goalkeeper David Seaman towers over the rest of the England team, 7 June 1997.*

Milla's heroes

England faced Cameroon, surprise packages of the tournament, who had been inspired by their prolific veteran centre forward Roger Milla. The African underdogs managed to go 2-1 up and put on a captivating performance before two late Gary Lineker penalties spared Robson's blushes and set the stage for a mouth-watering semi-final with old rivals West Germany.

Paying the penalty

The game proved a classic. A deflected Andreas Brehme free-kick put the Germans ahead, but Gary Lineker drew England level with a classic strike. The game was decided on penalties, as Stuart Pearce put his spot-kick too close to the keeper and Chris Waddle then lashed his over the bar to send England home empty-handed; West Germany went on to win the World Cup, but many felt England would have beaten Argentina in the Final had they progressed.

> *In Italia 90, Gary Lineker took England's match into extra-time when he converted a penalty nine minutes from time; he repeated the trick at the end of the first period of overtime to carry England into the semis.*

Geordie genius

Gascoigne cemented his place in folklore during the 1990-91 season. He had been outstanding all season, but was particularly rampant during Spurs' FA Cup semi-final with Arsenal at Wembley. He put Tottenham ahead with a brilliant 30-yard free-kick described at the time as one of the best the stadium had ever seen, and then set up Lineker for a crucial second goal that helped them win 3-1.

Reckless and wild

In the Final, however, he lived up to his billing for all the wrong reasons, and the other side of the Gazza phenomenon became all too apparent. For while he could be breath-taking on the pitch, he was always close to self-destruction; a notorious practical joker, darling of the tabloids for his drinking antics and seemingly in possession of a fearsome temper. Against Nottingham Forest in the Final, he charged around like a lunatic for a quarter of an hour and was lucky not to be sent off, before hacking into Gary Charles with a horrendous bone-crunching tackle on the edge of the box. Charles thankfully walked away unharmed, but Gazza was stretchered off with a very serious cruciate ligament injury.

Enter Gazza

Italia 90 also made a star of Paul Gascoigne, whose tears during the semi-final (after he picked up a booking which would have led to his missing the Final through suspension) were replayed throughout the world. Gazza was England's maestro, a talented central midfielder with the ability to coast through defences and an inspiring effect on the whole team. From a generation of Englishmen more noted for their all-round ability than their classic talent, he stood out a mile.

LEAGUE HOOLIGANISM

In January 1998, Linesman Edward Martin was beaten unconscious by a Sheffield United follower who attacked him during a First Division match against Portsmouth at Fratton Park.

▶ *Perhaps the most famous shot of Gazza – crying after England's defeat by West Germany in 1990.*

Paul Gascoigne in training at Bisham Abbey; before Glenn Hoddle dropped him from England's 1998 World Cup squad.

Italian adventure

Tottenham still managed to win the match 2-1 even without their wayward genius, but the incident was to have serious implications for Gascoigne. He had already agreed to join the Italian club Lazio, but the deal hung in the balance for the best part of a year while he attempted to recover. He never regained his best form when he did finally re-appear and had lost his sharpness and edge, although he remained a formidable talent. In Italy, however, a series of pranks and inconsistency on the pitch did little to endear him to the fans.

A wasted talent?

Gascoigne returned home to join Glasgow Rangers in 1995, and the lower standards of the Scottish game induced a mini-revival in form for club and country. Still he remained a controversial figure, and his 1998 move to Middlesbrough will test him to the full. As he enters his 30s, it remains to be seen whether he can recapture the promise he once showed or whether he will join George Best in the annals of squandered talent.

King Kenny abdicates

A more reserved figure kept Gascoigne out of the headlines during 1990-91. Kenny Dalglish shocked the game by quitting Liverpool two-thirds of the way through the season, as they chased yet another Championship title. He blamed the pressures of the job for his decision, and was begged by fans, directors and players to change his mind. The Merseysiders appointed Dalglish's former team-mate Graeme Souness to the Anfield hot seat weeks later, but the move did not pay off.

Gunners' glory

Liverpool lost the title to Arsenal, who lost only one match all season, and have never since reached the same dizzy heights. Souness – plagued by heart problems and poor dealings in the transfer market – lasted two full seasons, but the club dropped to the lower echelons of the top 10 and a visit to Anfield ceased to be quite as daunting as once it was. Roy Evans took over the job in 1994, but is still looking for a title-winning side.

ENGLAND HAVE CONTESTED NINE WORLD CUP FINALS SINCE 1950

Brazil	▶▶▶▶▶	1950
Switzerland	▶▶▶▶▶	1954
Sweden	▶▶▶▶▶	1958
Chile	▶▶▶▶▶	1962
England	▶▶▶▶▶	1966
Mexico	▶▶▶▶▶	1970
Spain	▶▶▶▶▶	1982
Mexico	▶▶▶▶▶	1986
Italy	▶▶▶▶▶	1990

Ferguson had felt a great deal of pressure during his five years in charge of the sleeping giants, but he repaid his chairman's faith in him by

▼ *Glenn Hoddle posing with models of his England squad in 1997.*

Fergie's fledglings

The time was ripe, back in 1991, for a new superteam to emerge, and all the signs were pointing to Manchester United. Alex

fashioning a brilliant squad of young players to rival the famous Busby Babes – Fergie's Fledglings. The wiser, older heads of Bryan Robson, Brian McClair and Mark Hughes led the side to the European Cup Winners' Cup in 1991, when two Hughes goals sealed an astonishing 2-1 victory over Barcelona.

FOOTBALL MILESTONES

1960	▶	League Cup introduced.
1965	▶	Substitutes allowed to replace injured players.
1966	▶	Substitutes permitted for any reason.
1981	▶	Three points for a win introduced.

The unprofessional foul

But United were not quite ready for the title yet – that honour was to fall in 1992 to Leeds, under the tutelage of Howard Wilkinson. It was the season the 'professional foul' was introduced, whereby any player who denied an

Hot-headed Frenchman

Cantona was an enigma in his native country, and had decided to retire after a series of run-ins with authority which ended in an explosive confrontation with a disciplinary committee, every member of which he personally branded an 'idiot'. He had first gone to Sheffield Wednesday, but they never took up the option of signing him, and it was Wilkinson who took a gamble on Cantona.

FOOTBALL MILESTONES

1990 ▶ **Player level with last defenders no longer offside.**

1990 ▶ **Professional fouls automatic sending-off offence.**

1992 ▶ **Premier League launched.**

1992 ▶ **Goalkeepers banned from picking up a back pass.**

1995 ▶ **Three substitutes allowed per match.**

1996 ▶ **Linesmen re-named "referee's assistants".**

1997 ▶ **Free-kick if goalkeeper handles a throw-in by team-mate.**

1997 ▶ **Goalkeepers can move along goal line for a penalty.**

1997 ▶ **Goal can be scored direct from goal kick.**

opponent a clear goalscoring opportunity by fouling him or handling the ball would be automatically sent off, and the early part of the season saw a huge rise in the numbers of dismissals as referees struggled to interpret the new ruling. Many clearly felt a red card was too harsh; others revealed dramatic inconsistencies among the men in the middle.

An intriguing blend

Leeds were a side fashioned around northern grit and Gallic flair. Gordon Strachan, sold by Ferguson, partnered David Batty in what was a fearsome midfield, while Lee Chapman provided height and firepower up front. They sealed their title on the final day of the season in what had been an open race, and owed a lot to their mercurial French signing Eric Cantona, who arrived late in the campaign to widespread acclaim.

In one of the quickest League goals, Huddersfield substitute Phil Starbuck hit the back of the net within three seconds of coming on against Wigan on 12 April 1993.

Gamble pays off

It paid off; the Frenchman was skilful, capable of scoring important goals and pleasing the crowds. He also had a penchant for winding up referees and becoming embroiled in controversy wherever he went. Alex Ferguson admired Cantona greatly, and signed him for a bargain £1.5 million in time for the start of the 1992-93 season. At Man United, he was to become a legend and a terrace idol, as well as a figure of derision for opposing fans.

Geordie Messiah

Just as Cantona was finding a new home, so was Kevin Keegan. The former Liverpool and England legend came out of retirement to manage Newcastle, and created a brilliant attack-minded side with Sir John Hall's money. Unfortunately, they could not pick up the trophies and Keegan eventually paid the ultimate price, but not without delighting supporters of the forlorn north-east club.

▶ *Hot-headed Cantona, star of Manchester United and France, kicked his way into the affections of British football fans.*

◀ A stricken Stuart Pearce, after missing his penalty shoot-out in England's World Cup semi-final against West Germany in 1990.

lower division clubs fearful of being forgotten.

Double-edged sword

At first glance, all this did not seem much of a revolution, but the revenue raised for the top sides enabled them to bring in some exhilarating talent and improve conditions for supporters. Striking a balance between the big clubs and their smaller neighbours is a difficult task, however. The huge cash injection from BSkyB, a satellite television company, has done wonders for the game, but many were worried at the prospect of having to watch live football through subscription services rather than on terrestrial television, and the introduction of weekly Sunday and Monday matches angered traditionalists. It took time to win over the footballing public.

Hereford player-manager Ian Bowyer and his 18-year-old son Gary played together in a 3-3 draw at Scunthorpe in Division Four on 21 April 1990.

Poor old Graham

Perhaps Keegan should have been made England boss; certainly, it seemed everyone else fancied having a go. When the FA appointed Aston Villa manager Graham Taylor – who had never played any higher than the Fourth Division – to the job after Italia 90, it was a surprising choice. Taylor was to become the most disliked and least successful England manager of all time, though in retrospect it is unfair to blame him entirely for his team's failings.

Swedes are sweet

The writing was on the wall after the 1992 European Championships in Sweden. England had qualified by the narrowest of margins, and Taylor was greatly criticized for his team selections; he blooded many new players, some of whom were clearly not of international quality. England drew with France and Denmark, before losing 2-1 to Sweden; there was uproar when skipper Gary Lineker was replaced on the hour as his country went down in what was to be his last ever game. It was most definitely a tournament to forget.

A new dawn

If there was a turning point in the decade, it came at the start of 1992-93 with the creation of the FA Premier League, which replaced the old First Division. The Premier League was viewed as a 'Super League' for the top clubs with the right to negotiate its own fees for merchandising and television, a move which prompted angry protests from

United make history

The advent of the Premier League – which would see the number of top-flight clubs reduced initially to 20 – coincided neatly with Manchester United's first title in over 25 years, an eagerly anticipated event at Old Trafford. They romped home with room to spare, fired by Cantona, skipper Steve Bruce, Danish goalkeeper Peter Schmeichel and the talented young winger Ryan Giggs, the latest to be hailed the new George Best.

▲ *Wonder-boy Ryan Giggs demonstrating the skills that put him into Manchester United's first team.*

Handy Andy

Arsenal helped themselves to the Cup in the last minute of extra-time in a replay with Sheffield Wednesday, defender Andy Linighan heading home to avoid the sceptre of the greatest footballing competition being decided on a penalty shoot-out. Brian Clough was less happy, announcing his retirement from Nottingham Forest as the club were relegated at the end of a miserable season.

Turnip Taylor

Perhaps Graham Taylor should have retired as well. If he had, he would have avoided the most

THE HIGHEST NUMBER OF DISMISSALS IN ONE FOOTBALLING SEASON TOOK PLACE IN 1994-95. THE TOTAL WAS 376.

vitriolic treatment any football manager has ever received from the tabloid press, a campaign which began in earnest after England lost 2-0 to the USA in a pre-season tournament. Already, one MP had tabled a motion calling for Taylor's dismissal after the European Championships debacle, and *The Sun* had dubbed him a 'Turnip' and ran the infamous headline 'Swedes 2 Turnips 1.' 'Yanks 2 Planks 0' was their response to the American result.

◄ *Rio Ferdinand's foolish conviction for drink-driving ruined any chance of playing for his country.*

▼ *England manager Terry Venables training his squad at Bisham Abbey, June 1996.*

Does he not like that

Things got worse after England lost 2-0 to Holland in Rotterdam in a World Cup qualifier. Taylor was unfortunate when Ronald Koeman was not red-carded for a clear professional foul and went on to score from a free-kick, but his own tactical naïveties were there for all to see, as was his nervous, comedic management style during a later television documentary, entitled *Do I Not Like That?* after his utterance as the second goal went in.

Sham Marino

England needed a minor miracle to make it to USA 94, and their final match in San Marino was a shambles; the home side, who had only scored once in a competitive fixture, found the net in the opening 10 seconds, though they went on to lose 7-1. Despite this victory, England were out of the tournament and Taylor's resignation was inevitable. He was replaced by ex-Spurs manager Terry Venables, who had left the London club after a series of public rows with chairman Alan Sugar. Venables was popular with the players and extremely knowledgeable, after spells with Crystal Palace and Barcelona in particular.

Parma's hard cheese

Spurs' rivals Arsenal overshadowed them again in 1993-94, beating Parma 1-0 to win the Cup Winners' Cup. Alan Smith scored the goal, and the Gunners gave a masterful display against the Italians.

Not quite as masterful, however, as Manchester United, whose years of perseverance finally bore fruit at the end of a brilliant season. Kenny Dalglish, now boss of newly-promoted Blackburn Rovers (after ending his self-imposed exile from the game), was unable to halt Alex Ferguson's side, and neither Liverpool nor Arsenal were capable of mounting sustained challenges. United took the Double, a year after re-entering the Championship record books, by beating Chelsea 4-0 at Wembley; Eric Cantona's brace of penalties made the difference between the two sides. United were becoming a superteam.

FA CUP FINAL ROYAL GUESTS

1981 ▶	Queen Mother
1981 ▶ replay	Prince Michael of Kent
1982 ▶	Princess Anne
1982 ▶ replay	Duke of Kent
1983 ▶	Duke of Kent
1983 ▶ replay	Princess Michael of Kent
1984 ▶	Duke and Duchess of Kent
1985 ▶	Duke of Kent
1986 ▶	Duchess of Kent
1987 ▶	Duchess of Kent
1988 ▶	Princess of Wales
1989 ▶	Duke and Duchess of Kent
1990 ▶	Duke and Duchess of Kent

MBEs

Kenny Dalglish	▶ (Celtic, Liverpool, Scotland)
Mike England	▶ (Blackburn Rovers, Tottenham Hotspur, Cardiff City, Wales)
Eddie Gray	▶ (Leeds United, Scotland)
Arfon Griffiths	▶ (Wrexham, Arsenal, Wales)
John Hollins	▶ (Chelsea, Queen's Park Rangers, Arsenal, England)
Mark Hughes	▶ (Manchester United, Barcelona, Chelsea, Wales)
Geoff Hurst	▶ (West Ham United, Stoke City, West Bromwich Albion, England)
Gary Mabbutt	▶ (Bristol Rovers, Tottenham Hotspur, England)

Throwing the game

With no World Cup interest for England, the summer of 1994 was a bleak one, and as a season of reconciliation began in earnest, events on the pitch were again overtaken by scandals and misdeeds off it. When the world woke up to tabloid newspaper revelations claiming players had fixed matches, it was a chilling throwback to the shame of 1915 and the Manchester United-Liverpool fixture. Liverpool goalkeeper Bruce Grobbelaar was implicated this time around, along with two Wimbledon stars – Hans Segers and John Fashanu.

Through the net

The Sun claimed Grobbelaar had accepted large amounts of money to let in goals deliberately, apparently from Far Eastern betting syndicates, and all three men were eventually sent to trial at Winchester Crown Court. The case was never proven, but the sceptre hung over the game for a good two years and left many fans badly disillusioned with football.

Bung 'em in

It was to be only the first blow in a wretched season; Arsenal sacked George Graham over his alleged involvement in transfer 'bungs', before, on a cold night at Selhurst Park, the madness reached a climax: Manchester United's French star Eric Cantona had been sent off against Crystal Palace and, as he left the field, lunged into the crowd with a two-footed karate kick on a jeering spectator.

The ensuing images were horrific and left a genuine sense of shock; how could a player so violently attack a fan, even if – as Cantona claimed – he was racially incited? Manager Alex Ferguson could not defend his star's actions, and Cantona himself went into hiding as resentment grew. The FA handed him an eight-month ban, and he was lucky to escape a jail sentence, but his club stuck by him and vowed he would continue to play for them when he returned.

Landsdowne riot

The crowd incident at Selhurst Park had not been the first of the year, either. The friendly game between Ireland and England at Landsdowne Road, Dublin, had to be abandoned after visiting thugs rained missiles on to home fans and the pitch. For a game which had begun to make steady progress, it was a harsh and timely reminder of the troubles of the past.

> **RUMBELOWS CUP**
> 1991
> **Sheffield Wednesday 1 v Manchester United 0**
> 1992
> **Manchester United 1 v Nottingham Forest 0**

PLAYER OF THE YEAR

1991	▶	**Mark Hughes (Manchester United)**
1992	▶	**Gary Pallister (Manchester United)**
1993	▶	**Paul McGrath (Aston Villa)**
1994	▶	**Eric Cantona (Manchester United)**
1995	▶	**Alan Shearer (Blackburn)**
1996	▶	**Les Ferdinand (Newcastle)**
1997	▶	**Alan Shearer (Newcastle)**

◄ Awards galore: (l-r) David Beckham with his Young Player of the Year award, Alan Shearer with his Players' Player award and Peter Beardsley with a merit award for Outstanding Contribution, 1997.

▶ Bruce Grobbelaar at a news conference after his release on bail, for alleged match-fixing offences, 1995.

Kenny's SAS

Without Cantona, United were powerless to stop Blackburn lifting the title thanks to their brilliant double 'SAS' strike force of Alan Shearer and Chris Sutton – another title for Dalglish and the culmination of a massive spending and investment spree by the club's benefactor Sir Jack Walker.

Eric lives again

United, however, were a side full of resilience and talent and bounced straight back in 1995-96. Kevin Keegan's Newcastle effectively ruled themselves out of the race with their attack-at-all-costs mentality, which proved suicidal, and Alex Ferguson's young team proved frighteningly dominant at Old Trafford. Cantona returned and stole the show at the Cup Final, scoring the only goal to beat Liverpool 1-0 and seal the 'Double Double' for his club. Having put his troubles behind him, he walked off with the Footballer Of The Year award for his part in a brilliant title triumph.

All change for England

England went into Euro 96 again knowing their coach would leave whatever the outcome. Terry Venables' outside business interests were deemed to be consuming too much of his time, and he stepped aside for Glenn Hoddle, England's youngest ever boss at 38. One of the finest players of his generation, Hoddle had managed Swindon to the Premier League and had been building an impressive squad at Chelsea.

Boom time

England's Euro 96 success in reaching the semi-finals finally vanquished the bitter aftertaste of those scandals a year previously, and the Manchester United players who proved so inspirational for their country shone as their club again raced to the title in 1996-97. David Beckham, the next starlet, a stylish midfielder with all-round ability and boy-next-door looks, scored from the halfway line against Wimbledon on the opening day of the season, and

▲ *Manchester United lift their Premiership trophy, 5 May 1996.*

▼*Arsenal's Dennis Bergkamp at the FA Carling Premiership match in 1997.*

there was rarely any doubt who would win the title.

The stars go out

Middlesbrough, under the leadership of Bryan Robson, signed the brilliant Brazilian Juninho and the temperamental Italian goalgrabber Fabrizio Ravanelli and made the Cup Final, where they lost to Ruud Gullit's Chelsea. Sadly, Robson's signings backfired as disunity and disarray saw the club relegated – had they not been docked two points by the FA for failing to

fulfil a fixture against Blackburn due to an illness epidemic, they would have stayed up.

Foreign fields

It was, however, boom time once again for the English game. The Premiership was graced by the cream of world football as clubs invested in overseas talent on the back of huge attendances and major investment. Gianfranco Zola was a star for Chelsea, while Dennis Bergkamp at Arsenal, the Colombian Faustino Asprilla and Italian Gianluca Vialli were all inspirational. Many felt the influx of foreigners would stifle up-and-coming English talent, but this has not been borne out.

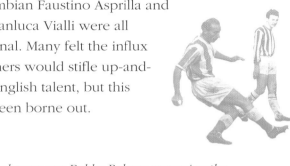

▶ *England manager Bobby Robson surveying the proceedings, June 1990.*

WORLD CUP SQUAD, ITALY – 1990
MANAGER: BOBBY ROBSON

POSITION	NAME	CLUB	AGE	CAPS	GOALS
Goalkeepers	David Beasant	Chelsea	31	2	0
	Peter Shilton	Derby	40	117	0
	Chris Woods	Rangers	30	16	0
Full-backs	Tony Dorigo	Chelsea	24	3	0
	Paul Parker	QPR	26	5	0
	Stuart Pearce	Notts Forest	28	23	1
	Gary Stevens	Rangers	27	38	0
Centre-backs	Terry Butcher	Rangers	31	71	3
	Des Walker	Notts Forest	24	17	0
	Mark Wright	Derby	26	23	0
Midfield	Paul Gascoigne	Tottenham	22	10	2
	Steve Hodge	Notts Forest	27	21	0
	Steve McMahon	Liverpool	28	12	0
	David Platt	Aston Villa	23	4	0
	Bryan Robson (c)	Manchester Utd	33	84	26
	Trevor Steven	Rangers	26	26	4
	Neil Webb	Manchester Utd	26	19	2
Forwards	John Barnes	Liverpool	26	52	10
	Peter Beardsley	Liverpool	29	39	7
	Steve Bull	Wolves	25	6	4
	Gary Lineker	Tottenham	29	50	31
	Chris Waddle	Marseilles	29	51	6

CHRIS WOODS, DAVID SEAMAN AND STEVE HODGE DID NOT PLAY.

Bosman revolution

The Bosman Ruling, under which players became free agents when their contracts expired, promised to keep a lid on huge transfer fees and attract big names to what had by now become Europe's most exciting league. Manchester United continued apace with a new crop of youngsters, but Liverpool, Arsenal, Chelsea and Blackburn were closing in on them while Spurs and Everton, two traditional giants, went into decline.

A crucial time

The end of the 20th century and the start of the next will be crucial years for English football, and could re-establish the national side as the best in the world. Supporters have never had it better, money is for once freely available and hooliganism would seem to be on the slide.

INDIVIDUAL TRAGEDIES

On 16 September 1972, referee Jim Finn suffered a fatal heart attack during a Fourth Division game between Exeter City and Stockport County, at St James' Park.

▼ *Mark Hughes* (left) *and David Beckham – a face of the future – battle it out on the pitch.*

PETER SHILTON: A LESSON IN LONGEVITY

A millennium of games

The Leyton Orient v Brighton Third Division clash in 1997 should have been notable only for the visitors' ongoing protests against chairman Bill Archer. Instead, another man was taking centre stage; Peter Shilton, goalkeeper par excellence and now a ripe old 47, was playing an incredible 1,000th game.

The prodigy

Shilton's longevity is far from his only credential; in his heyday, he was one of the world's greatest goalkeepers and an England cap between 1971 and 1990. A quiet and likeable man sent off only once in his career, he has set a superb example to younger players and struck an important blow for over-40s everywhere.

Out of the limelight

Shilton won a League title only once, when Forest lifted the trophy in 1978; he played the vast majority of his matches for Leicester, Stoke and Southampton, always placing his own enjoyment of the game above the need for glory. His 125 caps for his country stands as a record, and he was 40 years old when he won his last cap during Italia 90, a feat few believed any player post-Matthews could achieve.

England's number one

Ironically, he could have quit the national side aged 21, frustrated at being kept out by Ray Clemence, with whom he duelled for the number one shirt for the next 15 years. Had Clemence not competed with him, he might have made even more appearances; after all, he took Gordon Banks's place in the Leicester side while still in his teens.

▲ *Peter Shilton received an MBE for his services to British sport.*

ONE OF THE LONGEST-SERVING MANAGERS, SIR MATT BUSBY, WAS IN CHARGE OF MANCHESTER UNITED FOR 26 SEASONS – A POST-WAR RECORD.

Back for more?

Shilton kept fit and kept going well into his 40s, appearing for Derby and Orient among others, as well as an ill-fated

▲ *Shilton's spectacular defence against Ireland, June 1990.*

spell as Plymouth player-manager. Not only was he turning back the clock, he was still a quick and capable keeper who commanded his defence and made up for a slight lack of height with fantastic reflexes and agility. Who would be surprised to see him back for more as he enters his 50s?

MBEs

Frank McLintock
(Leicester City, Arsenal, Queen's Park Rangers, Scotland)
Mick Mills
(Ipswich Town, Southampton, Stoke City, England)
Alan Mullery
(Tottenham Hotspur, Fulham, England)
Terry Paine
(Southampton, Hereford United, England)
Steve Perryman
(Tottenham Hotspur, Oxford United, Brentford, England)
Martin Peters
(West Ham United, Tottenham Hotspur, Norwich City, Sheffield United, England)
Peter Shilton
(Leicester City, Stoke City, Nottingham Forest, Southampton, Derby County, Plymouth, Leyton Orient, West Ham United, England)
John Toshack
(Cardiff City, Liverpool, Swansea City, Wales)

MANCHESTER UNITED: TEAM OF THE 90S

▲ *Peter Schmeichel being crowned with the top of the Premiership trophy.*

Cole's goals

Andy Cole, a £7 million signing from Newcastle, took time to settle and was derided as a flop by the critics, but still managed a prolific goal rate and used his pace to full effect as he led the frontline following Eric Cantona's departure, flanked by Teddy Sheringham and Ole Gunnar Solskjaer. But it was the 'kids' – mocked by pundit Alan Hansen – who stole the headlines. Ryan Giggs became United's newest superstar when he made his debut in 1990. A tricky winger, he was inevitably compared to George Best but possessed a far cooler head and was far less prone to waste the ball, even if he did not possess the supreme skills of the Irishman.

Stick with him

Back in 1989, the writing could have been on the wall for Alex Ferguson, Manchester United's stalwart manager. He had been unable to take the club back to the top of the pile, and they were languishing instead in mid-table, an unacceptable position for such a huge club.

NON-LEAGUE GIANT-KILLERS

In 1924, during an amazing match, the strictly amateur club Corinthians beat League giants Blackburn Rovers 1-0.

Fortunately, United persevered with Ferguson because they knew he had a plan. The canny Scot had stopped the flow of ineffective big-money signings, and focused instead on rebuilding youth policy. The ploy worked, and United's young team were the outstanding side of the 1990s thanks to the allying of youth and experience.

Guiding lights

Older players, such as the dependable midfielder Brian McClair, versatile striker Mark Hughes and Peter Schmeichel, the Danish keeper rated the best in the world, kept cool heads and guided the youngsters through. Successive skippers Bryan Robson, Roy Keane and Gary Pallister were inspirational leaders.

Becks is best

David Beckham complemented Giggs when he burst on to the scene in 1994. A teenage idol with good looks and a pop star girlfriend, Beckham won hearts as well as matches, and showed an exciting penchant for long-range shooting, including a memorable goal from the halfway line against Wimbledon that seemed to defy the laws of science.

England's starlets

Ball-winner Nicky Butt and the intelligent Paul Scholes kept a lower profile but were just as integral, while brothers Gary and Phil Neville both made their England debuts after graduating from the United academy. It seemed there was no end to the production line of talent at Old Trafford, and there are more stars around the corner to keep United at the top of the Premiership for some time to come.

In February 1998, Manchester United's Michael Owen became the youngest international player of the twentieth century, at just 18 years of age.

▲ *Skipper Alex Ferguson picks up the Premiership trophy at Middlesbrough, 1996.*

ALAN SHEARER: A MODERN SUPERSTAR

A star without peers

One man, above all others, has come to symbolize the current state of English football, its astonishing propensity to generate money and its new-found excellence: Alan Shearer. In many ways, the quiet man from Newcastle is the archetypal centre-forward both on and off the pitch; a record-breaker, a diplomat and a legendary finisher possessing skills not seen in this country for many years.

length of the country to Southampton to sign pro forms and, on 9 April 1988, became the youngest ever player to score a top-flight hat-trick; he is currently pushing the 200-goal mark.

From the Dell to Euro 96

At Southampton, the young Shearer prospered and, just months after making his international debut against France, joined Blackburn Rovers and Kenny Dalglish in a £3.3 million deal. His Ewood Park partnership with Chris

▲ *Alan Shearer celebrates winning the FA Carling Premiership, with Blackburn Rovers' chairman Jack Walker.*

Money, money, money

When the 27-year-old returned to his native north-east in 1996, the astounding £15 million fee became a new world record. Yet the Shearer story started in much more humble surroundings. Overlooked by local clubs, he travelled the

Sutton became the most lethal in the Premiership and fired the unfashionable club to the championship. For England, he complemented Teddy Sheringham's deep-lying understanding of forward play and scored five goals to take his country to the semi-finals of Euro 96.

FOOTBALLER OF THE YEAR

1991 ▶ **Gordon Strachan (Leeds)**

1992 ▶ **Gary Lineker (Tottenham)**

1993 ▶ **Chris Waddle (Sheffield Wednesday)**

1994 ▶ **Alan Shearer (Blackburn)**

1995 ▶ **Jurgen Klinsmann (Tottenham)**

1996 ▶ **Eric Cantona (Manchester United)**

1997 ▶ **Gianfranco Zola (Chelsea)**

not fire the defensively naïve Newcastle side to silverware, but off the pitch he was everywhere, and his infamously un-controversial public persona could not prevent him from earning endorsements and deals worth hundreds of thousands.

DURING HIS TIME WITH BLACKBURN ROVERS, ALAN SHEARER NOTCHED UP 130 GOALS IN 165 GAMES.

Back to the beginning

Which is why, when Shearer left Lancashire for Kevin Keegan's Newcastle just a few weeks later, it sent shockwaves through the game. Blackburn supporters, in a show of devotion not seen in football since the days of Matthews and Finney, took back their newly purchased season tickets; while their Geordie counterparts flocked in their thousands to St James' Park for the mid-afternoon press conference confirming his arrival. The lad played a blinder, proclaiming: 'I'm just a sheet metal-worker's son from Newcastle,' and sending replica shirt sales spiralling to record levels.

A record-breaker

That an English player could command such a hefty fee was surprising enough. That an English club could afford to pay it was nothing short of flabbergasting. Shearer's arrival could

The final chapter?

It seems only injury can stop the one-man goal machine described by Terry Venables as 'one of the most magnificent strikers in the world' from further domination. A troublesome cruciate ligament injury curtailed his 1997-98 season, but his powers of recovery are legendary. Told to expect a year out by doctors, he was back in a little over five months. The World Cup will be his biggest crack yet at imposing himself globally; for a man of no vices, it was a huge gamble to profess himself fit to play so soon. However if he repeats his Euro 96 exploits at France 98, the sheet metal worker's son from Newcastle will become a superstar without parallel.

▲ *Top-scorer Alan Shearer sporting the kit of his home town.*

WHERE DO WE GO NOW?

▲ *The Aston Villa team of 1898 – a million miles away from the footballers of a century later.*

A whole new ball game

The early players and administrators of the game would struggle to recognize football today. The modern game is a multi-million pound worldwide industry and has arguably become the British Isles' most successful export throughout history yet football's participants 100 years from now will almost certainly be taking part in a sport very different from today's incarnation. For football will continue to evolve in both its priorities and its rules, and to keep up with the times the game needs to remain one step ahead.

A proud nation

It seems almost remarkable to consider today that, as recently as a decade ago, our national sport was seen less as a flagship for the country than as a millstone around its neck. The sceptre of hooliganism and the subsequent European ban drove staunch supporters away from the game in their thousands. Yet, as Euro 96 proved, England is still the home of football; the successes of that tournament both on and off the pitch sent an important message to the rest of the world. Where once we marvelled at the talents of the Brazilians and Italians we were re-learning an important pride in our home-grown superstars.

Sheffield FC, who still exist to this day in local leagues, lay claim to being the oldest football club in the world, having formed in 1857.

Fever pitch

With the advent of all-seater stadia, families flocked back to Premiership grounds and it seemed that every

▲ *The latest money-making deal – David Beckham launches his new Adidas boot.*

ASTON VILLA'S CHARLIE WALLACE WAS THE FIRST TO MISS AN FA CUP PENALTY IN 1913. VILLA STILL WENT ON TO BEAT LEAGUE CHAMPIONS SUNDERLAND 1-0.

newspaper, magazine and TV programme wanted to talk football as never before. New superstars like Alan Shearer and David Beckham became famed not only for their sporting ability but for their lives off the pitch and the huge multi-million pound operations that grew up around them. The advent of satellite, and eventually digital, television has helped the game reach a far larger audience than ever before and, indeed, made the presentation of football a slicker and more professional package. Yet the money from TV deals goes largely to the already-wealthy Premiership clubs, and even those at the top of the Nationwide League tree are sufficiently concerned about their future incomes to discuss the possibility of a second Premiership or even the regionalization of the lower divisions to provide fewer long journeys and more local derbies for the poorer clubs.

Striking a balance

There are those who are concerned about the changes in the game, and in particular the shifting power bases and changing demographics behind the scenes. As ticket prices rise year-on-year and many larger clubs have to turn fans away, it has been necessary for the first time to introduce a Government-sanctioned Football Task Force to examine striking a reasonable balance between the expectations of the shareholders and the worries and aspirations of the everyday fan. That balance is perhaps the greatest challenge the English game faces in the years that lie ahead, and the danger is that the ever-inflating market for football will eventually implode.

Fast and furious

So how will the game of the future differ from that of today? The 21st-century footballer will be an all-round athlete: fitter, stronger and faster than ever before, as the game itself will move at an increasingly frantic pace. The emphasis will be on physical excellence as well as

▲ *Chelsea's Ruud Gullit on the pitch – accompanied by mobile Sky TV cameras.*

▲ *Newcastle United fans in 1924 – an early version of the painted faces of today's supporters.*

ENGLAND INTERNATIONAL AND NEWCASTLE UNITED MEGASTAR ALAN SHEARER SCORED FIVE HAT-TRICKS FOR EX-TEAM BLACKBURN ROVERS IN 1995-96. JIMMY GREAVES CRACKED HOME SIX FOR CHELSEA IN 1960-61.

technical ability, and players who can today hope to continue careers well into their thirties may find their incomes curtailed before they are out of their twenties. Referees, too, will need to change with the times. We will almost certainly see professional men in the middle before the year 2000, and the ever-faster pace of football will lend itself to all manner of technical innovations, from action replays in the stands to aid officials to tennis-style line 'bleepers' to indicate when the ball is out of play or has crossed the goal-line. The game will frequently be stopped to allow contentious incidents to be viewed again by an independent adjudicator.

Money talks

Increasingly, the FA and other traditional power bases may find their responsibilities eroded by the demands of television and sponsors who demand radical alterations to the game. Large networks will want the game split into quarters for extra ad breaks, and the emphasis will be on vast pay-per-view audiences rather than paying spectators at grounds. The larger clubs may have even bigger

NON-LEAGUE GIANT-KILLERS

In 1920 Cardiff City beat Oldham Athletic 2-0 while Darlington toppled Sheffield Wednesday at Hillsborough by the same score-line.

◀ *A turnstile at Barnsley's home ground, Oakwell.*

MANCHESTER UNITED AND ENGLAND INTERNATIONAL PLAYER DAVID BECKHAM FIRST APPEARED FOR HIS CLUB AT THE TENDER AGE OF 12 – AS THE MASCOT FOR UNITED AT AN AWAY GAME AT UPTON PARK.

concerns than the Premiership or FA Cup. Discussions about a European Super League have been underway since the 1980s, and the likes of Milan, Barcelona and Bayern Munich see such a venture as crucial to their continued financial success. European games, which would replace the existing Champions Cup, could be played midweek to fit around a slightly reduced domestic schedule, and a worldwide television audience of millions would guarantee huge revenue for participants. For Manchester United, Newcastle and Arsenal, the Super League could open up a whole new pathway to the future.

Europe here we come

This break with tradition would be perhaps the most radical change the domestic game has seen since its formative years, but it may be the only way to satisfy the spiralling demands made on our top sides. A Europe-wide League, particularly when operated on a policy of limited promotion and relegation, would ensure the maximum possible financial benefits for those clubs dissatisfied with the limited potential of their domestic leagues. Silvio Berlusconi, the wealthy Milan president who has been among the scheme's most vocal supporters, would like to see it eventually extended to include American and Far Eastern sides, operating under a US-style franchise system.

Look out below

The effects of such changes would be seen most drastically at a grass-roots level. Smaller clubs would struggle to survive as their larger rivals grew ever bigger, and the effects of the Bosman Ruling – which will eventually lead to the complete abolition of transfer fees – would cut off a

vital route of income. The game's giants may sign up smaller fry to provide 'nursery' clubs, loaning out young players to the lower divisions in return for first refusal on bright young talents travelling in the opposite direction. But for many the future will be bleak, and a generation raised on the delights of Alex Ferguson's Manchester United are more likely than ever to eschew their home town clubs for the brighter lights of the top flight.

Too much, too young?

And the players themselves? The cream of the crop can only grow richer, with higher wages, kit sponsorships and off-screen endorsements making millionaires of tomorrow's George Bests before they are old enough to toast their success at the club bar. Tomorrow's superstars – from the exhilarating talent of Liverpool's Michael Owen to the defensive maturity of Rio Ferdinand – are a lucrative commodity coveted by agents and large corporations keen for a slice of the pie. For Alf Common and his record £1,000 transfer, at the time seen as a worrying trend in itself, it would be an incongruous sight, if an inevitable one.

To the future

Yet if all this sounds like a nightmare scenario, there is plenty of cause for optimism. Namely the players, managers, officials and fans the world over who have made football a game to be savoured, talked about, played, watched and loved in every country. It always has been – and always will be – the people's game, and nothing can change that.

▲ West Ham United's Rio Ferdinand playing against Newcastle United in the FA Premiership, 1997.

When Alf Common moved from Sunderland to Middlesbrough for £1,000 it set the tone for the modern transfer market, culminating in Alan Shearer's £15 million move from Blackburn Rovers to Newcastle United in July 1996.

FRANCE 98

After the ignominy of missing the World Cup in 1994, England stormed their way back into international football; first in Euro 96 and then at France 98. England manager Glenn Hoddle left the announcement of his squad until the very last minute.

Twenty-Two Lions

Goalkeepers: David Seaman (Arsenal), Nigel Martyn (Leeds United), Tim Flowers (Blackburn Rovers).

Strikers: Alan Shearer (Newcastle United), Paul Merson (Middlesbrough), Les Ferdinand (Tottenham Hotspur), Teddy Sheringham (Manchester United), Michael Owen (Liverpool).

Midfielders: Gareth Southgate (Aston Villa), David Beckham (Manchester United), Paul Ince (Liverpool), David Batty (Newcastle United), Steve McManaman (Liverpool), Paul Scholes (Manchester United).

Defenders: Gary Neville (Manchester United), Tony Adams (Arsenal), Martin Keown (Arsenal), Rio Ferdinand (West Ham), Sol Campbell (Tottenham Hotspur), Rob Lee (Newcastle United), Graeme Le Saux (Chelsea), Darren Anderton (Tottenham Hotspur).

Hoddle's Choices

Every England manager experiences public criticism and Hoddle was no exception. The expected combination of Seaman, Shearer and Gascoigne was scuppered by Hoddle's brave decision to drop Gazza (due to concern over his fitness level) – many fans were incensed. Hoddle also faced a choice between Owen and Sheringham. Both had played in the warm-ups, but Hoddle seemed to want to keep the faith in the classic striker combination of Sheringham and Shearer. The controversy continued over the choice of David Beckham, against contender Anderton (who had been out due to injury for months beforehand) with the media stirring up an Anderton/Beckham feud.

Despite all this, Hoddle's lads played magnificently together, storming to a 2-0 victory in their first match against Tunisia, with goals from Scholes and Shearer. Their 2-1 defeat by Romania was a shock, but there was a silver lining in the form of 18-year-old Owen. Substituted in the 73rd minute, he scored their only goal.

The Anderton/Beckham feud was laid to rest in the match against Colombia, with each man taking one goal to seal a 2-0 victory. Then they faced Argentina.

The Argentina Match

The match was touted as a revenge match for the 1986 'Hand of God' semi-final. Within minutes, Argentina were 1-0 up, but soon afterwards Shearer equalised. Once again, Owen left his opponents standing and scored a spectacular goal – by half-time, an England victory was a distinct possibility. But the first few minutes of the second half saw Beckham brought down by a tackle; he kicked out viciously, earning himself a red card. Even with ten men Hoddle's boys held out, and at full-time the score stood at 2-2. Extra-time passed without the Golden Goal and a penalty shoot-out was to decide the game. Owen, Shearer and Merson struck lucky, but a miss by Ince meant that Batty carried the weight of a nation on his shoulders. He missed.

The host nation went on to claim the trophy, and England came home earlier than they deserved to. But they had played, as always, with dignity and style, and a new star had been born. With Owen as part of the team's future, hope springs eternal.

▲ Owen's goal against Morrocco in one of the last warm-up matches before the onslaught of France 98

GLOSSARY

All-ticket
Matches where no tickets are sold on the day of the game.

Bosman Ruling
Out-of-contract players became free agents allowing them to move within the EC without a fee. It followed a case brought to the European Court of Justice in 1995 by Belgian midfielder Jean-Marc Bosman.

Cambridge Rules
The first set of modern rules drawn up at Cambridge University in 1846 by H. de Winton and J. C. Thring.

Captain Marvel
Nickname given to Bryan Robson by manager Ron Atkinson during his heyday with Manchester United and England.

The Double
Landing the League Championship or Premiership title and the FA Cup in the same season.

European Superleague
Proposed league including major European clubs from England, Scotland, Italy, Spain, Germany, Holland and Belgium.

Floodlights
Pylons with lights on top to illuminate night matches. First used for the Football League match between Portsmouth and Newcastle on 22 February, 1956.

Football Task Force
Government-backed body set up in 1997 and headed by former Tory MP David Mellor to investigate whether football fans are getting raw deals from the clubs they support.

Hacking
Cynical tackle from behind in which player's legs are swiped away by another's boot.

'Hand of God'
Infamous quote from Argentina skipper Diego Maradona after he fisted the opening goal past England's Peter Shilton in the 1986 Mexico World Cup Quarter-Final. He later claimed that the ball had been touched by the hand of God.

Injury time
Time added on by the referee at the end of 90 minutes to account for stoppages during normal play.

'It is now....'
Kenneth Wolstenholme's historic commentary at the end of England's 4-2 1966 World Cup triumph over West Germany. Fans were spilling on to the pitch as Geoff Hurst scored the fourth goal prompting the immortal phrase 'Some fans are on the pitch. They think it's all over.... It is now'.

Match-fixing
Players offered money by betting syndicates to guarantee results. Ten professionals, including England internationals Tony Kay and Peter Swan, were jailed in 1965 for taking part in English football's greatest fixing scandal.

Maximum wage
Money paid to players before 1961 could not exceed £20 a week.

Retain and transfer
Clubs were allowed to keep players at the end of their contracts against their will until 1963 when it was successfully challenged in the High Court by England international George Eastham.

Pay-per-view
Television viewers asked to pay to watch matches from their armchairs.

Pools
Weekly competition in which gamblers try to predict the outcome of league matches. Launched in 1923 by Littlewoods.

Pools panel
Team of experts called in to guess results of matches postponed due to weather, ensuring pools coupons are valid. First introduced in 1963.

Push and run
Players pass ball with inside of foot then move into space. Perfected by Liverpool under Bob Paisley in the 1980s.

Signing-on fee
Money paid to player moving to a new club.

Sweeper
Defender playing behind the traditional back four or three. Normally player with strong defensive qualities plus ability to move forward at will.

Transfer bung
When a manager takes money from an agent or player for securing a transfer.

Twin Towers
Distinctive pair of towers at the entrance to Wembley Stadium.

Wing-back
Players who perform role of winger and full back under 3-5-2 formation.

FURTHER READING

Brooking, Trevor, *Trevor Brooking's 100 Great British Footballers,* Queen Anne Press, London, 1988

Butler, Byron, *Official Illustrated History of the FA Cup,* Headline, London, 1996

Cameron, Colin, *Football, Fussball, Voetball,* BBC Books, London, 1995

Dalglish, Kenny, *My Autobiography,* Coronet, London, 1996

Davies, Hunter, *The Glory Game,* Mainstream, Edinburgh, 1996

Davies, Pete, *All Played Out,* Mandarin Press, London, 1991

Dunphy, Eamon, *Sir Matt Busby and Manchester United,* Heinemann, London, 1991

Faber Book of Soccer, Faber and Faber, London, 1992

Ferris, Ken, *The Double,* Two Heads Publishing, London, 1996

The Football League 1888-1988, Queen Anne Press, London 1987

Francis, Tony, *Clough – A Biography,* Stanley Paul, London, 1993

Freddi, Cris, *The Complete Book of the World Cup*, Harper Collins, London, 1998

Harding, John, *Football Wizard – The Billy Meredith Story,* Stanley Paul, London, 1998

Hornby, Nick, *Fever Pitch,* Indigo, London, 1993

Inglis, Simon, *Football Grounds of Great Britain,* Collins Willow, London, 1993

Inglis, Simon, *League Football and the Men Who Made It,* Collins Willow, 1988

Joannou, Paul, *United: The First 100 Years and More,* Polar Publishing, Leicester, 1995

Kelly, Stephen F., *Liverpool – The Official Illustrated History,* Hamlyn, London, 1995

Kelly, Stephen F., *Fergie – The Biography of Alex Ferguson,* London, 1992

Lopez, Sue, *Women on the Ball,* Scarlet Press, London, 1997

McIlvaney, Hugh, *McIlvaney on Football,* Mainstream Publishing, London, 1996

News of the World Football Annual 1997-1998, Invincible Press, London, 1997

Payne, Mike, *England – The Complete Post-War Record,* Breedon Books, 1993

People of Today, Debretts, London, 1998

Pringle, Andy and Neil Fissler, *Where Are They Now?,* Two Heads Publishing, London 1996

Rollin, Jack, *Soccer at War 1939-45,* Willow Books, London, 1985

Rothman's Football Yearbook 1997-98, Queen Anne Press, London, 1997

Russell, Dave, *Football and the English,* Carnegie Publishing, Preston, 1997

Sharpe, Graham, *Gambling on Goals,* Mainstream, Edinburgh, 1997

Soar, Philip and Martin Tyler, *Arsenal,* Hamlyn, London, 1994

Soccer Firsts, Guinness Superlatives, Enfield, 1986

Studd, Stephen, *Herbert Chapman – Football Emperor,* Souvenir Press, London, 1997

Superstars of the Premier League, Parragon, Bristol, 1995

Thompson, David, *4-2,* Bloomsbury, London, 1996

Thraves, Andrew, *The History of the Wembley FA Cup Final,* Weidenfeld and Nicolson, London, 1994

The World Cup: A Complete Record, Breedon Books, Derby, 1990

PICTURE CREDITS AND ACKNOWLEDGEMENTS

Ann Ronan at Image Select: 8, 14 (t), 15 (t), 17 (t), 24, 49, 101.

The Bridgeman Art Library: 10 (t), 78 (b), 80.

Christie's Images: 46, 60 (t), 68 (b), 105 (b).

Colorsport: 9, 19, 23, 30, 37, 41, 43, 51, 58, 64, 66, 75, 76 (t), 76 (b), 77, 79, 81(l), 85, 91, 98, 99, 108, 117, 121, 125, 126, 132, 135, 176 (t), 179, 182, 183, 186, 187 (b), 187 (t), 194, 195, 201, 202, 208, 245, 249, 250.

Empics Sports Photo Agency: 9, 21, 29, 31, 32, 33, 48, 63, 65, 67, 71, 88, 89, 90 (t), 90 (b), 92, 93, 104, 105 (t), 107, 112 (t), 113 (t), 113 (b), 130, 137, 143, 144 (t), 144 (b), 147, 149, 152, 153, 165, 168, 172, 173, 176 (b), 184, 185, 188 (b), 189, 203, 215, 216, 217, 218-219, 221, 225, 226, 227, 228 (b), 232 (b), 233, 246, 247, 248.

Hulton Getty Picture Collection: 10 (b)13, 22, 25, 40, 47, 73.

Mary Evans Picture Library: 11, 14 (b), 16, 18, 28, 34, 35 (t), 35 (b), 38, 53, 54, 56, 60 (b), 62, 68 (t), 69, 86, 120, 211.

Topham Picturepoint: 8, 26-27, 29 (t), 36, 39, 44, 45, 50, 55, 59, 61 (l), 61(r), 72, 74, 81 (r), 82, 83, 84, 87, 94, 95, 96-97, 100, 102, 103, 110, 111, 112 (b), 115, 116, 118, 119, 122, 128, 129, 131, 133, 134, 136, 139, 140, 141, 142, 145 (l), 145 (r), 146, 151, 154, 155, 156, 157, 158, 159, 160, 161, 162, 163, 164, 167, 170, 174, 178, 180, 181 (l), 181 (r), 188 (t), 190, 192, 193, 195 (t), 196, 198, 200, 204, 205, 206, 207, 209, 210, 212, 213, 214, 222, 223, 228 (t), 230, 231, 232 (t), 234, 235, 236, 237, 238, 239, 240, 241, 242, 243, 244.

With grateful thanks to Dave Jones for designing this book, to Lucinda Hawksley, Sonya Newland and Claire Dashwood for editorial work, to Lee Matthews and Ben Lee for valuable advice and production work, to Helen Tovey for proof-reading and to Helen Johnson, Josephine Cutts and Frances Banfield for picture research.

Thanks also to A. L. Digital Ltd., David Barber of the Football Association, Ray Spiller of the Association of Football League Statisticians and Ian Cole, Chairman of the Sports Writers' Association.

INDEX